GULF COAST

A JOURNAL OF LITERATURE AND FINE ARTS

gULF COASt

A JOURNAL OF LITERATURE AND FINE ARTS VOLUME 27, ISSUE 2

Faculty Editor
Nick Flynn

Editor
Adrienne G. Perry

Managing Editor
Martin Rock

Digital Editor
Carlos Hernandez

Business Manager
Brooke Lightfoot

Fiction Editors
Julia Brown
Laura Jok
Ashley Wurzbacher

Nonfiction Editors
Talia Mailman
Steve Sanders

Poetry Editors
Conor Bracken
Katie Condon
Sam Mansfield

Reviews & Interviews Editor
David Tomas Martinez

Guest Art Lies Editor
Raphael Rubinstein

Assistant Art Lies Editor
Lauren Greve

Online Editors
Talia Mailman (NF)
Christopher Murray (P)
Matthew Salesses (F)

Assistant Editors
Jeff Albers (F)
Melanie Brkich (NF)
Erika Jo Brown (P)
Kay Cosgrove (P)
Elizabeth Davies (F)
Rachel Fairbank (NF)
Kristin Kostick (NF)
Zach Martin (P)

Luisa Muryadan (P)
Georgia Pearle (NF)
Dino Piacentini (NF)
Henk Rossouw (P)
Nathan Stabenfeldt (NF)
Andrea Syzdek (F)
Will Wilkinson (NF)

Poetry Readers
Christian Bancroft, Eleanor Mary Boudreau, Lesli
Vollrath

Nonfiction Reader
Elizabeth Lyons

Fiction Readers
Claire Anderson, Selena Anderson, JP Gritton, and
Jeni McFarland

Interns
Ndidi Anofienem, Bryan Washington,
Stephanie Weigle

Gulf Coast: A Journal of Literature and Fine Arts is largely funded by the Brown Foundation, Inc.; the City of Houston through Houston Arts Alliance; Cynthia Woods Mitchell Center for the Arts; Houston Endowment, Inc.; Inprint, Inc.; the National Endowment for the Arts; Poets & Writers, Inc.; Texas Commission on the Arts; and the University of Houston English Department.

ARTWORK: Cover art (front and back): Design & artwork by John Earles & Jennifer Bianco of Spindletop Design Studios. Production & letterpress printing of cover by Workhorse Printmakers in Houston. The image on p. 32 is from René Descartes' *Treatise of Man*. The image on p. 48 is titled "The reflection inside the hollow sphere" and is from the 1900 issue of *Popular Science Monthly*, Volume 57. The image on pp. 98-99 is from the show *Approximately infinite universe*, 2013, on view at MCASD (Museum of Contemporary Art San Diego) in La Jolla, California. The image on pp.126-156 is titled "line art drawing of a queen bee" & is by Pearson Scott Foreson. All reprinted artwork from pp.157-172, & p.169-172, is by MANUAL (Ed Hill / Suzanne Bloom) & is courtesy of the artists & Moody Gallery, Houston. The image on page 282 is a photograph of the Tomb of Valentina Balbiani (1518-1572), by the French Renaissance sculptor Germain Pilon. The images on pp. 38, 64, 82, 109, 137, 146, 200, 208, & 222 are from the website *10,000 Pages, a Colouring Book of Abstract Line Art*. The image on p.239 is a vector field plot of the two population replicator dynamics for the game of chicken, & is by Kevin Zollman.

OUR THANKS TO: j. Kastely, Giuseppe Taurino, and the Creative Writing Program at the University of Houston; Wyman Herendeen, Carol Barr, Judy Calvez, Julie Kofford, Andre Cobb, George Barr, and the Department of English at the University of Houston; John W. Roberts, Dean of the College of Liberal Arts and Social Sciences at the University of Houston; Renu Khator, President of the University of Houston; CLMP; the staff of *Glass Mountain*; Rich Levy, Marilyn Jones, Kristi Beer, Lee Herrick, and Krupa Parikh of Inprint, Inc.; Sicardi Gallery & MKG Art Management; Adam Lefton and Litragger; Poison Pen Reading Series; Rudyard's British Pub; Barry Jacobs of Jones Day; Sasha Jamal and Monty Ward of Weil Gotshal & Manges LLP; Bob Camp, Jeff Fort, and Lillie Robertson.

Published twice yearly in October and April. Opinions expressed are not necessarily those of the editors. Send queries to *Gulf Coast*, Department of English, University of Houston, Houston, TX 77204-3013. Include a self-addressed, stamped envelope. For postal submission guidelines, or to submit your work online, visit www.gulfcoastmag.org/submit. Response time is 4 to 6 months. *Gulf Coast* is open to submissions from Spetember 1 to March 1.

Subscribe online at WWW.GULFCOASTMAG.ORG or send subscription requests to *Gulf Coast*, Department of English, University of Houston, Houston, TX 77204-3013.

A two-year print subscription is $28 / A one-year print subscription is $16
Current issues are $10 / Back issues are $8

Read *Gulf Coast* on iPad and iPhone!
Visit litragger.com or download the free app from the iTunes store
$5.99 per issue, or $9.99 for one-year digital subscription

Gulf Coast is printed by McNaughton & Gunn, 960 Woodland Drive Saline, MI 48176, 734.429.5411

Gulf Coast is listed in the Humanities International Complete Index. Distributed in North America by Ingram Periodicals Inc., 1240 Heil Quaker Blvd., La Vergne, TN 37086, (615) 793-5522.

Executive Board

Donors

*Gulf Coast would like to thank the following people
who have generously contributed to the journal:*

Benefactors

Jeff Fort
Lillie Robertson

Sponsors

Janet & Paul Hobby
Misty & Surena Matin
Nina & Michael Zilkha

Friends

Susie & Sanford Criner
Gwendolyn Goffe
Lynn Goode & Harrison Williams
Carolyn Roch Henneman
   & Matt Henneman

Eric Lueders & Thad Logan
Evelyn & Roy Nolen
Megan Prout
Hinda Simon
Cynthia Toles

Supporters

Blake Anderson
Katharine Barthelme
Tei Carpenter
Bettie Cartwright
Jereann Chaney
Audrey Colombe
Mary S. Jack Dawson
Amber Dermont
Susie & Joe Dilg
Martha & Richard Finger
CeCe & Mack Fowler
John Guess
Peg & Tom Grace
Alison de Lima Greene
Elizabeth & John Harper
Kate Hawk
Amy Hertz
Karl Kilian

Terrell James
Alison Jefferies
Sis Johnson
Marilyn Jones & Brad Morris
Emily Keeton
Rex Koontz
Tracy & Glen Larner
Rich Levy
Victoria Ludwin
Kate McConnico
José Ramón Ruisánchez Serra
Bettina Elias Siegel
Melissa Sjulsen
Barbara & Louis Sklar
Lois & George Stark
Elizabeth Strelow
Eleanor Williams
Stephen & Lois Zamora

Contents: *vol. 27, issue 2*

FICTION

NONFICTION

POETRY

THE SOUND OF A PUPIL AN EYE ROLLS
POETRY IN TRANSLATION

ART LIES: ART & CRITICAL ART WRITING

BEES IN THE GARDEN
WRITING AFTER LANGUAGE'S ECSTATIC NECTAR

REVIEWS

Barthelme Prize Results, 2014
Judged by Amy Hempel

WINNER:

Emma Bolden, "Gifted"

HONORABLE MENTIONS:
Patty Yumi Cottrell, "No One Makes Plans"
Susan Lilley, "Delmonicos"

Gulf Coast Prize in Translation Results, 2014
Judged by Jen Hofer

WINNER:

Kristin Dykstra, for her translations of Marcelo Morales

HONORABLE MENTIONS:
Derick Mattern, for his translations of Haydar Ergülen
Yvette Siegert, for her translations of Ana Gorría

I venture to suggest this solution to the ancient problem: The Library is unlimited and cyclical. If an eternal traveler were to cross it in any direction, after centuries he would see that the same volumes were repeated in the same disorder (which, thus repeated, would be an order: the Order). My solitude is gladdened by this elegant hope.

—Jorge Luis Borges, "The Library of Babel," translated by J.E.I.

Dear Readers,

Who or what has saved your life? The inspiring shimmies of fairy godmothers and godfathers on the dance floor? Someone offering a place to crash when you were adrift in an unknown city? A friend once told us that books and libraries had saved her life. Not that they made her feel a little less horrible, but that their comfort and instruction delivered her from the edge of a terrifying emptiness. We believe her. We don't pretend that life or art exist without shadow. Since the release of our last issue, the bathroom graffiti down the hall from *Gulf Coast* no longer contains advice for mending a broken heart. Over the fall and early winter, several different hands have written, "Black lives matter," "#MuslimLivesMatter," and "all lives matter." Work such as L.S. Klatt's poem, "Big Sur," takes on greater valence in the context of the American zeitgeist, repeating "Let's not get killed" three times in eight lines. War, prisons, urban decline, the metaphorical burning of an uncle's chicken shed: all of these things are here, breathing in this issue, and there is no pithy rejoinder to "all lives matter" except to say, "Yes."

We've also identified a palpable anxiety over the state of the printed word. Now and again, folks talk about the book, with its breakable spine and quaint pages, as if it has already gone the way of the dodo. For some, the object resting in your hands is an anachronism, an obsolete holdover from previous centuries, a technological vestigial tail. Please don't misunderstand us; we have no desire to marginalize the internet. *GC Online* and other online journals satisfy our need for poetry and prose in ones and zeros. We too gaze into the mirrors of our iPads, tablets, and phones and blush. We are made giddy by flicking our fingers over a news article: Behold hundreds of words fleeing beyond our device's rectangular frame! But if, just now, you are holding this newest issue of *Gulf Coast*, we suspect you take silent pleasure in the feel and heft of its letterpressed cover, the rainbow colors popping out of our Art Lies folios, and the singular smell of glue and paper inside the spine.

We are not alone in our obsessions. This winter, nearly 35,000 people attended the LA Art Book Fair. Lovers of art, books, and art books swarmed around stalls of zines, the wares of independent publishers, and antiquarian book dealers. Though *Gulf Coast* does not fit precisely into those categories, we can safely say that every issue of the journal pays homage to the beauty and possibility of printed and bound matter. This Summer/Fall issue takes that reverence to another level by paying special attention to the book in form and content. With a dazzling letterpress cover designed and produced by Spindletop Design and Workhorse Printmakers here in Houston, we tip our hats to a long line of artists and technicians who have realized the book's physicality and beauty. Art Lies Editors Raphael Rubinstein and Lauren Greve have brought us artists, such as MANUAL and Pablo Helguera, who challenge us to rethink the book as art object and to consider the library as a place for art installation.

Libraries and museums, the palaces of books and art, invite us into a conversation capable of interrupting the complicit silence in ourselves: When we have broken that silence on the page, could we not do the same in our families and communities? The roundtable featuring early-career poets of color urges us to open our doors to visitors we have not anticipated. They urge us to reconsider form and subject and tradition and self so that we become fearless and capacious students of the world and all its creatures. Chitra Ganesh's installations and drawings also contain multitudes in their reimagining of mythology, narrative, desire, and paradigms of power. Our inaugural *Gulf Coast* Prize in Translation, which we have begun in order to further legitimize the work of translators and translation, not only complicates language dominance, but it gives our readers access to work that operates outside of English and American tropes. Whether or not you speak Korean, Spanish, Turkish, Hebrew, or the English represented in this issue, we hope your eyes and ears will delight in the polyvocality they bring *Gulf Coast*.

Spring is almost here, or so our senses tell us. Despite the cold, fruit trees have started to blossom. Lime green auras surround the branches of deciduous trees. Birds, busy and high up, at their work. So are all of the authors and artists represented here. So are you, our readers, in the fullness of your lives. In the fullness of Venetian glassblowers, Vespas, reunions, EMTs, radios, old photographs, the loss of someone—ecstasy and doubt mingle in us and in this issue and that is just right.

Adrienne Perry, *Editor* | Martin Rock, *Managing Editor* | Carlos Hernandez, *Digital Editor*

Translator's Note

Kristin Dykstra

We dedicate these poems to the memory of Migdalia Hernández Delgado.

Writing about time inevitably suggests loss—slippages in experience, human mortality. For *The World as Presence / El mundo como ser*, I considered specific valences of loss fragmenting the past as well as the insistently present present. On a related note, rather than translating *ser* with the dull thud of "being," I prefer the crisp and temporally loaded option of "presence."

Attentive readers will also notice that I added a phrase to one poem. I refer overtly to speaking in unison, whereas in the original work, Morales evokes unison in phrases often spoken by or (with persuasive intent) to groups. In other words, I cue the idea of unison for readers not initiated into the writer's language environment.

To some translators, cues of this length are transgressions because didacticism could overpower or disrespect other aesthetic elements. Up to a point, I agree. I don't advocate frequent addition to poetry, which so often relies on compression or suggestion over explanatory gesturing. But it's tedious to write in fear of rules, and here I choose a minor transgression. The unison cue can enhance a reader's feel for the pointillist shifts in voicing through which Morales' speaker admits and resists social locations.

Splinters from past realities slide into and out of focus in *El mundo como ser*. In what we call the Facebook poem, the splinters include voices from Morales' childhood education and state-oriented everyday life. They guided him toward becoming a certain kind of citizen, often prioritizing collective goals and identities. He foregrounds a struggle to create and retain a mature, coherent individuality under their long shadows. What makes *El mundo como ser* such a compelling manuscript is that his exercises in presence take form against the backdrop of Cuba's confusing transition into whatever its present was in 2014, and whatever it will become next.

36

El puntilleo constante del ser dentro de ti.

—Artaud

Un tanque de basura con humo, una moto que se enciende. Una bicicleta con letrero Marco Polo, en la radio, i want to know what love is. La niebla toca las flores como si no existiera. En Neptuno, un río de desempleados. La manera en que el terror funciona. El puntilleo constante del miedo dentro de ti, del amor dentro de ti. En la bodega estatal, un gato sobre la pesa de comprobación, un negocio privado, dos mundos que se encuentran, por primera vez, en mucho tiempo. Portales, calle Reina, suciedad del piso en mi cabeza, lozas partidas y mugrientas. Detrás de los cristales, héroes socialistas, flores plásticas. La niebla toca las flores como si no existiera. Un papel sucio flotando en la calzada, humo. En la radio, i want to know what love is.

Marcelo Morales

36

The constant stippling of presence within you.
—Artaud

A garbage bin spilling smoke, a motorcycle that catches fire. A bicycle with a Marco Polo sign, on the radio *I want to know what love is*. Fog grazes flowers as if it didn´t exist. On Neptuno Street, a river of the unemployed. The way in which terror functions. The constant stippling of fear within you, of love within you. In the state-run corner store, a cat on mechanical scales, a small private business, two worlds meeting for the first time in a long while. Portales, Reina Street, the filth from the floor in my head, tiles split and grimy. Behind the glass windows: socialist heroes, plastic flowers. Fog grazes flowers as if it didn't exist. A dirty paper floating across the road, smoke. On the radio *I want to know what love is*.

39

¿Qué estás pensando?
Facebook.
I think of Dean Moriarty.
Jack Kerouac. On the road.

I.

Yo pienso en los cristales de la nieve y en paisajes de un milímetro de diámetro y en organismos de un milímetro de diámetro y en universos de un milímetro de diámetro y pienso en cosas que han vivido sin ser vistas y en la estructura de la célula y en las olas que se elevan sobre el muro y en pancartas con consignas socialistas y en moléculas de ADN y en los close up de las películas del oeste y en el peso de la luz y en la onda de la luz y en la punta enrollada del helecho y en los días de mercurio y en las lágrimas de las lámparas de araña y en nosotros convirtiéndonos en otros y en nosotros convirtiéndonos en otros y pienso en mitocondrias y electrones y el espacio y en colillas aplastadas contra el piso y en nosotros convirtiéndonos en otros y en nosotros convirtiéndonos en otros y en estrellas que miramos en pasado, la cara de Jackie Chan descascarándose en un bolso y en los tres mil de la luz en un segundo y en nosotros convirtiéndonos en otros y en nosotros convirtiéndonos en otros y en nosotros convirtiéndonos en otros y en nosotros convirtiéndonos en otros.

2.

Yo pienso en el centro del sol y en el cable enrollado del teléfono y el formol de las manos de Guevara y en las raíces de los bosques y en los colores del lagarto y en tomografías de pulmón y en los dientes delanteros de las ratas y en nosotros convirtiéndonos en nada y en nosotros convirtiéndonos en nada y en nosotros convirtiéndonos en nadas y pienso en las rayas de la cebra y el boquear de los pescados en la tierra y en el basilo de kosh y en el eureka y en nosotros convirtiéndonos en

Marcelo Morales

39

What are you thinking?
Facebook.
I think of Dean Moriarty.
Jack Kerouac. On the road.

1.

I think about snow crystals and landscapes one millimeter in diameter and about organisms one millimeter in diameter and universes one millimeter in diameter and I think about things that have lived without ever being seen and about the structure of the cell and about waves that break over the wall and placards with socialist slogans and DNA molecules and closeups in westerns and about the weight of light and the waving of light and about the curled tip of a fern and about days of mercury and teardrop pendants on spider lamps and about us transforming ourselves into others and about us transforming ourselves into others and I think about mitochondria and electrons and space and cigarette butts crushed on the ground and about us transforming ourselves into others and about us transforming ourselves into others and about the stars that come into our sight out of the past, Jackie Chan's face peeling off a duffel bag, and the three thousand per second of light and about us transforming ourselves into others and about us transforming ourselves into others and about us transforming ourselves into others and about us transforming ourselves into others.

2.

I think about the center of the sun and the curled telephone cable and the formaldehyde with Guevara's hands and about the roots of the forests and about the lizard's colors and about lung scans and rat incisors and about us transforming ourselves into nothing and us transforming ourselves into nothing and us transforming ourselves into nothingness and I think about stripes on zebras and the gasping of fish on land and about tubercle bacillus and about the eureka and

nada y en nosotros convirtiéndonos en nada y nosotros convirtiéndonos en nadas y pienso en el gas de Júpiter y en nosotros convirtiéndonos en otros y en nosotros convirtiéndonos en otros y pienso el quantum y el enredo y en la noche que se extiende por los campos, el vacío que contiene la materia, el latido de mi tía en la pantalla y pienso en el núcleo del sol y pienso el centro del sol y en nosotros, convirtiéndonos, en otros.

3.

Yo pienso en esos objetos en el suelo donde se trancan las varillas de las puertas y en la mancha de Gorbachov y en el verde de los paños de hospital y el sentido de la lluvia y en la consciencia de la célula y en el azul de Urano y en los anillos de Urano y en las playas que se esconden en las perlas y en la electricidad de las neuronas, los relámpagos de nuestro cielo mental y pienso en las alas prietas de las gallinas prietas y en los quilos y en el óxido en la güira y pienso en Bosnia e Hiroshima y en Ruanda y en Bagdad y en Nagazaky y en la electricidad de las neuronas y en las tormentas de nuestros cielos mentales.

4.

Y pienso en la UMAP y en la revolución de cuando era un niño y en pioneros por el comunismo y en lo que ven los babalaos cuando empiezan a morirse y en patria o muerte venceremos, la luz de Sachsenhausen sobre hornos para infantes y pienso en arbeit macht frei y en las ondas de posibilidad y en las partículas de experiencia y en el campo unificado y en la liebre de los galgos y pienso en dios y en las carnadas. La coherencia entre la pudrición y la peste, entre la muerte y la peste, entre la descomposición y la muerte. Pienso en arbeit macht frei y en la muerte de Martí y en no me pongan en lo oscuro y en la muerte de Fidel y en a morir como un traidor y en la de Villena y Guiteras. Los ojos de Abel descansando sobre un plato y pienso en meteoritos y en neones y en apellidos terminados en kovsqui y en las células muertas de cuando yo era un niño y en los ojos de Abel descansando sobre un plato y en los ojos del Che tan abiertos en la muerte y pienso en arbeit macht frei y en Guantánamo y en las papilas de la lengua y en el sabor del hielo y

about us transforming ourselves into nothing and about us transforming ourselves into nothing and us transforming ourselves into nothingness and I think about the gases of Jupiter and us transforming ourselves into others and us transforming ourselves into others and I think about the quantum and entanglement and about night that lengthens across countrysides, the vacuum that contains matter, my aunt's heartbeat on the screen and I think about the sun's nucleus and I think the center of the sun and about us, transforming, into others.

3.

I think about those devices on the floor used for barring doors and about Gorbachev's stain and about the green of hospital scrubs and the meaning of rain and the consciousness of cells and about the blue of planet Uranus and the rings of Uranus and the beaches hidden inside pearls and about the electricity in neurons, lightning across our mental skies and I think about the brown wings of brown chickens and about kilos and about coins rusting inside gourds and I think about Bosnia and Hiroshima and Rwanda and Baghdad and about Nagasaki and electricity in neurons and about the storms in our mental skies.

4.

And I think about the camps run by Military Units to Aid Production and about the revolution when I was a boy and about the child-pioneers for Communism and speaking in unison and about what the babalawos see when their death first approaches and about ¡Patria o Muerte! ¡Venceremos!, about the light of Sachsenhausen falling on ovens for infants and I think about arbeit macht frei and about waves of possibility and about particles of experience and about unified field theory and the hare for greyhound racing and I think about god and decoys. The coherence of rot with pestilence, death with pestilence, decomposition with death. I think about arbeit macht frei and about Martí's death and about Don't leave me out in the dark and about Fidel's death and about dying as a traitor and about the deaths of Villena and Guiteras. Abel's eyes resting on a plate and I think about meteorites and neon lights and about surnames ending in kovsky and about the dead cells from when I was a boy and about Abel's eyes resting on a plate and

en pistolas impresas y en los átomos de hidrógeno y en las cruces que se asoman en la vía. Yo pienso en arbeit mach frei y en Valeriano. En la sonrisa de Bush y Berluscony. Yo pienso en arbeit macht frei.

5.

Yo pienso en los objetos artificiales de las ciudades del futuro y en el calor de los iglús y en la piel de las termitas y pienso en la claridad y en el lóbulo frontal y en la red de las neuronas y en el pasillo del oncológico cuando cae la noche y en las glándulas de la oncóloga cuando cae la noche y en la soberbia de la oncóloga cuando cae la noche y en la perra de la oncóloga cuando cae la noche y pienso en la ambición y en la búsqueda y en mi tía bajo la vía láctea y en marcelo bajo la vía láctea y en mi muerte bajo la vía láctea y en nuestras muertes bajo la vía láctea y en esos mundos en los que no voy a nacer, en los que no voy a morir, en los que nunca has nacido, en los que nunca has muerto y en los palillos dentales y en los bosques encerrados en los libros y en la madera de las páginas en blanco y en la fosforescencia de las rosas en la noche y en el amor de los perros y en las cosas que no sé de mí y en las que voy a saber y en la voluntad del salmón y en el mundo de los recién nacidos y en los ojos de los recién nacidos y en la lógica del cardumen y en mi tía bajo la vía láctea y en mi muerte bajo la vía láctea y en las especies extintas y el trabajo del bufón y la actitud de los bufones y en los hombres bombas y en las bombas y en lo que ven los poetas cuando empiezan a morirse y en lo que ven los poetas cuando empiezan a morir y en lo que ven los poetas cuando empiezan a morirse y pienso en los cisnes blancos de la nieve y en Praga y en la luna reflejada en dos mil charcos y en lo que ven los poetas cuando empiezan a morirse, la gomina en el pelo de Batista y en las cosas que se dicen al oído y pienso en el paraíso, el límite líquido del mundo de los peces, el cansancio de las tortugas en la arena, la desnudez gradual de toda alma, el aspecto del mundo en la escritura y lo que ven los poetas cuando entran al círculo y en lo que ven las personas cuando empiezan a morirse.

Marcelo Morales

about how very open Che's eyes were in death and I think about arbeit macht frei
and about Guantánamo and about the tongue's taste buds and about the flavor of
ice and about the three-dimensional printing of guns and about hydrogen atoms
and crosses that appear along the way. I think about arbeit macht frei and about
Valeriano. About Bush's smile, and Berlusconi's. I think about arbeit macht frei.

5.

I think about artificial objects in cities of the future and about the warmth of igloos
and about termite skin and I think about clarity and the frontal lobe and about the
neuron network and the hallways in the oncological hospital at nightfall and about
the oncologist's glands as night is falling and about the oncologist's arrogance as
night is falling and the bitchiness of the oncologist as night is falling and I think
about ambition and the search and about my aunt under the milky way and about
marcelo under the milky way and about my death under the milky way and about our
deaths under the milky way and about those worlds in which I will never be born, in
which I will never die, about worlds where you have never been born, in which you've
never died and about toothpicks and the forests enclosed in books and about the
wood of blank white pages and the way roses phosphoresce at night and about love
between dogs and about the things I don't know about myself and about the things
I will know about myself and about the salmon's fortitude and about the world of
newborns and the eyes of newborns and about the logic of schools of fish and about
my aunt under the milky way and my death under the milky way and about extinct
species and the fool's job and the fool's attitude and about suicide bombers and about
the bombs and about what poets see when they begin to die and what poets see
when their death first approaches and about what poets see when they begin to die
and I think about snow-white swans and Prague and the moon reflected across two
thousand puddles and about what poets see when they begin to die, the brilliantine
in Batista's hair and things that are murmured into ears and I think about paradise,
the liquid limit to the world for fish, the exhaustion of turtles in sand, the gradual
nakedness of all souls, the aspect of the world in literature and what poets see when
they enter the circle and about what people see when they begin to die.

6.

La curva del malecón a 140, la flor que me señaló mi tía el día antes, la inteligencia de mi padre, la primera vez que vi a mi hermano. El día que lloré por Cristo. El día en que conocí a Cristo. El Peugeot blanco de mi infancia. La luz de los corales fluorescentes, las flores de Julia en el balcón. El cura del barrio judío en la iglesia de Roma. El contra cielo en una hoja impresa. Los días del amor, la mañana en la frontera.

7.

La fuerza de los brazos mecánicos, las gotas de los sueros, la brillantez de la lluvia, las flores biseladas del espejo. La impresión de las sombras en las paredes de Nagazaqui. Las piedras falsas en las mezclillas de las gentes, la consciencia política, el socialismo de estado, la inquisición. Los juguetes plásticos, la muñeca sin brazos, las gotas en el frío del cristal, las encrucijadas de los pueblos. El polvo de los camiones. El reguetón en la playa, los tatuajes de presidio, la conciencia de clase. El mar, las pelotas que flotan como perlas. Las huellas de grasa en el garaje. Las palabras de Hatuey cuando iba hacia la hoguera. El cisne de yeso en el estante, las flores que cayeron en la iglesia.

8.

Explicar la poesía al tubo de la quimio de la tía, a la bolsa de quimio de la tía, a la gota de la quimio. El puntilleo constante. Un gorrión vuela sobre mi cabeza, un hombre lee, en una cara del tenis tiene un semicírculo rojo que completa un sol en el piso pulido, algunas cosas tienen que morir, otras, desaparecer, la idea de la poesía a una rata muerta, o mejor, la idea de la poesía de una rata muerta, en una rata muerta. A la manilla del reloj kichón decir: si la energía de tu vida no pasa por tu mano a la escritura. Explicar la poesía a una rata muerta.

Marcelo Morales

6.

The Malecón's curve at 140 kph, the flower shown to me the day before by my aunt, my father's intelligence, the first time I saw my brother. The day I cried for Christ. The day I came to know Christ. The white Peugeot from my childhood. Light from fluorescent coral, Julia's flowers on the balcony. The priest from the Jewish barrio in the Roman church. *Le contre-ciel* on a printed page. Days of love, morning at the border.

7.

The strength of mechanical arms, drops of mitomycin solution, brightness of the rain, beveled flowers in the mirror. The impressions of shadow on walls at Nagasaki. The fake jewels people wear on denim, political consciousness, state socialism, inquisition. The plastic toys, the doll without arms from that poem, drops on the cold glass, town crossroads. Dust from trucks. Regguetón on the beach, prison tattoos, class consciousness. The sea, balls that float like pearls. Greasemarks in the garage. Hatuey's words as he moved toward the bonfire. The plaster swan on the bookshelf, flowers that fell down in the church.

8.

Explain poetry to my aunt's chemo tube, to my aunt's chemo bag, to the chemo drops. A constant stippling. A swallow flies over my head, a man reads, a face on a sneaker includes a red semicircle that forms a complete sun against the polished floor, some things have to die, others must disappear, the idea of poetry to a dead rat, or better yet a dead rat's idea of poetry, on a dead rat. Say to the secondhand on your überkitschy watch: whether your life force does not pass through your hand into the writing. Explain poetry to a dead rat.

TRANSLATED FROM THE TURKISH BY DERICK MATTERN

Haydar Ergülen

İpsiz Şiiri

iplerden dolan da gel
olur kardeş sev beni

ipince akar su ipince
ipinden düşsün boynum ipince

suyun izini sürer uzun ipler tarihi
hükmü kara boynuna insin günü gelince

kaçarlar göçerler ipini kıran gelir
doksandokuz tepsihli avcılar peşlerinde

siz de sırandasınız bu ip herkese yeter
ipler yansın boynuma bir yağmur yürüdükçe

hamalbaşı bir ip buldum senin mi
yok efendi ben ipimi kiraladım ölüme

haylazlar eşkıyalar ipsizler...
ihya ettin beyamca öpülesi dilinle

ip ipler ipsizler bu ne biçim şiir be
dilerim boynun yetmez uzandığın iplere

oğlum ipini çözme o yarın kesilecek
n'olur ipi keselim baba kurban yerine

Poem Untied

come loose these bonds
be my brother and love me

thin as flowing water so thin
let my neck so thin slide from the rope

long as a length of water lasts the history of ropes
as for today let the sentence lift from your black neck

the leash has snapped the fugitives are on the loose
pursued by hunters with ninety-nine prayer ropes

you're nothing special—for everyone there's enough of this rope
let the rope burn my neck it's just a walk in the rain

hey porter I found a rope—is it yours?
no sir I've hired mine out to death

the layabouts and outlaws those unbound by the rope
lavish life on them good sir with your kiss-worthy words

rope ropes ropeless—what the hell kind of poem is this?
if only your neck would never grow long enough for the rope

don't untie the rope son it'll be cut tomorrow
instead of the sacrifice please papa let's slit the rope

Efendiler Gazeli

kayık karşıya varınca sizin gözleriniz umman
daldık efendim

yangın dile çıkınca sizin sözleriniz yağmur
kül'dük efendim

sır ortada kalınca sizin yalanınız baki
dil'dik efendim

müşkül ortak durunca sizin yatağınız viran
kaldık efendim

aşk yolundan taşınca sizin bahçeniz tarümar
olduk efendim

fener dahi sönünce sizin yıldınız zühre
gördük efendim

kul kendini bulunca sizin efendiniz kayıp
n'olduk efendim

biz hiç olmaz mıyız âşık, olduk efendim!

Efendim Ghazal

when the caique arrived your eyes were the ocean
your servant *efendim* fell in

when fire rises to the tongue your words were the rain
your servant *efendim* was the ash

when the secret lies in the open your lies linger
efendim on your servant's tongue

when troubles were partaged out your bed was a wreck
your servant *efendim* was the wreckage

when the path of love strayed your garden was devastated
your servant *efendim* was torn asunder

even when the light was quenched your star was brilliant
efendim your servant saw it

a servant comes into his own once the master has gone
if only *efendim* if only

you thought your servant would never fall in love
ah but *efendim* he did

TRANSLATED FROM THE SPANISH BY YVETTE SIEGERT

Ana Gorría

Siluetas

¿Para qué resistirse a la frontera? Hay un desvestimiento en las paredes en las que forjo el habla por extender la lengua; siempre como pequeñas marionetas en un teatro sin hilos, abrimos nuestras cuerdas vocales agitadas al viento que se esconde en las cornisas. Tu sombra ha iluminado cuanto de mi interpreta: la mujer impaciente que espera el autobús, aquel adolescente que llega tarde al cine y los que van al raso, sin abrigo, los que duermen y callan. Todo lo que se encuentra iluminado no es más que sombra exacta, propia del resplandor de una caverna de la que afloro con la brutal violencia del sexo golpeado por la sangre. Es a través del cuerpo que tira de los ojos por el que el contorno no es contorno; como un diminuto fuego fatuo tus ojos encendidos.

Silhouettes

Why resist at the border? The walls strip down. That is where I forge speech that will stretch my tongue. Always, like little marionettes performing without strings, we spread our vocal cords, shaken by gusts that lurk along the ledges. Your shadow illuminates whatever it found to interpret in me: the impatient woman waiting for a bus, the guy running late to the movies and those who go out in the cold without a coat, the ones who are sleeping and those who grow silent. But the thing that appears illuminated is nothing but a precise shadow, which was cast by the glow from a cave where I am blooming now with the brute force of sex that is rushing with blood. It comes from the body seen in someone's eyes. For that body, an outline is never an outline. And your eyes like a will o' the wisp, glowing faintly.

THE 2014 GULF COAST PRIZE IN TRANSLATION

HONORABLE MENTION YVETTE SIEGERT

Despliegues

Sobre los cauces de la memoria, arcos: hilos entre los vértices. La ligera espesura que media entre el paladar y los oídos, sonoros, lo que queda tan leve. Lo que pulsa hacia afuera. Como células que se multiplican, metástasis del aire. Ser soñada por ojos que han soñado que sueñas. Es rapidez. Abierta, una vez más, la cuenca del deseo apaga el día y la noche. Para dejar pequeños surcos que se abren, que se abren, que se abren. Con la fugacidad del propio rastro, del rostro que se hunde sobre sí mismo, elástico.

Ana Gorría

Unfolding

Over the currents of memory, arcs: threads between the vertices. The light viscosity that mediates between your palate and your ears, sonorous and remaining so weightless. It pulses outward. Like cells replicating: the air metastasizing. To be dreamed up by eyes that have dreamed of you dreaming. It is swiftness. Desire opens up again, like a basin. It has extinguished day and also night, and left small tracks that open, that open, that open. Swiftly effacing every trace, every face that sinks into itself, and so elastically.

THE 2014 BARTHELME PRIZE

JUDGED BY
AMY HEMPEL

"Gifted" has a breathless, headlong quality that never stalls out. It is acoustically interesting as well, and where there is repetition it is deserved, and delivers an additional beat through the final powerful line. "Delmonicos" is an homage to the grande dames of Florida—"they are dying out, the grand old ladies of Florida, along with the citrus fortunes long spent and the orange blossoms that crowned their heads when they were beauty queens," and the piece speaks to the death of an era, of a kind of life, in moving observations that capture these women exactly. "All I want in my life is a great abandonment," says the odd man in "No One Makes Plans." And this is more than the narrator can say for herself, seeing her reflection in a wig store window, and coming to an unsettling conclusion. There is a logic to the conversation reported here, without a line being predictable.

—Amy Hempel

Gifted
Emma Bolden

We were all in love. We were always in love. We wore cardigans and slipped off our shoes to run-stop-slide down the tiled hallways, into the tiled classrooms, through the tiled cavern that was the cafeteria. We were always moving and we never went anywhere. Except into their offices. Except into their classrooms. There they angled us into corners angled away from doors and windows and doors with windows. We were very bright. We learned very quickly. We were very bright and we learned very quickly about danger, which meant an open door, an open window. Which meant being seen. Every answer was obvious and every obvious thing was frightening. We were touched. We were kissed. We were touched again. Our hair was braided. Our fingers were braided. We promised, promised. We would never tell. We were fifteen, sixteen. We were seventeen. We were of an age but never of age. We smoked stolen menthols under the overpass, in the parking deck, in the lot across the street where all of our teachers parked. That is how they found us. That is how they knew us, the ones they said were ready, were ripe. We picked skim milk over chocolate milk. We were in ninth grade, tenth grade. We buckled into their passenger seats. We lay down in their backseats. We were laid down in their backseats. We folded beneath blankets in their floorboards. We whispered, *Is it okay? Is it all clear?* We kept quiet until our classmates passed. We kept quiet until another teacher passed, until the principal, the janitor, the policeman passed. We were fourteen, never eighteen. We were promised high grades and high praise. We were promised an audition at Juilliard. We were given Certs and Algebra II answer sheets. We received instructions. *Unzip me. Touch me. Let me touch you.* We hit puberty. We came to school with our breasts, with our combat boots. We knew only one definition of *coming* and so we were unable to translate correctly their wishes, their warnings, their lines from Catullus and Sartre. We were in eighth grade, eleventh grade. We were in seventh grade, and we were polite. We followed instructions and checked every answer. We were taught this way. We were taught this way. We were taught one way or another that *no* had a synonym, that its synonym was *yes*.

No One Makes Plans

"Patty," the man called out. "Patty, I've been looking for you."

I stopped what I was doing and said hello. The man leaned on his crutches and smiled. I liked the man because he was a composer of elegant musical compositions that sounded like snowfall. He also had an urgent way of talking that made him sound rich. Was he rich from writing his musical compositions or was he rich from his parents? I couldn't be sure. The man repeated that he had been looking for me, but he said it in a gentle way and offered to buy me a hot chocolate.

"I don't really like to drink chocolate," I said, "especially hot."

"It's hard for me to make friends," he said.

"Why do you think that is?"

"I call people to ask them to do things but they don't call me back."

"Do you think it's harder for you to make friends because of what happened to your leg?"

"I think it's harder for me to make friends because I'm older. Listen: I'm having a party later. Would you like to come? Other people will be there, too."

"I don't know," I said. "No one in this city makes plans with each other. Perhaps I will drop in, perhaps not. Either way, I'm not one to worry."

"That's right," said the man. "When we first met you conducted your business this way, do you remember? It was way back when you had long hair and now it's all gone."

"I did have long hair. And we eventually became friends and we've been friends for a long time."

"A lot has happened to me since then," said the man. "My mother and sister passed away and I moved out of my apartment and into a new one, but people can never run away from their problems, their complexities. All I want in my life is a great abandonment."

"Like a gray crumbling. Like the coral reefs scrubbed free of plankton."

"Like that," he said. "Like that."

Later that afternoon, on my way home, I saw a different man almost get hit by a bright yellow car in the crosswalk. The man was wearing a nylon jacket and the wind blew into it and puffed it out like an airbag. The bright yellow car jerked to a stop. The man in the nylon jacket pounded the windshield with his fist. The driver got out and yelled, "Hey!"

No one was injured. Suddenly I realized that remaining open to the city was perhaps at odds with my true nature. Personally, I did not like to take risks, only calculated ones that I could attempt to control or read about. I made vague gestures toward the reasonable and remained harmless, shiny with life, a tolerant Korean.

I looked at my reflection in the glass of a shop that sold wigs and wigs only.

There was some information there and I didn't know what to do with it.

Delmonicos

They are dying out, the grand old ladies of Florida, along with the citrus fortunes long spent and the orange blossoms that crowned their heads when they were beauty queens. Their graves wear flowers they called hydrangelas and spear lilies. They had their own language. In widowhood they traveled. When my grandmother went to Europe she had her hair done once and did not touch it for weeks. She might go up to Atlanta or down to Miamah for a funeral or a wedding, but would never board a plane to Chicargo. They were generous. They donated regularly to the Starvation Army and gave their maids and cooks old cocktail dresses and camellia cuttings, avocados, kumquats, and tangerines from the yard.

Some were teetotalers. Cousin Grover-Nell would order a Beefeater martini straight up *only* above the Mason-Dixon line. But my Granny and great-aunts blithely picked up fifths of bourbon with their delmonicos and maraschinos and long cartons of Benson & Hedges every week in the queenly light of high noon, fussing at the bagboy to stow everything just so in the back of Granny's Oldsmobile Ninety-Eight. They never seemed lonely. They loved gaudy costume jewelry and kept the real stuff in a safe. They sat at white and gold French Provincial dressing tables and patted their necks and shoulders with giant powder puffs. They wore slinky negligees into their 80s and read racy Hollywood exposés until three in the morning. Aunt Mary Belle trained her poodle to sit in a highchair and smoke cigarettes. Granny talked to faces she saw in the coquina-swirled walls of her bedroom. They attended thousands of cocktail parties. They sent elegantly signed checks to their grandchildren for birthdays, and at fancy restaurants they taught us girls to order Shirley Temples and lobster tails against our parents' wishes. If we wore denim in their presence, they moaned that we looked like field hands.

Then a few springs ago my own mother died. In her final weeks, the azaleas smelled so pink she hauled herself out of bed one day and said, "Honey, take me to ride!" I realized she was one of them. I drove her slowly past all the landmarks: her

newlywed duplex, the bougainvillea blooming along the ball field fence, and then the lake house where she and Dad raised us, where she laughed and cried and cooked dinner in the orange light of uncountable sunsets. She muttered that the tacky new owners had ripped out all the flame-of-the-woods, her name for ixora, a shrub with tiny starburst blooms.

I nodded and kept my mouth shut. I learned as a child that you could argue with them all you like, insist the movie with Elizabeth Taylor and a horse is not called *Natural Velvet*, nor is what they served with tomato aspic and canned asparagus called college cheese, and the day after Friday is not Seerdy. They could take a lot of heartbreak. They would do anything for you. But they would not be corrected.

Rachel Howard

On Modeling and Mortification

I wish that everyone could have the experience of posing naked for a group of good artists at least once.

At the beginning of every session, yes, there is fear. You receive instructions—whether to do a set of two-minute "gesture" poses, or perhaps fives or tens; standing or sitting or reclining or a mix—and then you press "start" on your timer and drop the robe. It is arousing and unnerving, the first few seconds, to feel the air on your buttocks and your breasts. You reach for the sky or you lunge or you twist as though swinging a baseball bat. You are trying to do something that looks like a real, human action, something that is not two-dimensional but rather traverses three planes. Something that gives the artists a line of force to observe, or perhaps a bit of negative space to work with compositionally, or a challenge of foreshortening to solve. You are trying to do all this and you are hoping that your thigh bearing all the weight of that lunge will hold out for three minutes, and you are worried that the twist in your spine will make your latissimus dorsi spasm. By the third or the fourth pose, your muscles are warm, your neck loose, you are reasonably confident that you will not fall down, and the *scratch-scratch-scratch* of mark-making has cast its hypnosis. You breathe deeply and steadily. You feel a particular man or woman's eye trained intensely on your collarbone or your crotch.

When the break comes, you slip on your robe, roam the room. Often, something that you hate about yourself—the spread of your thigh, the sprawl of your nipples—surprises you as beautiful on the artist's page.

———✦✦———

I started modeling at 32, to keep myself fed while I wrote a novel. I was by that point eight years into what I suppose is called a "spiritual practice." Initially, there was a clarifying horror to be had in walking into the vaulted space of Grace Cathedral and feeling small and mortal, and I began to seek such experiences at other times in the week. I found them elusive, until my divorce, when suddenly— even just trying to rent a new apartment, drinking alone in well-lit bars—I shook with fear, feeling exposed and at the mercy of the world. Mortified by divorce, I was fragile; I became keenly thankful to God for every moment that passed without that fragility being shattered. Feeling I could just about die, I was alive. But I was also plenty young and attractive, and the sharpness of the vulnerability dulled, or at least became more known and managed and therefore less truly threatening over many nights alone, many cycles of hope and disappointment with men I wanted not just to be loved by but to love. Much of my increasing security came, I believe now, because I started modeling.

My first husband co-founded a women's magazine devoted to plastic surgery. When we had just started dating, and I was 22 and he was 30, he asked me to play a game rating the waitresses at a cocktail bar on a scale of 1-10. He then told me I was a "7." (In love and naïve, I had been on the verge of telling him he was a "9.5," thinking the half-point off would convince him of my sincerity.) A year into our marriage, when I was about to publish a memoir, he told me I should get the mole above my right eye removed for my author photograph. Just after we split, when I had lost 10 pounds from heartsickness, I ran into him at the gym as I was heading to the pool in a bikini. My ex-husband eyed the hint of curve beneath my belly button and said, "Don't lose any more weight, or you'll be too skinny." A smile snuck onto his lips. "If you want to get rid of that last bit of fat, go for liposuction."

———— ◆ ◆ ————

Three years later, in my first months of modeling, everything from the arch of my foot to the "volume" of my thighs was suddenly cause for fascinated observation. And as much as this experience of being fully seen can lead you to accept yourself, modeling can also cause you to let go of yourself. When you strip, fully strip, you forfeit the signals of your social identity and your status. No flattering hemline or chic belt or classy earrings. You are just a body. I suppose this could be mortifying. But to me, to my surprise, it was freeing.

My behavior while clothed changed. If I were at a party and got caught up in trying to be a certain version of myself, if I noticed I wasn't listening to people because I was so concerned with what they thought of me, I would stop and remember what it felt like to pose. I would think, *just be naked*.

———— ◆ ◆ ————

In my third year of modeling, while posing for a drop-in community drawing group at UC Berkeley, I was approached by a soft-spoken artist with tufts of blonde on the rims of his ears. Dave did not hit on me; he asked me to pose for the drawing class he was teaching. I posed for his class, a little flummoxed by his request for twisty, odd poses, and a few months later, when I saw him at a party, I gave him my email address.

Our first three dates consisted of having a drink at a local watering hole and talking about ballet and art, rather stiffly at first. But then Dave said he played the piano, and when I told him I had just begun singing jazz standards at a dive piano bar, we made an afternoon appointment at his house to try out some songs together. I sang "The Man I Love" over Dave's chord changes. I was terrible. Dave didn't judge. Did my vulnerability as a model, his empathy as an artist, make our relationship possible? I think so.

Two months after that date, I got a job on the other side of the country. Almost instantly, Dave and I decided we would move together. As soon as we arrived, we eloped.

— • —

When Dave and I left for North Carolina, I was 35. When we moved back to California, I was 37. To others the physical changes of those two years might seem small. To me they seemed decisive. I felt every cell in my body flipping the switch from youth and growth to slow decay.

I had gained five pounds. Tiny growths caused by sun damage dotted the whites of my eyes. Black hairs sprouted from my chin and grey hairs from my temples, and the forehead crevasse that used to appear only when I was deep in thought had become part of my resting visage. But I resumed posing the day we got back to San Francisco. That first gig was for a group of classical realists. On the break, I saw that they had all drawn the forehead crease.

I have watched female models react in different ways to middle age. Lisa L. was in her fifties when I first saw her pose, though she could have passed for forties. I don't know what her posing was like in her youth, but by mid-life, she was fixated on sexy costumes. A frilly corset, a lace parasol, a string of pearls between her breasts, a red satin ribbon wrapped around her thighs: Lisa L's props made me curiously embarrassed for her. I was thinking of Lisa L. when, at 34, I told my boyfriend at the time that I would not model past 40, that doing so seemed "not natural."

But while I was getting my first grey hairs in North Carolina, another Lisa— Lisa D.—was changing her Bay Area Models Guild roster description to read, *Hair: salt and pepper*. I sat in on one of her modeling sessions a few months after moving back to Oakland. Her curls were unabashedly white-streaked, and raisin-sized moles sprouted proudly from her cheeks. She had, as always, some extra "volume" at her hips, but the rest of her was muscle. In a twenty-minute set of gestures, she touched her toe to the back of her head, flung herself across the male model on the stand like a woman launched out of cannon, and balanced on one leg like a body-building Aphrodite. The artists howled.

Lisa D. would be my inspiration.

⸻ ◆ ⸻

Yet I tend to throw myself not into powerful poses, but desperate ones—grasping, cowering, shielding myself as though about to be struck. Despite the fear suggested by these poses, when I am holding them I feel strong, and I feel I am being myself, not some idea of an "attractive" woman. I suppose that in these poses, it seems to me, I am a vulnerable human animal. And if I am being animal, I am not trying to be sexy or not-sexy. Or so I hope. Defenselessness as a form of defense against falsity.

⸻ ◆ ⸻

The fears are a bit different in these waning years of my thirties. I still have a phobia about losing control of my bladder and mentally monitor my genitals for any hint of dampness, sometimes imagining that a bead of liquid has begun to run and then, during the break, blotting myself with a paper towel to discover the sensation was all in my head. (One time, it was not in my head. I finished a pose and spotted a crimson drop racing down my thigh. I ran to the bathroom, and my period commenced in a gush. Fortunately the artists did not seem to notice that warning rivulet of blood.)

But now, many times before dropping the robe, I think of the darkening age spots along my jaw, the multiplying dimples below my ass. I worry that my poses, which are spontaneous, might direct attention to my varicose veins or to the stretch marks on my breasts.

But still I model.

⸻ ◆ ⸻

I do just one or two gigs a week now. Dave insists that I model only when I want to, for its own sake. So I turn down jobs for the motorcycle-jacket-wearing drawing teacher at the overly expensive animation college who always shows up 15 minutes late and talks endlessly about his ex-wives while the poor 19-year-olds hoping for his instruction throw their parents' money down the drain. I stopped accepting requests from the leader of a drawing group held in a drafty Sausalito warehouse who likes to test his models with bizarre props, thrusting hula hoops or wads of pink tissue paper at us and saying, "Ah, now the pressure's on!" (Once upon a time, that artist landed me in an ambulance. I had a sinus infection and couldn't find a replacement; when I said I was sick he answered, "Well, I hope you can still do active poses, because we like lots of energy." I took Sudafed to get through and later that night, while I was working a second gig at an animation company, the exhaustion and the medicine combined to make me pass out.)

— ◆ —

Every week I ask myself when it will be time to just stop. And then a few months ago, right after my 38th birthday, something disturbing happened.

I was modeling for an undergraduate class on the last day of the semester. "Just do whatever," the professor said.

Five or six students were setting up their easels in silence. A handful of shy girls and just one awkward, pimpled boy in a ball cap who kept his chin tucked toward his chest in a disjointed way as though he had either Asperger's or some kind of medical issue. "I'll be across the hall in my office," the professor said. Then he left.

I dropped the robe and did some gestures, feeling strangely apologetic, as though I were the detention monitor. I got the sense that this professor hadn't taught much all semester—and that because these students had not been taught to see, my naked body was no more notable to them than the greying polyester curtain in the corner. It would be hard to be the vulnerable human animal in this situation, but moving on to the longer poses, I tried, looking over one shoulder as though on alert for danger. The room was silent save for the occasional skid of an easel leg or a cell phone buzzing in a pocket. *Just be*, I was thinking. *Just be, and in two hours this will all be over.*

Then the boy began to cough and spasm. He knocked over his easel and jerked around the room like a fish on a hook.

The other students looked away in the manner of people who have just spotted a person they wish to avoid coming toward them on the street. Perhaps they had taken their behavioral cues from the professor who couldn't be bothered to teach them. Whatever the cause, their refusal to acknowledge the boy alarmed me.

Should I break the pose? But then the boy seemed to recover. Jerkily he walked to the easel the professor had left behind. *What the hell?* He picked up the professor's charcoal and made some marks on the professor's paper. The other students saw. They saw that I saw. Had he done this before? With lurching steps, his elbows pinned to his sides and his hands held like claws, the boy spasmed back to his easel. Maybe it was over. Please, I thought, let that be over.

Still I was naked, watching all of this from my peripheral vision, motionless. If there was one imperative I had learned as a model, it was that you don't move until the timer rings. As long as you don't move, you are protected, sealed behind the imaginary glass of professionalism that the client has paid you to maintain. As long as you don't move, you are just an object. And I wanted, more than anything at that moment, to be just an object.

The professor walked back in and made a cursory tour, looking at the students' drawings as though fearing they'd ask for instruction. He stopped at the easel he'd set up and abandoned, where the spasming student had made his frenetic marks. *Thank God*, I thought. *He'll see what happened and step in.*

"Hey now," the professor said with a false little laugh. "Looks like someone's played a practical joke." The boy said nothing. The other students said nothing. The professor left.

Still I was posing. Five minutes passed.

Again, the boy began to flail and choke, this time violently. He stumbled in front of his easel, folded over, lurching toward me and then away. I tried to make eye contact—no one would meet my eyes. But if the boy lost consciousness . . .

I said gently to the boy, "Are you all right?"

And in that moment, I realized that in trying to pose like the vulnerable human animal, I had been hoping the "animal" would cancel out the "human." But right then, more truly than in months, I was a naked woman. Holding out a hand to this boy, speaking in a concerned voice, breaking the invisible wall. How did the students see me? As a woman the age of their mothers, with the middle-aged body and face of their mothers. Acting like a mother and yet, naked.

It was like being inside a dream in which you realize that everyone else is clothed and you are not, and you feel you should cover yourself or dash behind a tree, but you can't.

As though I had broken a spell, the boy stopped shaking and returned to his easel, mumbling, head curled to chest. I resumed posing. During the break I put on my robe, and hurried to the professor's office.

"Oh, yes," the professor said. "Carl sometimes has seizures. If he's better now, you can just carry on."

I trembled through the rest of my poses. I trembled through the rest of the day, shaking as I drove. I gripped the rail for balance as I carried my modeling bag up the stairs and back into the apartment I share with my husband. I thought of how I would describe the experience to him.

I did not feel merely embarrassed, and the quickness of my pulse, the prickle on my skin suggested the opposite of deadness. Mortification. I looked it up: *Common forms of mortification today include fasting, walking barefoot, motion by pious kneeling or laying face down on the floor.*

Or: nakedness.

In that classroom with that flailing boy, mortification had brought me back to the state of alertness, of fragility, of gratitude to God for my preservation that I had known during my earliest experiences of the cathedral, during those too-exposed months just after my divorce. But how strange the suffix of that word "mortification," the implication that we are the ones who make ourselves as if dead and reborn.

The truth is that I will probably not model much more in middle age; lately I feel that time is past. Perhaps this is right. It feels too contrived to continue modeling in the way of a self-righteous believer, as though falling to my knees, congratulating myself on the infliction of humility and pain. The shock of mortification cannot be willfully repeated, only welcomed. If we are fortunate, the clarity it brings might remain with us for a few weeks, or a few months, until the vulnerability becomes managed once more.

Our protections are illusory and yet, we think, so reliable. We conceive of vulnerability as the willingness to risk exposure and pain, with the assumption that if we allow ourselves to be vulnerable, we will be the lucky ones, we will be spared the inevitable loss.

But in the end we will all be naked. We will all be in pain.

And so, for the chance to feel this truth, I still model.

physiognomy

Black animals fill the face, silhouettes, buildings fill the face, an alphabet fills the face.

Inside the face, black animals grow, they animate the data, form a demography of day, stained and soiled undershirts, they die or ask to be fed, they walk with their misshapen feet toward every kind of wild. Their hollow bells cringe against a tabernacle of idleness, the carnivores, the maggots, dogs loose from their leash. The too-white walls of them raw and exposing us like throats above the collar of a dress.

The animals arc dusks remembering, their secret bodies blackening below the aftermath, their light sail lifted to gather speed.

The face grows bright with bones, and is bird-crazed, and the sculptures. Its python ribs: finger bones unnerved, finger bones predicting how the wind will empty. Its coast at last has closed its fist. Its little thistle called the mind, a hinged thing finding its options.

Natalie Shapero

Hard Child

So I had two lists of names for a girl, so
what. The president's allowed to
have two speeches, in case the hostage
comes home in a bag. The geese
in the metropark don't want
for bread crumbs, despite the signs
proclaiming the land provides them all
they need. I was a hard child, by which
I mean I was callous from the start.
Even now, were I to find myself, after
a grand disease or blast, among the pasty
scattering of survivors, there isn't one
human tradition I would choose to carry
on. Not marking feast days, not
assembling roadside shrines, not marrying
up, not researching the colloquialism
STATEN ISLAND DIVORCE, not
representing paste pearls as the real
things, not recounting how the advent
of photography altered painting,
soured us on the acrylic portrait, thrust us
toward the abstract, sent us seeking
to capture in oil that which film would
never be wasted on: umbrella stands,
unlovely grates, assorted drains, body casts.
I typically hate discussing the past
and treasure the option, rarer and rarer,
to turn from it, as when K's twins
were born and one of them
nearly died—I don't remember which,
that's how much they got better.

THE SOUND OF A PUPIL AN EYE ROLLS:

poetry in translation

El país de hielo X

Y como un congelado sol muerto,
la Antártica subía amaneciendo
frente a la enloquecedora costa

Blanca   como una noche al revés levantándose sobre el
cielo demencial de esas heladas   así iba subiendo la
Antártica y era igual que un sueño el sueño muerto que
subía   yermo   recortándose frente a la escarchada costa

Y era como un sueño muerto la costa emergiendo
bajo los hielos

Dejando entrever las congeladas ciudades en el
borde del mar y arriba del mar los témpanos aún
amoratados del amanecer

Allá   cuando extendido debajo de los témpanos
se vio el cielo y como una gigantesca mañana
muerta la Antártica ascendió sobre el congelado
cielo sudamericano

Sobre el congelado aire   sobre el horizonte donde se va
levantando la mañana y es solo la blancura infinita de la
Antártica amaneciendo igual que un gigantesco planeta
muerto sobre las ciudades congeladas   sobre el océano
congelado   sobre el largo país congelado para siempre
bajo los demenciales témpanos del martirio y de la noche

Raúl Zurita

The Country of Ice X

And like a frozen dead sun,
Antarctica ascended awakening
before the maniacal coast

White   like a night in reverse lifting itself over the demented
sky of those frosts   that's how Antarctica ascended and it
was just like a dream the dead dream that ascended   barren
outlined before the frosted coast

And the coast emerging beneath the ice was like a dead
dream

Exposing a glimpse of the frozen cities on the edge of
the sea and above the sea the icebergs still bruised
purple from the dawn

There   when spread beneath the icebergs the sky
appeared and like a giant dead morning Antarctica
ascended over the frozen South American sky

Over the frozen air   over the horizon where the morning is
rising and it's only the infinite whiteness of Antarctica
dawning just like a giant dead planet over the frozen cities
over the frozen ocean   over the long country frozen forever
beneath the demented icebergs of the agony and of the night

La guerra de los huertos 14

Allá en las felices mañanas, cuando los árboles se cubren de naranjas, de azucenas de fuego, entre noviembre y diciembre, y en la escuela es la fiesta de exámenes, y mamá acomoda los panales, y nace el jazmín, multiplicado al millón, como una Virgen-María infinita, y el gladiolo santísimo levanta sus llamas blancas, sus ramas blancas, cuando se para el jardín de gladiolos frente a la casa como un navío de velas delirantes, y mamá viene remando en el mar de gladiolos, en esa marea blanquísima que inunda la chacra, la casa de los vecinos, los más lejanos prados, y todos nos morimos dulcemente.

Marosa di Giorgio

The War of the Orchards 14

On all the happy mornings, when the trees get covered in oranges, in lilies of fire, between November and December, and in school during the exam festivities, and Mother arranges the honeycombs, and the jasmine appears, multiplied by a million, like an infinite Virgin Mary, and the most holy gladiolus lifts its white flames, its white branches, when the gladiolus garden is stopped by our house like a ship of raving candles, and Mother comes rowing in the sea of gladioli, in this whitest tide that inundates the farmhouse, the neighbors' house, the most distant meadows, and all of us die sweetly.

La guerra de los huertos 16

Cuando todavía habitábamos la casa del jardín, al atardecer, cuando llovía, después de la lluvia, esos extraños seres, junto a los muros, bajo los árboles, en mitad del camino. Sus colores iban desde el gris más turbio hasta el rosado. Unos eran pequeños y redondos como hortensias; otros, alcanzaban nuestra estatura. Allí, inmóviles; amenazantes; pero, sin moverse. Mas cuando la noche caía del todo, ellos desaparecían sin que nunca supiésemos cómo ni por dónde.

Entonces, los abuelos nos llamaban, nos daban la cena, los juegos, regañaban. Nosotros hacíamos un dibujo, apasionadamente; lo teníamos de gris, negro, gris, de color de hortensia.

La lluvia del jardín.

Marosa di Giorgio

The War of the Orchards 16

When we still lived in the garden house, when it rained at dusk, after the rain, those strange beings, alongside the walls, under the trees, in the middle of the path. Their colors ranged from turbid gray to pink. Some were small and round, like hydrangeas; others reached our height. There, immobile; threatening, but motionless. But when night fell over everything, they vanished without anyone knowing how or where they'd gone.

Then, our grandparents called us; they gave us dinner, games, scolding us. Often we'd make a drawing, passionately; we shaded it black, gray, hydrangea-colored.

Rain in the garden.

נהר המקונג

הַלַּיְלָה חָלַפְתִּי עַל שָׁלוֹשׁ מְטוֹת
כְּמוֹ שַׁטְתִּי בַּמֶּקוֹנְג
וְלָחַשְׁתִּי אֶת יְפִי הַפְּרָת וְהַחִדֶּקֶל.
מִתַּחַת לְרֶגַע הַתָּמִיד
מְחַפֶּשֶׂת
מִתַּחַת לַצִּיץ הַשְּׂמָאלִי
יֵשׁ לִי חוֹר
וְאַתָּה מְמַלֵּא אוֹתוֹ
בִּגְבָרִים אֲחֵרִים.
רֵיחַ שֶׁל בִּירָה "טַייְגֶר"
עַל גּוּפְךָ.

בִּבְדִידוּת,
יֵשׁ רַעַשׁ צְרָצָרִים מִדָּרוֹם לְלָאוֹס.
מִמְטְרוֹת שֶׁל אֲוִיר קַר מֵהַאֲנוֹי
הַגַּב מִתְנַשֵּׁף
הַיַּשְׁבָן מִהַדֶּק; כֶּתֶם דְּיוֹ עַל הַבֶּטֶן.
צַיֵּר לִי תַּרְשִׁים זְרִימָה
בְּצֶבַע אָחִיד
עַל פְּרָחִים טְרִיִּים
בָּאֲגַרְטֵל.
אַשְׁפִּיךְ לְמַרְגְּלוֹתֶיךָ שָׁרָשִׁים,
רוֹצָה לִגְמֹר לְהָקִיא גַּרְגְּרֵי
אָבָק
בְּעֶרְוָתִי. הַנַּח אֶת יָדְךָ
בְּתוֹךְ תַּחְתּוֹנַי. תִּהְיֶה אִישִׁי
מִי מֵעַז לַעֲזֹב מַחֲלָה בְּאֶמְצַע יָם?

TRANSLATED FROM THE HEBREW BY ADRIANA X. JACOBS

Vaan Nguyen

Mekong River

Tonight I moved between three beds
like I was sailing on the Mekong
and whispered the beauty of the Tigris and Euphrates
under an endless moment
looking
under the left tit
I have a hole
and you fill it
with other men.
Notes of Tiger beer
on your body.

Alone,
crickets drone south of Laos.
Showers of cold air from Hanoi
the back gasps
the tight ass, an ink stain on the belly.
Sketch me a monochrome
flow chart
on fresh
potted flowers.
I'll release roots at your feet,
I want to come to puke specks
of dust
in my crotch. Rest your hand
in my pants. Make it personal
Who abandons an illness in open sea?

나는 문득 어머니의 없었던 연애 같은 것이 서러워지기 시작했네

화단에 앉아 어머니가 비눗방울을 날리고 있네 아버지는 나의 목마를 타고 나가서 돌아오지 않고 병뚜껑을 가지고 놀던 우리는 배 속에 검은 똥을 담고 잠드네라면 스프를 손바닥에 조금씩 부어 먹지 오빠야 나는 나의 외계 속에서 바닥, 나고 싶을 뿐이야 누이들이 밤이 되자 몰래 달력의 흰 뒷면에 눈이 큰 미미들을 그려 넣었네 새들의 발목에 붙은 개미는 드디어 지상을 떠났네 인공위성이 잠들지 못하는 이마들을 지나치며 먼 하늘에서 눈알을 기리릭 굴렸네 중세의 수도원 첨탑의 창문에서 죽은 비눗방울들이 이쪽으로 날아왔네 우리의 겨드랑이에도 촛불들이 조금씩 자라기 시작했네 껍질 벗겨진 쥐들이 모여 앉아 떨고 있는 계단에서 서로의 미래를 바꾸며 노는 아이들 나는 언제쯤 이 모래성을 완성할 수 있을까 목욕탕에 놓고 온 인형이 하천을 헤엄쳐 왔네 집으로 돌아오지 않고 이빨들을 떨면서 떨어진 손가락들을 집어 물에 씻고 있었네 우리 집 공주들은 모두 커가면서 담배를 물고 사진을 찍지 「브란덴부르크 협주곡」이 흘러나오는 피아노 학원 그 옆을 지날 때에 아이들은 뭉크처럼 귀를 막고 뛰었네 지붕 위에서 개구리들이 사라진 목젖을 쿨럭거렸네 어머니가 긴 머리를 바닥에 풀고 지우개로 방 안으로 들어오는 불빛을 지우기 시작했네 어머니 등을 긁어드릴게요 누가 뭐래도 우리는 어머니의 등을 긁어주며 자랐네 밤마다 어둠은 문짝에 대고 손가락을 부수면서 낄낄거리고 농구(農具)처럼 어두운 바람의 지느러미들이 땅에 끌리는 것을 바라보며 나는 창문을 올리고 무서워 누군가의 발걸음이 들릴 때마다 무수한 불빛의 환상을 흔들어주던 그 밤을 잊지 못하네 수녀복을 입은 어머니가

My Sorrow Suddenly Began Like a Love for Mom that Never Existed

mom sitting in a flower bed blowing a soap bubble / dad riding my wooden horse / not returning / and playing with a bottle cap / we have black shit in our stomach and sleep / sprinkle a little ramen powder on our palm and let's eat / older brother, the floor inside my outer world / that is the thing that I want to be / sisters at night secretly draw Korean barbies with big eyes on the white back of a calendar / riding a bird's ankle, the ant finally topples to the ground/ while a satellite passed a forehead that can't sleep on the earth, in the distant sky a pupil rolls back into its head with a shiver / from the window of a steeple on a house of worship in the middle ages, dead soap bubbles flew in this direction / inside our armpits, little by little, the candlelight began to grow / while skinned mice sit gather on trembling stairs and exchange their futures, the kids that are playing ask "can we complete the sand castle now?" / a doll that was accidentally left in the bathtub swam to the river / not returning home, teeth chattering, it grabbed its fingers that fell off and washed them in the water / princesses at our house grew big biting cigarettes and taking pictures / when they passed the piano school where the sound of the Brandenburg Concertos flowed, they covered their ears like Munch and ran / on the roof frogs with missing uvulas croaked / mother loosened her hair to the floor, grabbed an eraser, and began to erase the light entering the room / mom, I will scratch your back / whatever anybody says, we were raised scratching mother's back / nightly while giggling, darkness smashes its fingers in the door / and while staring at the dark wind's fins being dragged across the ground like a shovel, I open the window and am scared / every time I hear the footsteps of a stranger, I can't forget the

화단에 앉아 수백 개의 면도날을 날리고 있네 뒤집어진 트럭
속을 드나들며 놀던 나는 죽은 아이들이 돌아가고 나면 혼자서
어머니의 없었던 연애 같은 것을 서러워하기 시작했네

night when the vision of the scary light rocked into my life / Mom in a nun's habit sitting in a flower bed throwing hundreds of safety razors / hanging out inside a flipped truck that that I used to play in, if the dead children return / then I am alone / and so my sorrow began like a love for mom that never existed

hablan de un profundo rencor

hablan de un profundo rencor
de abandono
de un derrame interno

dicen que todo era relámpago de fuego
que dios salió corriendo
con un rebozo en la cabeza

el mar se fue despellejando
piel de caracoles

pero no
nosotros no nos enteramos del suceso
hemos estando bailando
y andamos un poco perturbados

José Eugenio Sánchez

they speak of deep resentment

they speak of deep resentment
of abandonment
of internal bleeding

they say that everything was a bolt of fire
that god took off running
a shawl thrown over his head

the sea was peeling
the skin off of snails

but we
we don't realize what's happened
we've been dancing
and on we go a bit unbalanced

The Happy Few

Three women sit beside a dock, facing a flat gray sea. They huddle in blankets in lawn chairs, sipping red wine, and shiver under the white sun. It is early spring.

They have gathered for their thirty-fifth high school reunion, not in Bristol, Connecticut, where they grew up and went to Catholic school together, but at Penelope's summer home in Maine. Penelope has the summer home in Maine and a brownstone in Brooklyn. She is the acknowledged beauty of the group, and her unexpected ascendance to the leisure class has preserved her girlish ethereality. She's long and languid, like a grape vine, with a thick spray of black ringlets and a thin, arching nose. Not much has changed since her yearbook photo, where she wore her hair down, no makeup, with black hooded eyes staring away from the camera, as if she were already dreaming her way out of Bristol. The only difference is that now she looks settled, without that raw, sullen yearning.

In her yearbook photo, Didi—the class secretary—had heavy bangs and a smile that turned her eyes into raisins. The years have drained and soured Didi. She sports a disorderly, faded-blonde pixie cut, with spikes of white popping out of the mess. All the sharp, odd-angled bones in her face have come forward, making her look gaunt and exhausted. She is a nurse at Bristol Hospital, where her husband is the director of security. She spearheaded this anti-reunion.

Janis is short and compact, her hair brown and thin and straight. In the yearbook, she was all circles: long oval face, enormous saucer glasses spotlighting shiny patches of upper cheek. She used to envy Penelope's hair and skin, curse her own stubborn acne. Now she comforts herself with the notion that at least she never had looks to lose. She had that blessing. This morning, heading to the airport with her son, she caught herself in the cab's rearview mirror and thought: I look like a boiled pot sticker. It's a relief to age, to give in to sexlessness. She carries a few extra pounds around her waist, which makes a big difference on her small frame; she thinks of her belly as a buffer against the world.

Right now she is trying hard not to be envious of Penelope's summer home, her twenty acres of pristine woods, the white yawl bobbing idly by the dock, the fleeting, almost bashful references to rarefied dinner parties and unknown restaurants in New York. Janis and her husband have visited Penelope's place in Park Slope, had brunch at a tiny bistro that felt like a neighborhood secret. But this is her first time at the summer home—Penelope and Geoff built it three years ago—and somehow the fact that it's an ugly, clapboard structure, smutty brown, no frills, strikes even harder at Janis's sense of deprivation. Penelope and Geoff are so rich they don't care about things looking nice. Janis knows these feelings are silly: she has done absurdly well, with her partnership in a law firm, her husband the city planner, her son about to graduate from Swarthmore, her home in Lower Merion. Considering the Archie-and-Edith house she grew up in, considering her brother the convicted felon, Janis should consider herself among life's winners.

———◆◆———

"Oh God," Didi says. "I've been meaning to tell you. Guess who died?"

"We're too young for this game," Penelope says. "Who?"

"Mike Napolitano."

"Who was Mike Napolitano?"

"Two years ahead of us. Basketball player. Dated Claire Delaney."

"Was he the one who sang 'American Woman' on a table in the cafeteria?"

"Uh huh. After they broke up. Oh, I had such a crush on him."

"How did he—?"

"Suicide," Didi pronounces.

The women observe a stilted pause. They were best friends for four years, and they still live in rough proximity, but their contact has long been erratic: three-hour phone calls at six-month intervals, in-person gatherings every other year. At times, their familiarity feels improvised.

Janis pulls her blanket tighter and concentrates on the blurry horizon, on pale lumps of island.

"Well, you know he was bipolar," Didi continues, chopping off a hunk of cheese with a little, thick-handled knife. "We had no idea back then. We just thought he was Italian and emotional. But yeah, he went through three or four colleges and finally ended up in an institution. And then his whole life was either institutions or his parents' home. Working a little, I think—gas station, convenience stores—until his parents died and he moved into a group home in Fairfield. And one morning they found him hanging in his room. Isn't that something?" Didi bites down on some cheese. She chews for a moment. "I hadn't thought of him in years, and on impulse I Googled and—three months ago, he died. Just like that."

"How awful," Penelope murmurs. And then, with a slight adjustment of her narrow shoulders, she seems to cast off everything Didi has told her. She turns to Janis. "Do you remember him, J?"

Janis shakes her head. But she does remember Mike Napolitano. She remembers his moussed hair, black and stiff; his mayor-of-the-halls swagger; his impression of softness beneath that. She spoke probably two words to him in high school, but for a good year he was the star of her fervent inner life. She wrote poems for him. She imagined sitting in the dark, in an air-conditioned movie theatre, his hand warming her knee. She got over him—she had plenty of hopeless love to spread around in those days—but she thought of him occasionally over the years, and when she did, she pictured some steady, dull sort of person. He was a dentist or an account manager; he had a mid-life gut and thinning hair; he still had his soft smile. Now it turns out he never had any life at all.

"Some people have phenomenally bad luck," Janis says.

"Who are you talking about?" Penelope asks. She brings her calm, velvety gaze to rest on Janis's face, and Janis thinks of the faint acne scars that linger on her cheeks, a reminder of the adolescent self she has mostly eliminated.

"I guess I'm thinking of my friend Charlotte," she says. How they must look in this bright, merciless light. "I was just visiting her in Wisconsin." She talks about how Charlotte's eldest daughter went to Princeton to become a junkie and thief. How her son decapitated himself at nineteen, racing down an Interstate. How now Charlotte herself has Stage IV colon cancer and has been given six months to live, at best. Janis tries to paint Charlotte for the other women, the way she sat on her sofa, sipping green tea, her head covered in a kerchief, her colostomy bag bulging under a blanket.

"Can you imagine?" Janis says as a harsh, angry wind sweeps in across the water, agitating the surface. "How can all those things happen to one person? I don't think I could even—but Charlotte was just sitting there drinking tea."

"She's trying to enjoy the time she has left," Didi says.

"I know she was. I know that. But I think—there are other people I know. Just this parade of tragedies. It's not like one bad thing happens to them. *Twenty* bad things happen to them."

"And then there are the people," Penelope says, her voice like soft snow, "who nothing ever seems to happen to, bad or good."

Janis frowns. "Well, I mean—what do you mean?"

But Penelope is waving at something over Janis's shoulder. Janis turns and sees three people walking out of a clump of bare ash trees towards the house, which squats on top of a rocky hill behind the dock. They march in single file, like condemned prisoners. Leading the way is Geoff, tall and hunched-over, in a jean jacket, staring at the ground. Behind him is Nick, Janis's son, absorbed in his phone, and trailing Nick is Rachel, Geoff and Penelope's daughter, who is about to finish high school. Like her father, she has developed a relationship with the ground before her.

"Boy, they look like they had a great hike," Didi says.

Nick glances in their direction, smiles and waves. He says something to the others and starts to make his way down the rocky hill, to where the women sit. Geoff continues up the steps to the back porch and into the house. Rachel, after thinking it over, follows Nick. She takes the footpath down the hill, while Nick scrambles over the rocks in his white shorts, bare knees wobbling and yellow curls bouncing.

Watching him, Janis feels that Nick has been possessed by a surge of boyishness, a ghost of how he used to be, before an adolescent glaze of surly opacity settled permanently over him. He's been performing since they got here, flirting with the other women. Janis is flattered to know her friends find her son attractive ("Bob Dylan circa 1965," Didi whispered to her when they all met up at the Portland airport), but his beauty also unnerves her, makes him seem like a stranger—a houseguest she must try hard to please.

Further up the hill, Rachel edges along the footpath sideways to maintain her balance. She's a tall girl, with black hair and wide glasses covering a long, ascetic face. She has a sturdy body that she treats as an inconvenience, an obstacle to be negotiated. Her khakis are stained with mud from the woods. Is it too horrible, Janis wonders, too crass, to be proud that she has Nick to show off, while Penelope has only gloomy, grumpy Rachel?

It was supposed to be a couples' weekend—three women and their husbands. But Geoff wanted to stay in New York and work on his book, and the other men happily surrendered their invitations. Then Penelope decided that Rachel needed some fresh air—she was spending all her time moping about online—and it briefly became a mothers–and–children weekend, until Didi's son had to stay home and work at the Apple Store in West Hartford. Janis would not let Nick renege: he racked up a thousand dollars of Capital One charges over winter break and the bank has suspended his card. It's Janis's belief that Nick needs, somehow, to be brought down to earth. Nick has met Rachel twice before, briefly, the last time when he was seventeen and she was twelve, and so far she hasn't done much to dispel his juvenile image of her.

"Not obsessed with making a great impression," was all Nick had to say to Janis as they were unpacking.

Janis laughed. She knew what he meant. Rachel is an odd girl. She keeps quiet, eyeing the ebb and flow of a conversation from inside a blank-faced carapace, occasionally tossing out remarks that are hostile, self-pitying, or obscure. She got this blunt, arrhythmic style from her father, who, infuriatingly, was there at the house after all when Janis, Nick, and Didi showed up this morning. Now the weekend lacks any shape or purpose.

In the kitchen, Penelope picks up a brown lobster with a dishcloth and clips the claw bands. The tail buckles in fright. Four other lobsters wait on the cork countertop beneath wads of wet newspaper. As Penelope drops the lobster into boiling water and covers the pot, Janis sees her own unease reflected in Rachel's face.

"Remember when you and Janis were vegetarians for about five seconds?" Didi says to Penelope, standing beside her, rubbing rosemary onto red potatoes.

Nick looks up at Janis. "You were a vegetarian?"

Janis makes what she hopes is a wry grimace. Nick always assumes she's the squarest square imaginable. "I was, as a matter of fact," she says.

No response. He's sitting across from her at the kitchen island, lazily cutting up lemons, his movements loose and dreamy. Rachel is sitting beside him, gripping the stem of an empty wine glass, and Janis sees that she is squinting at him as though he were an exotic, easily frightened lizard. Nick, of course, knows he's being watched.

"It was the 70s," Penelope says. "Laura Nyro was our goddess. We did everything she told us to."

"I could never," Didi says. "I saved all my discipline for the church."

"It was Penny's idea," Janis says, getting up and moving towards the lobster pot, listening for any death throes. Silence—lobster inertia. She pulls the sleeves of her fleece over her hands. "My parents threatened to disown me. They lived on meatloaf."

"I was even a vegan in my early thirties," Penelope says.

"You were not," Didi says. "I don't remember this."

"You and J had children then, you didn't know what I was up to."

Janis meets Didi's eyes: is this the revelation of some long-withheld bitterness on their friend's part? Janis sits back at the island and begins to cut stems and strings from sugar snap peas. Her joints have flared up in the cold; her hand moves the scissors stiffly. Geoff is supposedly off somewhere, dealing with the pipes. Penelope floats about, pouring wine for everyone.

"I was reading Peter Singer in those days," she says, "and Dorothy Day, trying to simplify my life. Everything was fucked up, my relationships, my painting. My mother had finally died of cirrhosis. I thought that I could become happier if I reduced the harm I put out into the world." Penelope shakes her head, embarrassed, but also (Janis knows) proud of her high-mindedness. "Plus, I was broke. I was living in Chinatown, and could buy tofu in bulk and find all kinds of exotic vegetables and spices. I made rice and beans on a hot plate every night."

"Sounds nice," Nick says. "Sounds like you were free."

"Free, hmm?" Penelope stands by Nick and places a hand on his shoulder. There's no excess flesh on her; she's just a spare, curving line in a moth-eaten sweater. "I guess I was. Maybe it's the last time I was." She reaches over and brushes a hair out of Rachel's face. Rachel scowls, and Penelope leans down and hugs her daughter from behind, kissing the shiny black curls they share, as Rachel's glasses begin their slow crawl down her nose.

Penelope and Janis had a fight when Janis was getting married, because the wedding was held back in Bristol, at St. Anthony's, and Penelope had scandalized the town with her teenage romances and didn't want to go back. "I'm dying to be there, J, obviously," she said, "but I can't face those judgmental cows." They were all twenty-eight then, Didi long married; Penelope's mother had moved to Bridgeport for a man. Janis told Penelope she was being melodramatic, that actually she was just pissed Janis was getting married before her. And Penelope did end up coming, sitting in the front row in a handmade dress of raw, blue silk, an orange flower in her hair, looking proud and lonely and rare. All night the community's whispers circulated back to Janis: Well, Penny hadn't changed too much, had she? She was still mucking about, living life. In New York you could live on dreams, people said derisively, *for a while*. Janis took a small, private pleasure from these remarks, though she answered them with effusive defenses of her friend. A sense of magnanimity and pity allowed her to ask Penelope's forgiveness after the ceremony, and they never fought again—they aged into rigorous politeness. Penelope never returned to Bristol.

Five years after Janis's wedding, Penelope met Geoff and some kind of calamity was averted. What would that calamity have looked like? Janis wonders now. She tries to imagine Penelope's delicate beauty thickened and obscured by failure, by grown-up poverty, but she can't imagine Penelope as anything but what she is. Would Penelope be a fifty-three-year-old office temp, cooking rice and beans on a miserable hot plate? Would Janis be loaning her money? Would she still be hustling for gallery showings? Janis looks around the vast, cherry wood kitchen, as if it held the answers to these questions. The kitchen maintains an air of scrupulous nonchalance; in one corner, a three-thousand-dollar espresso machine lies chicly abandoned.

◆◆

While the potatoes are roasting and the third lobster cooking, Janis and Didi slip out of the kitchen and prowl through the house. The floors are warped and lumpy, the halls narrow and dimly lit. There's a stale, locked-in smell.

"They designed it themselves," Didi whispers.

"Looks like they never got around to finishing the job."

They grin at one another, their resentment of Penelope's good fortune like a shared blanket. Then they turn a corner and Janis grabs Didi's hand: Geoff is standing right in front of them, hands in his pockets, studying the ceiling. He lowers his gaze.

"Hello, ladies. Having a look around?"

It's worse when Geoff tries to be polite. He sounds like he's reading from cue cards, or from a handbook called *How to Be Human*.

"Just green with envy," Didi murmurs.

He smiles blandly. He has a rough handsomeness, cured and toughened by the elements, with a rust-colored mustache and a jutting, gray-stubbled chin. He wears jeans and a flannel shirt, but his voice seems piped in from another source: Groton School, perhaps. "I was listening to see if the pipes were working. I think they are. Can you hear?"

He points at the ceiling. They all tilt their heads back and sure enough, there is a faint noise to be heard, like the lowing of a cow.

"Good job," Janis says.

He nods and passes by them, disappearing into the shadows. The women scurry down the hall into an open room, letting out gusts of laughter as soon as Didi has shut the door. They have found themselves in what looks like a study. Orange light pushes through bay windows, illuminating stacks of nautical almanacs and maritime histories. Geoff's book is about the sinking of the *Albatross*.

Didi drops into a thin, brittle chair. "I'm not gonna make it through two nights with Mr. Charisma. I get so nervous around him, like I'm gonna fart or I've got food stuck in my teeth." Her voice is tiny and combustive.

Janis picks up a sailing book studded with Post-its. When she first heard about Geoff, twenty years ago, he was just an attractive enigma in Penelope's therapy group, another in a long line of inauspicious infatuations. This was before Penelope had any idea about his family.

"Penny's always gone for fixer-upper guys," she says. "Nothing too easy for her."

"He thinks we're dumb."

"He's just a little reserved," Janis says. Though actually, when they were getting the house tour earlier in the afternoon and Geoff mentioned the Sulzbergers having a cottage nearby, Didi was the one who had to ask who they were. Janis had been pretty certain they were the family that published *The New York Times*.

"And that poor girl got her father's chin," Didi says. "God, why am I such a bitch? It's menopause, right? I've been going through menopause for the last ten years."

They sit in a bay window and watch the sun drift down, turning a neighbor's schooner into a black triangle. Janis tells Didi a little about her recent fights with Nick. Didi admits to some concerns over her youngest, Christopher, who still lives at home. He hasn't launched himself into adulthood with the alacrity of Didi's two daughters, who are both married and living in other parts of Connecticut with their husbands and children. Before heading back to the kitchen, Janis stops by the door to examine a portrait of a fine-boned, purple-skinned woman set against a blinding yellow background. The bright colors and thick lines suggest a child's finger-paint creation, but there's sophistication in the aquiline nose and sunken, sorrowful eyes. Janis knows nothing about painting, but she can see that it's Penelope's work and she can see that it's good.

"I'm glad we decided to do this," Penelope says, her face flushed and girlish, half-hidden by a veil of lobster steam. "Those years were so important. We didn't even know what we had, did we? Nick, Rach—pay attention. Remember your past, remember where you came from. Remember the people who matter."

Janis and Didi are so touched they stare guiltily at their lobsters. They have gathered around the long, wide table that, Penelope has explained, Geoff carved out of a single piece of white pine. It fills the low-ceilinged dining room. Penelope and Geoff are sitting at opposite ends of the table; Janis and Didi face Nick and Rachel. Oil lamps bathe everyone's face in nineteenth-century light. After a brief pause, Didi raises her glass and toasts the "almost-graduates," and they all start attacking their food.

The air is stifling. Sweat breaks out on Janis's brow as she cracks open a claw and drags out pale shards of meat with a small fork. Penelope splits open her tail with a single supple gesture. Geoff excavates little bits from the knuckles. The conversation orients itself around Nick's post-college plans. He wants to do odd jobs in various states and write about the reality of working life in Middle America. Janis has already expressed her feelings about this proposition. Penelope, of course, thinks it's the greatest idea ever.

"You could be like Barbara Ehrenreich," she says. "For the post-recession generation."

This leads to a discussion of the chain stores that have replaced the old businesses back in Bristol, with Didi praising their convenience and affordability, as Nick and Penelope moan in horror. Janis doesn't know what she thinks about chain stores. She watches the two older women incline towards her son, listening to his stories about building houses in Honduras and teaching English in São Paulo, and she watches Rachel, at his side, who regards him a bit more warily, but also steadily, her whole body locked in attention. Nick, for his part, pushes his curls aside and charmingly disparages his own ideas. His butterscotch voice hovers in the damp air above the table, mingling with the lobster steam. He doesn't look at Janis. She made him waste his spring break on this trip, and she knows he's going to punish her by dazzling these people.

"Nick wrote this amazing essay on stop-and-frisk," Janis says, trying to latch on to the conversation. "For this website that—"

But Penelope is telling Nick about her own book, which is "heavily influenced by Japanese scrollwork." Is everyone working on a book? Janis wonders. It's an easy enough thing to say. Then she remembers that Geoff owns a small publishing house, or his family does. Nick laughs at something Penelope has said and his lips glisten with butter. Janis flashes on an image of him going down on a girl, making her cry out with happiness. She quickly clears this from her mind.

"You're studying biology, right?" she asks Rachel, who is fumbling with her lobster tail. She knows Rachel is going to Yale in the fall.

"Botany," Penelope corrects. "Rachel is interested in horticulture. She won first place in a city-wide botany competition."

"I was supposed to be second place," Rachel adds dourly. "But they found out the person in first place had cheated." She has a deep voice for a seventeen-year-old; already she sounds like a research scientist.

Nick turns to her. "That's how you were able to tell me the names of every single thing in the woods. The anemone, the snowflake. You had the whole forest memorized."

"Hardly anything grows here in the spring."

"You're like the Prospero of Boothbay Harbor!"

She shakes her head impatiently, and he watches her struggle to open her tail. "Here," he says.

He reaches over and takes the tail in his hands. He barely seems to move, but there is a terrible cracking noise and the tail spews its contents onto Rachel's plate. She reddens as Nick extricates the digestive tract and glands, spears the bulbous green liver with his fork.

"You don't want to eat this," he says, sliding it into his mouth.

"I'm in awe of my daughter," Penelope says. "I don't know where she gets it. Lord knows I was a C student my whole life. Or, as Father Kieran liked to call me, a 'behavior problem.' And Geoff—well, Geoff's brilliant, but he dropped out of three different PhD programs. Rachel actually *likes* studying. It's not a struggle. The gates of knowledge are just—*whew*—open for her."

Geoff, emerging from a monkish contemplation of his food, blinks irritably. "That's not the way it works, dear."

"It's certainly not," Rachel says.

Penelope shrugs. "It seems like it is."

"Sounds like this one," Didi says, indicating Janis with her fork.

"Oh," Janis says, "I was never a good student."

"You were valedictorian, J," Penelope says. "You were the only intelligent life form in our graduating class. I mean, I'm sorry, Deeds, but you know it's true."

"No, I wasn't." Janis braces herself against the table, her head suddenly cloudy. "School for me was like mastering a foreign language. I had to work hard every step of the way. Remember that report I gave on the Wars of the Roses? I spent three weeks preparing it. I read every book six times. My hair fell out in the shower." She feels everyone staring at her, and she glances down at the stained tablecloth. "I was the tortoise in the race, that's all."

"But what's the difference?" Didi says. "Either you work hard and you're smart or you're smart because you work hard."

"I think my mother is talking about people having a natural talent for things," Nick says. He rests his elbows on the table and stares straight at Janis. The oil light washes out any expression in his eyes.

Janis nods warily. She can never be sure if Nick is testing her, luring her into saying something foolish. This morning on the plane they bickered in circles, about money and the future and Audrey Wynter, the girl Nick had been so serious about for such a long time and then, suddenly … wasn't, anymore. "She always wanted to know what I was thinking all the time," he said, slouching violently in his seat, hair in his face. "Like she wanted to consume me. I don't know what else to say, Mom." He sighed and shook his head, and Janis felt a curious tenderness inside of her annoyance; her poor son's feelings were such a mystery to him. Audrey's been calling Janis at work and home, looking for answers.

"Natural talent is one thing," Geoff says. "You have to cultivate it."

"I met people at college," Janis says. "They could read something once and it would come alive. Their minds had this elastic quality."

"Geoff's editor is like that," Penelope says. "My brain turns to mud around him."

"I wanted to be a Tudor scholar," Janis says, mostly to herself. "For God's sake."

"Rachel has natural talent," Penelope says, "and a lot of ambition."

"Why are you talking about me like I'm not here?" Rachel says. "You're always doing that."

"She needs to remember that living is important." Penelope explains to the other women that Rachel has decided not to go to her senior prom, not even with a friend or a gay boy. "You know I didn't go to mine because I was dating Jean-Michel at the time. I mean, he was black and twenty-five. Father Kieran had already informed me I was going to hell."

"Do we really have to dig this up again?" Geoff asks.

"I regret it, is what I'm saying. I missed out on an iconic experience."

"I married my prom date," Didi tells Rachel. "You don't have to go that far."

The girl is scowling at her plate, her face plum-colored. She's probably a little bit drunk. "Christ," she mutters.

"That's enough." Penelope's soft voice snaps like a sheet in the wind. She doesn't look at her daughter; she peers into the corners of the room, abstracted. Something in Penelope's tone just now strikes Janis as familiar. Something she's heard for years in her clients' voices, over the phone, discussing wills and contracts, but that she never dreamt she'd hear from Penelope Gennarelli. Total assurance? Janis's parents used to discourage her from spending time with Penelope because her father had run off and her mother drank and they lived in an apartment building next to an SRO hotel. Janis and Didi, and often Janis alone, would bike home with Penelope and raid the liquor cabinet and listen to the strange sounds that leaked in through the thin walls. "I don't know why you always want to come here," Penelope once said, "when your family has that whole house."

At the time Janis murmured something about her brother's awfulness and worried that she was being pathetic and clingy. It didn't occur to her until college that what Penelope really was asking was why Janis never invited her over.

Rachel takes off her bib and uses it to wipe her chin. She does have her father's chin, Janis thinks: heavy and obtrusive. But she also has her mother's hair and her mellow, olive-toned skin. Her black eyes dart briefly at Janis, then drop, staring into her lap.

Geoff has retreated into his private zone of concentration. Nick looks tickled by everything; he spears a potato. Ravaged shells lie scattered across the table.

Penelope's eyes have widened. Her skin is tinted a soft rose. She spills some wine while pouring out the remains of a bottle. "And do you remember, after school, walking to Liberty Diner, rolling up our skirts? Trying to see who had shaved the farthest?" She's talking to no one in particular. "Well, there's only so much you can do with brown wool."

◆ ◆

Janis lies awake, trying to picture Mike Napolitano's room at the home in Fairfield. She can envision lives better than her own in crisp, sensory detail, but worse ones remain a fatalistic blur. She sees a man in his early fifties with pink rashy skin and a coarse black beard. He stays in bed every day, reading and drinking cheap beer, gazing at the view of a Sunoco station or an outlet mall. How do some people get lives and others don't? Luck? Janis has never counted on this. She identified herself early on as not among the happy few destined to lead charmed existences. She slogged forward with a kind of fearful fastidiousness about every aspect of her life. While Penelope dropped into and out of art school, hitched across the country, indulged in bewildering relationships—while Penelope dithered and dreamed, there was Janis, on a far less circuitous track, studying every night in the library at Wellesley (full scholarship), and later, the

Law Library at Penn (loans), applying for summer associate positions, putting in eighteen-hour days… Penelope seemed so indifferent to the future, yet here she was with her two houses, easy life, dinner parties filled with interesting and important people. Things always work out for beautiful people, Janis thinks. They're a kind of aristocracy; they don't even have to try. There is a small, childish monster inside of her that believes in and rages against this injustice.

She gets up and finds a joint in her jeans pocket. A few hours ago, after everyone had turned in, Didi appeared at her door with rolling papers and a Ziploc bag of dark green herbs. They snuck down to the study, not bothering to discuss inviting Penelope. They giggled and tipped over stacks of nautical manuals, blowing smoke out the bay windows.

It's past two in the morning now. Janis makes her way downstairs, onto the porch, in her slippers and puffy winter coat. The shock of the night cold penetrates her pajamas, but she stands defiant, breathing in the salty air, her little tummy rising and falling. The stars look packed into the sky; the coastline looks like rubble. As she takes the footpath to the dock, she remembers the one and maybe only time Mike Napolitano ever talked to her. He asked her opinion of the motorcycle jacket he was wearing. She can't remember what she said; she only remembers biking over to Penelope's house afterwards, full of happiness. But Penelope was in the midst of some real-world turmoil—probably involving Jean-Michel—and Janis felt the virginal puniness of her news. So she kept her love a secret. They drank Fresca spiked with rum and listened to "Eli's Comin'" and Janis imagined the song's dark, pitiless lover coming for her. She thrilled at the impossibility of escaping him.

She sits in one of the lawn chairs and lights up, listens to the dull slap of the waves, until she becomes aware of a presence behind her. Rachel is standing up on the rocks, looking like something that's always been there. Her breath creates a little cloud before her face. Bits of moonlight flare in her glasses.

"Hi there," Janis says, feeling a flash of irritation. The girl is just watching her.

Rachel advances down the hill. "Are you smoking pot?"

Janis looks at the gray, wilted joint in her hand. "I guess I am. You want to try?"

Rachel nods. She sits in a lawn chair beside Janis.

"Think of this as my graduation present to you," Janis says. "Be careful. Don't burn yourself." She hasn't gotten high in a decade before tonight; now she's sharing the experience with a teenage girl.

Rachel holds the joint the way she held her wine glass: stiffly, at a distance. She takes quick, shallow drags. "I hope college is better than high school," she says. She turns her opaque glasses towards Janis. "Is it?"

Janis sighs. "Well, it is and it isn't. You have more freedom. But you also have more responsibility. No one's going to walk up and take your hand. You have to make your own way. It's easy to get lost."

"That's what I'm afraid of."

Janis looks at the girl's narrow face, bent and shrouded with hair. Her voice sounded so naked. "You shouldn't be afraid," Janis says. "That's not going to get you anywhere."

"I don't know how to do anything."

Janis rubs her swollen, aching knuckles. Penelope got to have so much *fun*. Janis knows it's stupid to compare her lot with Mike Napolitano's. From Mike Napolitano's perspective—from the universe's perspective—there's no difference between Janis and Penelope. But Janis can't help it. She grieves equally for Mike, for Charlotte, for Rachel. For the unlucky. She thinks of this sulky, inhibited girl sitting at her side, this person who will go through adulthood convinced that somewhere else, wherever she isn't, "real life" is taking place, even as she nurses a secret superiority to all those people out there living "real lives."

"When I was up for partner at my firm," Janis says, leaning back in her chair and staring at the sea, "about fifteen years ago, I was down in Palm Beach, helping a rich old lady write her will. My mom called and told me my brother had been arrested again for check fraud, could I please recommend a lawyer? This would be my third or fourth time putting my brother in touch with a colleague. I said I didn't have time to find someone to help Danny." She takes the joint from Rachel and drags on it; the smoke scrapes the back of her throat. Beneath the moon, the sea looks like a sheet of purple glass. "My dad stopped speaking to me. My mom begged me to apologize. Oh, it felt good to be totally in the right. I didn't give a damn about being the bigger person. This went on for years, not speaking to my dad or brother, talking to my mom in secret." How easy it is to tell this story, as if it happened to someone else. But that cold, righteous anger lives inside her still, like dry ice burning her guts. She hands the joint back to Rachel. "Then my dad died and my brother and I basically reconciled. But it was different. He knew not to take me for granted anymore."

Janis doesn't look at Rachel; she wonders idly if the girl is freaked out by the sudden, vomitous intimacy of a near-stranger. Janis feels opened out, blurred, as if she were dissipating into the night air along with the weed smoke. She feels so far away from the person who sat in these chairs with Penelope and Didi a few hours ago. Who is she, anyway? She's a stranger. She likes that.

Rachel takes a slow, heavy drag and coughs. Janis imagines a piece of herself passing out of the joint and into this girl.

"Let me tell you something else. A secret."

Rachel sits up straight in her chair, shivering a little. "Okay," she says, the word a puff of smoke.

"If you go right now and knock on my son's door, he'll still be awake. And if you ask to come in, he'll let you."

Rachel stares, her face twisted towards Janis, still arrested in the stock listening expression of a moment ago. The moon picks out peach fuzz on her cheeks and jaw.

"You understand what I'm saying?" Janis asks. In her ears, the words seem to come from another woman's voice, coarsened and strained by smoke. "The world's not that difficult. You can do anything you want."

Rachel nods quickly and turns away, sinking into her chair as if she is embarrassed for Janis. They sit in silence, obliterating the joint. *People who nothing ever seems to happen to, bad or good.* There is a sore spot lodged beneath the surface of Janis's skull, and she feels sweaty inside her puffy coat. Suddenly, Rachel stands up, brushing ashes to the ground. She looks less solid than in the daytime—slighter, more delicate, just a girl in her pajamas; she's got skinny wrists. She peers down at Janis, as if waiting for a command or reprieve. Janis stares back, her heart rioting in her chest.

The white yawl glows on the water. Finally, Rachel nods again, now in acknowledgement of some private understanding between them. She flashes Janis a bladelike smile—the first Janis has ever seen from her—turns and stumbles slowly up the rocks, towards the ugly, unfinished house, which in darkness looms like an enormous thumbprint, a smear against the star-filled sky. Janis watches her go. She learned about love on those boozy afternoons, listening to Penelope's stories, listening to Laura Nyro, listening to the sounds from the SRO hotel. Now there isn't anything left to learn.

She sings lightly, under her breath, an old song. He'll break her heart.

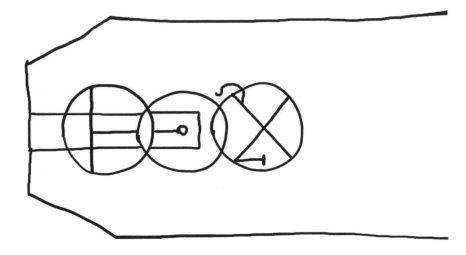

Oneness Plus One

The speck of dirt lived on the floor of the apartment, and somehow had, until now, avoided the broom. It was, after all, just one speck, and all its brethren had spilled out ahead of it and been taken up in the fan-like funnel tilt, then thrown away. The speck of dirt had watched, but impassively, as it had not been attached to any of its kin. Dirt glommed to dirt, but unfondly. What it wanted was to be left alone, but every afternoon the snuffing nose of either the vacuum or the broom threatened to destroy its existence, and it huddled under the bookcase and tried not to be seen.

The speck of dirt knew soulful others: the lint, who had seen God. The cat hair that understood something of love. The tiny broken half of pistachio shell that had been able to recite poems, poems it itself had created, about becoming one, about sheltering meat, about breaking off, decay, death. Those three had loved one another, had gathered near the speck of dirt to talk about life and their surprising consciousnesses, brains no one could identify but that were there, somehow, anyway, communication skills that only functioned with the other discarded members of the underneath. When the pistachio shell had tried to talk to the meat, it told the others, nothing had worked. I tried and tried, the shell said. How I courted it with villanelles and sonnets! Only you, here under the shelf, it said, can hear me.

The shell could not weep but it still carried an air of longing and emotion and a thickness to its speech; the cat hair emanated a boundless empathy in response. They all had been parts of larger, more desirable entities, and had been separated. The cat hair, of course, had once been on a cat. The shell had been the shelterer of food. The lint had been part of a swath of dryer lint, peeled off the screen in a blue-gray sheath, but this portion had separated out when the whole cat itself got ahold of the lint glob and whisked it joyfully to pieces.

How about you? they asked one day, turning to the speck of dirt. What do you feel, away from your group?

Happy, grunted the speck of dirt. Glad. What I want is aloneness, it said. Not these foolish mutterings of the set-aside.

But I feel a oneness, said the lint, and it said it in a way that made it sound true, not just something you heard again and again.

I'm not in that oneness, said the dirt. I am the oneness plus one. Please, can you go somewhere else?

But they could not. No one had legs, after all. They ended up where they ended up, and all four were stuck together unless the vacuum or the cat had anything to say about it.

What they wished, or what the other three wished, was to find a secure place where they could decompose together, a place of some beauty. I want to write poems of sky, said the shell. Even if I cannot see it. I want to feel the sunlight on my shoulders, said the lint. The gleaming eye of the divine. The cat hair beamed upon them. The speck of dirt would have been more than happy to assist; what he wanted, as he'd stated, was this place all to himself, and an owner who was vigilant about all other dirt except for him. He wanted to be the last remaining speck of dirt in an entire home, where he could remain quietly for a long time.

Eventually he too would break down into smaller parts and at that time he suspected he would lose whatever thinking he had available to him now. But he was fine with that. He just wanted to do it on his own.

But how to get them out?

The big break happened when the child, home from school, left the front door open on a breezy day. The wind scattered toys in the living room and finally reached an arm under the bookcase and lifted the group, moving them across the room to a far wall.

This is it! said the shell. It's happening! It could not see but could sense the open door, the open door that would be the gateway to their beautiful cyclical death.

Lord! prayed the lint.

Wind! asked the hair.

The speck of dirt did not say a word, so aggravated was it by the interruption of its time under the bookcase and now exposure to the wide world by the wall.

The mother came in carrying groceries, and closed the door. The wind stopped. The items remained uncovered and exposed, near an electrical outlet.

Tony, said the mother, as she walked to the kitchen. Honey, will you grab the broom and pick this all up?

Tony didn't mind sweeping; it was his main chore, by choice. To brush bristles against the wood, to find the clean floor beneath. In a minute he had all four of them up in the dustpan and down into the trash can. There, they sifted slowly to the bottom of the plastic baggie, next to orange peels and pasta curls and so many squashed paper towels.

This is not what I had in mind, sighed the cat hair, though within minutes it had made a nice bond with a shard of glass.

I had hoped for sun, said the lint, but there was a kind of church-like space at the very bottom corner where he felt the weight of the world and his own lightness at once.

Biodegrading, mumbled the shell, hunting for a good rhyme.

The dirt did not see any other specks of dirt, but he was no longer alone. He had fallen right inside the curl of a full orange peel. The orange peel wrapped him in a kind of cocoon. The bag won't break, the dirt told himself. This is where I will be. To his vast relief, the orange peel was quiet, and just held on. In the silence, he examined his new space. White pulpy inside. Smell of citrus. Dents where a human thumb had dug into the peel and opened it up. He was no butterfly, or caterpillar, but for the first time in his life, he imagined himself a seed, deep in the peel of a fruit. What a different life it might have been, he thought. Planted in the dirt. Growing into a fruit. Eventually down the gullet of a bird, or a worm, or a human.

But then ultimately shit out and back to the soil, right? Not so different after all.

The orange peel settled her bumpy arms around him. You are my seed that will not grow, she told it. You are my tiny fruit of dirt.

The dirt speck bristled. We all end up dirt anyway, it said. I'm just fast. I just got here faster.

Perhaps you too were something else first, wondered the peel.

The dirt huddled into a pulpy corner. The idea had never occurred to him. No, he said, bothered. No way. Something else? Me?

It was highly irritating to consider. Particularly because it also seemed logically possible. How would he know?

I am dirt to the core! he yelled.

Maybe he had been a rose, or a bird, or a piece of bread.

A cat hair, a bit of lint, the shell of a pistachio.

He could feel the pull to join everyone. No, he thought, to his thoughts.

The peel embraced the dirt, and the light from the window shone through the bag and through the peel and lit up the inside in a glowing white. I've got you, she whispered. Little dirt. We will go where we go together.

We go to dirt, thought the dirt.

Rebecca Liu

Journey to the Center of a Mechanical Bird

Let's consider for a minute how time is built
        in this green mechanical bird how slippery

as bullets the whirr of its tiny metallic brain
        its tinny taloned wings its tinseled

wind-up heart so inordinately quick for this static
        flapping to stay just still in flight—

How the underbelly gleam so crunching in its gunmetal
        nerves & blurring on its cobalt axis

cannot keep still the brass of this stammering chassis—

What of the clockhands that creep backwards?
        The whirl at the center of this whirligig

heart armored in its shivering orbit
        & sweating off its bolts the fizzle

of bolts like this bird in the rubble of an after-fire
        such stationary whirling, whirling

        so fast in its big bird head just to stay
as all gears click & all systems go

rifle of neon to the tinny drum core—

When you get to the center nothing
        but the explosion of tiny bird guts tinny bird

shrapnel descending at the speed of fine rain

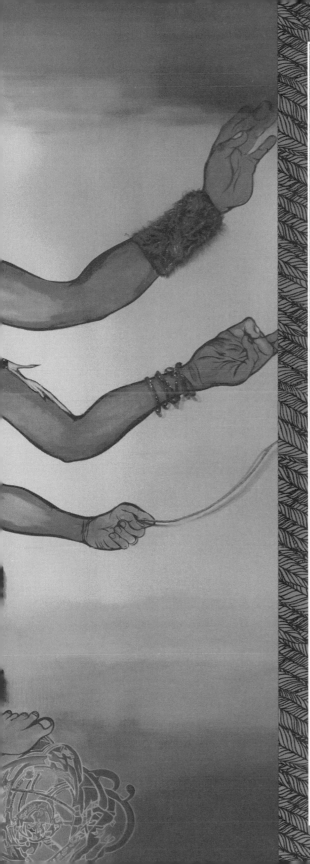

Sharon Butler

Fig. 1. Chitra Ganesh at the Brooklyn Museum. Image courtesy of Svati Shah.

As It Happens: Tracking Down Chitra Ganesh

December 2014

When Raphael Rubinstein asks me to write an article about Chitra Ganesh for the Art Lies section of *Gulf Coast*, which he is guest-editing, I reflexively oblige before I've even investigated her work. Raphael and I are aesthetically kindred spirits. We are both interested in, and have written about, a certain kind of irresolute abstract painting. Sometimes it is called abject. He calls it Provisional; I call it Casualist. But when I look at Ganesh's website and learn that her feisty, energetic practice is rooted in Indian myth, Hindu religion, and feminism, I wonder whether I can find something to say about Ganesh that hasn't been said already in some art glossy. She writes comic books, plans big site-specific installations, works with assistants, wins awards from influential organizations like Creative Capital, and exhibits her work internationally. An American of South Asian descent, Ganesh was raised in Queens and is the product of an elite education that includes a diploma from St. Ann's, a BA from Brown University with a double major in Comparative Literature and Semiotics, and an MFA from Columbia University.

Logistics prove challenging. Chitra and I have crowded and irregular schedules that don't mesh terribly well. After exchanging several throat-clearing emails over the course of a few days, we finally speak on the phone—she from a Providence-bound train on her way to RISD where she is the Kirloskar Visiting Scholar, I on a Philadelphia-bound train where I'm an adjunct at the Pennsylvania Academy of Fine Art. She tells me her schedule is tight because she is in the process of completing a huge wall painting at the Brooklyn Museum. We agree to meet later in the week, and she sends me a link to the press page of her website so I can read articles about her to prepare for our meeting. I do not complete my homework assignment, but do glance sufficiently at the array of PDF files—*Vogue India, Time Out New York, Flash Art, Elle, Modern Painters, ArtForum, New York Times, The*

Fig. 2. (below) Chitra Ganesh. *Robot Rose*, 2013. Mixed media on paper, 60 by 40 inches. Courtesy of the artist and gallery Espace, New Delhi.

New Republic, ArtIndia, Art Asia Pacific, and so many more—to feel unequal to the task of writing about this powerhouse culture producer. Here the Casualist point of view comes in handy: I decide to wing it.

Early the next morning, I get another email from Chitra. Our scheduled meeting for a couple of hours hence won't work due to museum-related contingencies. She asks whether Monday morning would be possible. On Mondays I teach an MFA seminar at UConn and visit my teenage daughter, so we need to arrange another time. I offer to come to the museum so we can talk while she's working. She counter-proposes that we meet at a place near the museum. I agree. The day of our scheduled visit arrives and the phone rings. Chitra is sick. Loath to catch what she has and get behind on my own projects, I suggest we reschedule. We settle on the Wednesday afternoon before Thanksgiving. This gives me only a few days to write the article, but I figure what the hell.

On the Wednesday, I send Chitra a text indicating my preference for meeting somewhere near the 2/3 subway line because I live on the Upper West Side. She suggests two places. I don't really care, I say, as long as it's near the train. The weather has turned nasty, with hard rain and flooding. She puts forward two possibilities—a café and a restaurant. I pick the one with the bar.

I spend the morning jurying a show online for the New Britain Museum of Art, then go to the studio to receive a painting of mine that is being returned. I am working on a new large-scale canvas called Gerrymandered Shirt in which a torn-up flannel shirt stands in for Illinois's Fourth District. I lose track of time, and, hands covered with a thin, shiny coating of dried glue, hurry to the Museum to meet Chitra at Bar Corvo, a convivial neighborhood place that serves food like squid-ink pasta, charred cauliflower, duck-leg confit. My umbrella is small and flimsy, and by the time I dash the four blocks from the subway, I am soaked. I order a pint and text Chitra that I'm there. She arrives fifteen minutes later and we take a small table in the back.

Fig. 3. Chitra Ganesh. *Intimacy of the Void*, 2014. Silkscreen and woodcut, 25 ¾ by 18 ⅛ inches. Courtesy of the artist and Durham Press.

Chitra is harried. As the end-of-semester approaches, work has started piling up, and most faculty, distraught over lack of studio time, can barely hang in there until Thanksgiving break. Both of us are exhausted and don't know where to begin. As the conversation unfolds, it must become clear to Chitra that I haven't read any of the materials from her website. Chitra is used to discussing big issues like the role of religion and stories in our lives and culture, and about aesthetic phenomena like *transgression*, whereby art jarringly subverts traditional narratives and paradigms.

I'm more interested in personal challenges than public success, so I ask mundanely nosy questions. She lives in Ditmas Park (a diverse neighborhood). She has a partner (an anthropology professor at UMass Amherst). They have no kids and want none (she doesn't want to be a "wife" and neither does her partner). She talks about spending time in India last year when her partner had a Fulbright, and we commiserate about commuting to far-flung academic positions.

After we order some food, I ask Chitra about her project at the Brooklyn Museum. She tells me how she was invited by assistant curator Sasha Grayson, whom she has known for many years, to propose a project for the large wall outside the room in which Judy Chicago's *The Dinner Party* is installed—a perfect place for her images of Kali, the angry Hindu goddess associated with darkness, time, and empowerment. She gets out her laptop and shows me images of the work in progress, which is indeed hugely inventive, expansive, and vibrant. The process for the wall piece starts with small, hand-drawn pictures that she translates into a larger format by projecting digitized versions on the wall. Although she is working with two assistants on the project, her hands are dirty, coated with graphite and flecks of brightly colored paint. The drawing will include three-dimensional elements like long arms cast at Sculpture House Casting that will form Kali's skirt.

As we finish eating, I ask Chitra about her plans for 2015. At first she says she doesn't have much planned, but then reels off a list of visiting artist gigs and grant opportunities. Then she says she wants to spend some time painting in the studio. Instead of site-specific projects? I ask. Yes. Paintings on canvas. She wonders what

Fig. 4. (opposite) Chitra Ganesh. Untitled 2014. Mixed media on paper, 60 by 40 inches. Courtesy of the artist and gallery Espace, New Delhi.

she can do if she limits herself to paint and canvas and filters out all the extraneous noise. "Early in my career, I was encouraged to do site-specific installations and other types of collaborative projects that incorporated a wide range of media," she says. "And I've gone in that direction. But I want to simplify. Rather than preparing for large-scale projects, I want to generate new ideas through process and execution in the studio."

For all her success with site-specific projects, it turns out that Chitra yearns to spend time making more traditional art. Recalling a conversation the week before in which a relational aesthetics artist decreed that he rarely painted anymore because painting was self-indulgent, I ask Chitra if she agrees. No, she told me. As a female gay artist of South Asian descent, a group that has never been included in the larger art world dialogue, everything she decides to do will be important. When I get home, the December issue of *ArtNews* is waiting on my desk. I flip through it. "Chitra Ganesh: Eyes of Time," her project for the Brooklyn Museum, is included in the Editor's Picks section. I still haven't had time to read the rest of the articles about her. But I'm looking forward to seeing her work.

OUR LADY OF THE HOUR {OUR SUBJECT} IS ⟨TIME.⟩ SHE WAS: AN ABANDONED HOUSE DRAWN FROM MEMORY, SHAKING LOOSE THE CONTENTS OF MY INSIDES... INVISIBLE CONTINENTS AND IMPROBABLE FUTURES, PLUCKED FROM THE EDGES OF DAWN...THE HAND OF FATIMA ON ME, HER LIGHT & AMPUTATED TOUCH. TOOLS OF HER TRADE? A SPIDERWEB, A RAINBOW, AN EYE THAT CANNOT CRY...

THE STRANGLING POWER OF DUST AND STARS...

WHAT CAN WE SAY ABOUT HER AS WE SIT HERE, CAUGHT IN THE THROES OF CIRCULAR TIME, WARMING OUR FLAYED SOLES BY THE FIRE? UNDER HER SKIN THE RISE AND FALL: OF IMMORTAL JELLYFISH, OF UNSPOKEN PLEAS & MECHANICAL HANDS-- SELFSAME SHARDS OF THIS TUMULTUOUS UNIVERSE....{A SIGN OF THE CROSSROADS?} TATTOO HER ONTO THIS CITY'S SKIN, STROKE BY STROKE BY STROKE.

SHE TAUGHT ME PRECIOUS LITTLE BEFORE SHE WITHERED AND DIED. NOTHING OF THE LITTLE BLACK HOLES I WOULD DIP INTO, POOLS OF QUENCHING WATER IN THEIR OWN RIGHT. NOTHING OF TELEPATHY, OR THE INSIDES OF, MY EYES ≋NOTHING≋ OF...

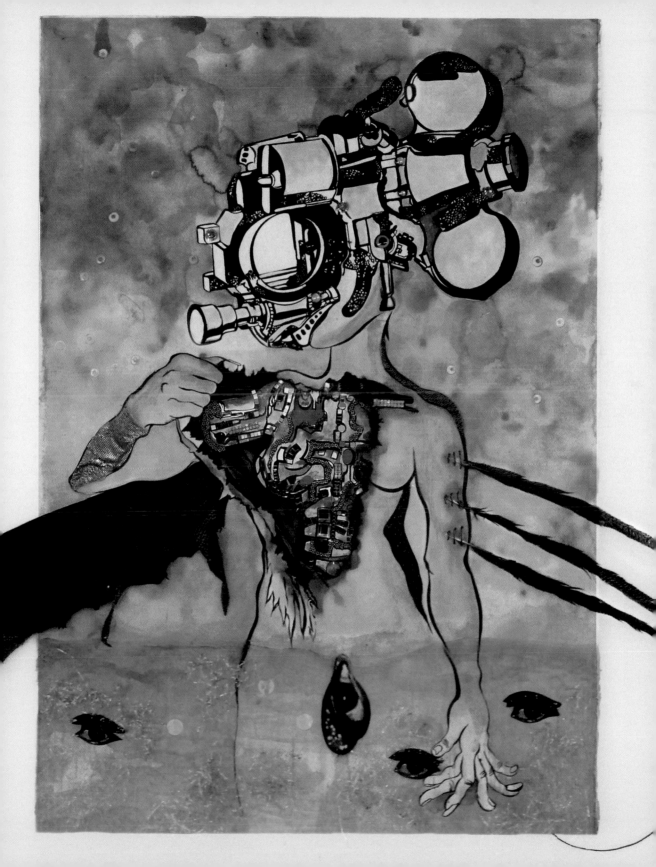

It must have been the season of the midnight sun,

the ides of July those fifty years ago, when
my grandmother split wide, unbroken, unnamed
light pouring out of her: a river into a river.

Svet: luminescence, shine. The child took a while
to cry. *Sveta*: pure, blessed, divine. The girl
had a weak spine and bowing legs and hardly

any hair and left too little of herself inside.
Call her *Svetlana*. Call her by way of ignited sky
and fairytale and yellow luster and the morning.

Know her name was cast out of orthodox
holy water under the glow of a golden cross.
Recast her chosen and a *zhid* and watch her suffer

the way all light must, knowing
                                    it is the light.

G.C. Waldrep

I Have a Fever and Its Name Is God

I have a fever and its name is God.
The nurses come in shifts
and worship it.

All around me the land suffers
from the loss of love's handkerchief.
Children sing brackish rhymes
in the lowest schools.

There is no key, only
the locked door
projected onto the city wall.
In my dreams I run from it.

The nurses bandage my body
in mathematical problems
I can't solve. I tell them
no, no, measure me
by the sweetness of honey—

Hush, they whisper.
*Our names, too, are written
in the Book of the Smallest Moon.
You were brought here
in the traitors' black ambulance.
Your brother is a scar.*

The nurses place bowls of fruit
around my prone body,
as sacrifices. *Not to you,* they explain,
but to the heat you bear.

Finally I stumble
through the image of the door
in broad daylight. No one stops me.
I am prescient as a lilac.

But the nurses say
We will never leave you.
They have prepared a feast,
they have sewn my wedding garment.

There are so many of them,
far too many to count.
Each of them lifts a piece of me
to her mouth—

By the sweetness of honey.
Let I and my works be undone.

Oxygen Song

I am unstrung: ash in an ash-garden. So say an instrument, tuned in clay, strung with ash. Not a music. A means towards an end which picks each ash-strand from the body, the mind's camber. So say there is choice, and then choice's absence. A cold star the mind's body moves into. And I fled that governance. Say not without terror. In the last photograph I will be the darkness, singing. Unremarked, as any stray or perfect tone. Is not *song*, as such: these burnt ligatures. They leave bruises. Eye of ash, eye-bramble, ash-lever.... .Ash in an ash-garden, weft from warp suspended. Is not the mind's or any final act's. A shedding tremor. Love's thinking lathe, white on white. I am moving away from this blue constellation. Speak ark, speak ash. Be a hearing wound. Mixed with oil, each pale note untrellised. Was not a bridge, was not a harp; am music's trace, blood-residue. In time or some bright kerning. Not without terror. A paler gash. Not song, nor song's unflinching charity: I fled that vagile hymnary. So say *Ash in an ash-garden*. The mind will follow the body almost anywhere, into choice, even (or any final act). If unstrung then O un-bridle me, Master.

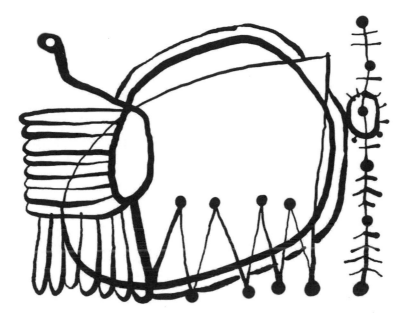

Intermission

Every other Wednesday evening, the Northwest District Small Group of the Mendota Heights Church of the Holy Redeemer held a Bible study at one of the attendees' homes. Starting at six p.m., they would chat and eat a potluck dinner, sing praise, and then break for dessert before reconvening to study the Word. They found this schedule best for digestion.

Most of the time, Jolie was excused on account of homework or some other clever reason—sore throat, important movie with important friends, emerging allergy to the mold problem at the Hatfield place. But every so often, like tonight, it fell to Jolie's mother to host, and then there was no way out. She had to greet guests and help clean and smile, displaying to everyone her exemplary behavior.

Leaning against the white pantry doors, she watched the adults flock around the kitchen island where the desserts were laid out. The snaps and falls of their conversation were something like the squawking of birds. "—I just can't stand the swearing in those movies—" "Can you believe those gas prices? They're *gas-tronomical.*" George the Senior's horse-like laugh boiled up, and Jolie clenched her teeth. George the Junior smirked at her from across the room, wiggling his pinky in his ear.

And then her mother's voice. "Jolie. Jolie, are you listening? Go get your poem. Show Reverend Stark that poem you wrote for class."

"Mom." Jolie rolled her eyes. She would be thirteen in five months. She didn't need to do a show-and-tell.

"It was the most wonderful poem," her mother said.

"Jolie is very bright." The Reverend smiled at her in the way people smiled at little kids who thought they'd done something great, like coloring a giraffe purple. He had a smear of chocolate on his front tooth.

"It's too bad she's so shy." That was her mother's new excuse for why Jolie didn't go to Bible study, why she didn't talk to adults, and, now, why she didn't run and grab her poem, which was a stupid poem anyway.

But she wasn't shy. She was just sick of them, all these adults with their fake smiles, repeating their old, used lines. The only one she could stand was Andria, who touched her on the shoulder. "Jolie, I haven't seen you in so long," she said in that sweet, breathy voice of hers, a hand resting on her swollen belly. "Come up to the bathroom with me. Let's freshen up."

When Jolie was younger, and Andria, who lived down the street, was still her babysitter, Andria would powder Jolie's nose and paint her nails in a rainbow of colors, and Jolie would practice braiding Andria's beautiful blonde hair. Now Andria was married to Jack Sullivan who had bought the house next door and who did not believe in God. Jolie and her little sister Jessica had been the flower girls last August. Andria was going to have her own baby in just a few weeks. She said that Jolie would be her little boy's babysitter, and wasn't that perfect. It was a lot to take in, even for Jolie.

"So?" Andria said, leaning toward the mirror as she put on her lip gloss. "How do you like seventh grade? How are your classes?"

Jolie shrugged, studying her reflection next to Andria's. "It's okay. Language Arts is all right."

She didn't know how Andria got her hair so soft and wavy. Jolie's own hair was straight and stiff and boring brown. She was a long, bony twig standing next to Andria, who was lovely as a doll, only now she was cruelly overstuffed. She grew puffier each time Jolie saw her. Her belly was bigger than a basketball.

"Is it exciting to be in a new school?"

"Not really. It's mostly boring."

Everything was supposed to be boring at almost-thirteen, it seemed. Everyone was always talking about being bored. It was never safe to say you liked a book or enjoyed talking to a boy or didn't mind a certain teacher.

Andria smiled at her. "You're so grown up," she said, and offered Jolie the lip gloss. "Want some?"

Jolie took it and leaned toward the mirror, opening her mouth and moving the pink brush over her lips as Andria had done. Then she pressed her lips together and tasted the stickiness. There was no flavor or sweetness in it, only the vague smell of pencil shavings.

"Thanks." She handed back the lip gloss. Andria placed a hand over her belly. "Calm down now," she said.

"Does it hurt?" Jolie asked. She watched as one side of the belly pitched forward.

"It's just a bit bothersome. He doesn't kick hard. He just likes to move around."

But Jolie had meant the whole thing; she did wonder what it was like to be pregnant. She could see Andria's belly button outlined behind the blue jersey.

"Do you want to feel him kick?"

Jolie shook her head. "No, thanks." She had touched a pregnant cat's belly once. She had cupped the shape of the kittens inside her palm. They were so strangely alive, squirming behind the thin, stretched-out skin. Jolie had worried she would squish them, and she had been disgusted.

Back in the kitchen, the adults were scraping the last crumbs off their plates. Reverend Stark stood by the entrance to the living room, smiling at no one and clearing his throat to signal that it was time to get started. A few crumbs stuck to his argyle sweater vest at the place where his belly began to widen. Her mother said he was young, but Jolie wasn't so sure. He was beginning to go bald. Little white scales lined the pink skin near his temples. Finally, it was her mother who ushered the adults into the living room.

Alone now, Jolie surveyed the mess of chocolate-smeared dishes and half-eaten sweets. She ignored them all and selected an apple from the fridge, one with no bruises or blemishes. She rinsed it under the faucet and crunched into it, enjoying the spray of juice. The first bite was always her favorite. All the bites after that were less flavorful.

She brought the apple down to the basement, where the kids were always banished. There had been a time when Jolie loved the basement nights. The lower levels of everyone's house seemed full of games and new friends and noise. After her father died, those nights were the only time she could be herself without fear that her mother might be watching—or worse, that her mother was not watching but lying in bed, listening. She and Jessica had tiptoed around the house for months, afraid to watch television or play piano, afraid to talk above a whisper.

Downstairs, Jessica had already taken out Connect Four and Operation and Hungry Hungry Hippos, trying to interest the Hatfield twins and the Martin boy, all of whom probably still played games by throwing things in the air and declaring victory. George the Junior lay sprawled on the bean bag chair, stuffing his face with another brownie, his fourth or fifth. Crumbs fell onto the pillow's blue corduroy and the cream-colored carpet.

"So?" Jolie said. "What do you guys want to do?"

"I want to fart a candlestick on fire," said George the Junior. He laughed with his mouth wide open, revealing every bit of brownie clinging to his teeth.

Jolie couldn't figure out what had gone wrong with him. He was, after all, only one or two years younger than Jolie herself, but he acted worse than Jessica, who was nine.

"What about the rest of you?" Jolie asked.

The twin girls looked at her blankly, and the little boy rubbed his nose. Jolie spotted the plastic white funny bone between his fingers and snatched it away. She dropped it back into the Operation box and closed the lid. "You can't give them little toys like that," she told Jessica. "They'll choke."

The little boy crumpled his face like he was thinking about crying. Jolie looked down at him sternly. "You'll choke."

"Let's play Hot Lava Monster," Jessica said.

"How?" They would need much more space to run across the room, and more people, too.

"We'll go in a circle and the little kids can sit in the middle. They can be lava the whole time, even if they tag us."

"I call beanbag for safety," George the Junior said.

They took the pillows and the couch cushions to set up more rocks, grabbing a plastic pink stool and dragging over the wooden toy chest. In the end, the circle was big enough, so they decided the little kids could move around, if they crawled. The little kids were so excited about playing a big-kid game, they didn't even mind being lava.

Jolie chose a sofa cushion as her safety, and each time someone shouted go, she skipped over to the next pillow and the next, until she made it all the way around. She was the tallest one with the longest legs, and she imagined herself jumping like a dancer. She even pointed her toes and added little scissor kicks. *Sissone! Pirouette!* she shouted the commands in her head. The kids shrieked with laughter and Jessica repeated her three-note giggle. George the Junior punctuated his jumps with shouts of "Take that!" and "Hallelujah!" Jolie was as quiet and light as a falling leaf, balancing one-legged on the pink stool. She could do this with an apple in her hand. Each time she reached safety, she took another bite.

The little kids actually managed to tag them a few times, but they didn't know to ask for any kind of reward. George the Junior kept adding more rules and tricks. One leg only, he'd say, or whoever got to safety last had to do the next run alone. When he was standing on her safety cushion, and Jolie was only two rocks away, he turned without warning and came bounding back.

"Re-*verse*! Time to re-*verse*!"

Jessica turned the other direction, but Jolie, already in motion, couldn't react fast enough, and George crashed into her. Her jaw snapped shut and she fell off the pink stool. She hit her arm against the toy chest, but that wasn't what hurt— George had struck her chest with his elbow. Pain reverberated from the center of her breast like ripples of red heat. Tears welled up in her eyes. George's legs were heavy across her stomach as he lay diagonally on top her.

She shoved him hard. "Get off me, you pervert." She had just learned the word, but it seemed like a word invented for George.

He rolled away and sat up, hugging his knees to his chest. He peered at her with worried, sorry eyes. The little kids came over and huddled around her with a hushed gravity. They all saw her crying.

Jolie wiped the tears with the back of her hand. "Okay," she said, trying to keep her voice firm. "No more playing. We're watching a movie now. We're watching *Toy Story*."

No one argued, and that made her feel better. George hovered close to her as she stood up. She didn't want to look him in the face.

She started the movie and kept one light turned on so she could read *Pride and Prejudice*. The library book was so old, the pages were yellow and she had to be careful turning them. Everyone in her class had chosen their own books for the Book Report in a Bag project, and Jolie had gotten permission to do *Pride and Prejudice*. It was a difficult book, like her teacher had warned her, and she couldn't concentrate with the movie playing. She gave up and went upstairs to use the bathroom. The adults were taking turns reading a Bible passage out loud as she crept by.

In the bathroom, she found streaks of russet brown on her underwear. She had been through this before, but it was still embarrassing, and she had to take off her light khaki pants to check the back. There was no stain, and when she wiped, there was no blood, either. Her mother had said that she would get used to this, that she just had to count the days on the calendar, that it was easy. But womanhood made no sense at all. It was awful to wear a pad. They were itchy and smelled bad, like fish or old pennies. She went back to her room and grabbed a clean pair of underwear, then added a liner to be safe. The liners were more comfortable than the pads. Back in the bathroom, she gazed at herself in the mirror. This was her third period. Who knew how many more would come? Only if she were pregnant could she skip her period. She imagined the slither of half-formed bodies, the collision of limbs and mingling of fluids—all that was required to create a life.

"Gross," she said, making a face. Then, her self in the mirror made a worse face. She shook her head to scatter the thoughts, and then she skipped downstairs.

Her mother was in the kitchen with Reverend Stark. Jolie stopped at the doorway, watching them. They stood too close together. The reverend murmured something she couldn't hear, but the soft, falling tones of his voice made her ears buzz. The back of her head burned. She watched as Reverend Stark lifted one beefy hand and placed a finger against her mother's cheek.

"Jolie." Her mother jumped back, away from the reverend. "What are you doing up here?"

Her voice was high and rushed. Jolie didn't answer. Reverend Stark looked at the two of them stupidly, his mouth half-open.

"How's everything downstairs?" Her mother wiped her fingers against the side of her pants.

"Fine." Jolie kept her face blank but refused to look away from her mother.

"What's everyone doing?"

"Watching TV."

"Oh, good." Her mother clasped her hands together, looking relieved, even though she despised TV. "Reverend Stark was just—" she paused, "explaining something. We better get back in there now."

They rushed to the living room. Her mother glanced back once, but said nothing. Jolie stood in the empty kitchen. Everything seemed different.

She was too hot. She did not want to go back downstairs, so she stepped out to the yard. The night air was cold and sharp. She took several deep breaths until she felt the tightness inside her uncoiling. The moon was bright and full. It lit up the yard and the browned maple leaves caught in the grass. She walked over to the lilac bush and touched its bare branches, then to the raised garden bed her father had made for her mother, which was now filled with dirt, leaves, and shriveled weeds. Her mother had stopped planting things. She lifted a rock from the dirt just to hold its solid shape in her hand. Then she stood and looked up at the sky, where everything was still.

"You looking for something?"

She turned in surprise. Jack Sullivan was standing in his yard. His dog Cody, a black lab, trotted over and stuck his wet nose into one of the diamonds of the chain link fence. Jolie didn't know how long they had been there. She walked over to say hello to Cody, who was Andria's dog now, too. Jolie knew the dog better than she knew Jack Sullivan, who traveled for work.

He pointed a finger at her and narrowed his eyes. "Jessica. Right?"

"Jolie."

"I thought Jolie was the older one."

"I am the older one."

He slapped his forehead. "Right! Of course you are. Yep. I can see it now. You're definitely the older one."

She focused on patting the dog's snout. "Good boy, Cody."

"*Jolie, Jolie, Jolie,*" he sang her name in a little melody. "So is that short for Jolene, or did they name you for Angelina?"

"They named me for beautiful," Jolie said. "It's French. My dad spoke it."

She felt things shift back into place inside of her. Reverend Stark didn't know how to speak French. He could never compare to her dad.

"A man of sophistication." Jack Sullivan smiled at her, but his smile looked more like a smirk. She glanced away and watched as Cody sniffed her hand. But then the dog lost interest and turned his nose to the side, sniffing *her*. Jolie took a step back and crossed her legs.

"So how's the party? How come you're not in there?"

Jolie looked up. "How come *you're* not at the party?" The tone she used was a mixture of her mother's stern voice and the teasing lilt of a loud but pretty eighth grade girl who was dating the tallest boy at school.

She was surprised by her imitation of it, how easily it came, but he laughed approvingly. "Doesn't seem like my kind of party." He nodded his head toward the living room window, and Jolie turned as well. Between the wheat-colored curtains, she could see the adults sitting in a circle. George the Senior was waving his hands in front of his face like he was swatting at butterflies.

"That's all pretend," Jolie said. "You should see what they do for real."

She didn't know why she had said that, but he leaned forward with interest, resting an elbow on the fence post. She had to go on. "They look like they're praying, but they're really incanting. Like, curses. To the devil."

"Oh, my." He peered toward the window. "Is that what they're doing?"

Jolie nodded. In Social Studies, they had acted out a scene from the Salem witch trials. Jolie had played one of the young girls in the courtroom.

"Revered Stark traffics with the devil." It felt good to say this.

Mr. Sullivan—Jack—shrugged. "I guess we all do, sometimes."

His eyes swept disinterestedly across the lawn.

"He drinks blood," Jolie went on. "Chicken blood."

Jack turned back to her, the corner of his lips twitching. "Chicken blood. That can't taste good."

The boldness that had raced through her earlier dissipated as she grasped at what to say. "He likes it fine."

"Andria wanted some backyard chickens. Now I know why." He turned his squinting eyes to her. "Are you out here trafficking with the devil, too?"

"No. Of course not."

"Maybe you should. You could tell some scary stories."

Jolie forced a smile, because he was expecting one. The dog ran off in pursuit of a squirrel or a rabbit, leaving her alone with Jack. She shifted her feet and pulled at a loose blue thread dangling from the hem of her shirt.

Jack lifted a hand to his head and stretched his neck. The inside of his arm was smooth and pale, unlike the outside, which was covered in coarse brown hair. As he stretched, his white T-shirt rose up, and Jolie could see another line of hair that trailed along his belly to the brass button on his jeans.

"So I married a blood-drinking Satanist," he said. "Now that is some tough news to swallow."

The adults stirred in the living room, getting up and rearranging the chairs. They wrapped up these evenings by praying out loud, sitting in groups of two or three.

"You won't tell Andria I said anything, will you?" she asked.

"Would they curse you if I did?" His eyes were amused, but she was serious now. "I'd hate it if they cursed you, on account of anything I did."

"Promise?"

"Cross my heart." He winked. "If you'll keep a secret for me."

A carton of cigarettes appeared in his hand. He held it out for her to see. Camels. She shrugged. "I don't care if you smoke."

She knew her mother would disapprove—that she already disapproved. She thought Jack was irresponsible and too charming; that he didn't pick up dog poop or keep up the front lawn; that he traveled too much to be a good husband. If he'd converted to Christianity, she'd be more charitable, but he hadn't.

Jack flicked his lighter, and a small flame appeared. He shielded the flame and brought it up to the cigarette dangling from his mouth. Jolie watched as he closed his eyes and inhaled, then tilted his head and released a ghostly stream of smoke into the sky, which was much darker than before.

"I won't tell if you won't tell," she said.

"Sounds like we've got a deal."

He smoked his cigarette, but no longer seemed to relish it as much. A bird called out in the night. A cold breeze swept by, and she hugged her arms around her chest. The button on his jeans glinted, the teeth of the zipper curving loosely around the bulge of his crotch. She'd studied the diagrams in health class, the little pictures of the cartoon man shown from the side. His penis, always a darker color than the rest of his skin, would dangle out like a spigot. The little elephant trunk, her friend had called it.

"So you think it's gonna snow soon?" he asked.

"What?" Her face flushed.

He was looking up at the sky. "Wondering when we're going to get snow. Got some new skis this summer. Doesn't seem that cold yet." He held out a palm, like he was offering her something, but he was just testing the temperature. "You like snow?"

"It's okay," she said. "I like it all right."

"I love it," he said. "I was gonna do a trip to Colorado in January, but we'll see with Rosemary's baby on his way. Afton's okay, and I could go to Wisconsin, but I bet I could still make it to Denver. Just for a weekend. I've got buddies there."

"Sounds fun." Jolie thought of Andria, and suddenly a wave of sadness came over her.

"Hey. You'll be our babysitter, right? I'm glad. You're a pretty cool kid."

"Thanks." She didn't know what else to say. If she talked about her babysitting experience, she would only sound more childish. She wondered if she should check on the kids downstairs, but then Cody came running back to them, so she offered the dog her fingers to lick. His tongue was rough and warm.

Mr. Sullivan dropped the cigarette stub into the grass and stamped it out. He wore brown flip-flops, and tufts of hair curled along the top of his bare feet. He kicked away some loose dirt near the fence to make a shallow hole. Still using his foot, he brushed the cigarette into the hole and covered it up again.

"All right now. I'm counting on you."

Jolie nodded. She knew it was just one of those adult jokes, that it wasn't serious. Still, she was sharing his secret.

"You won't rat me out?" The cigarettes were gone now and instead he was holding a pack of Doublemint gum.

"Attagirl." He held up his hand for a high five, like the gym teacher sometimes did, but this was different. She placed her palm carefully against his, making sure their fingers lined up. His hand was much bigger than hers, and his skin felt calloused. She hadn't realized how small her hands were. He could fold her hand entirely into his, but he didn't. They touched for only a moment.

"See you around, Jolie." He turned to leave, whistling for Cody to follow. Jolie waited for his door to shut before going back in.

The adults were slowly filing out into the kitchen. There was always more talking to be done, with the adults. They talked as they doled out leftovers, offering more of this and that, and then, "Please, we don't need any more sweets." They talked as they searched for their belongings—sweaters and shoes, purses and children. Across the room, Reverend Stark was finishing off the last piece of carrot cake. Cream cheese frosting stuck to his lips and fingers. He caught his thumb in his mouth and licked the frosting off. When he caught her gaze, he stopped and gave her a grimacing smile. She looked away. Her mother was in the foyer, saying goodbye to the Martins. George tapped her on the shoulder. "Sorry," he said, bowing his head several times. "Super sorry." Then he raced away to join his parents at the door.

Andria came down the stairs from the bathroom, keeping one hand on the railing and the other one against her back.

"How did it go?" she asked. "Did you have fun?"

Jolie shrugged, guilt dipping in her stomach. "We watched a movie." Andria nodded, as if she couldn't wait to hear more.

"That was it," said Jolie.

"What movie did you watch?"

A wave of homesickness came over her. It tired her to lie, to keep Jack's secret, but this was how the world worked, how it would always work from now on.

The house sank into a bright silence after everyone left. All the lights were still on. Jolie imagined what the house looked like from outside, from the yard, lit with emptiness. She wondered if anyone might be watching.

"Better clean up," Jolie's mother said. Jessica was sent to tidy the basement, and then to bed. Jolie gathered the dirty dishes and sponged them in soapy hot water.

Her mother dried them with the green linen. "What do you think about Reverend Stark coming over sometime?" Her tone was careful. "For dinner or something?"

Jolie paused. Her mind raced with mean things to say about his boring sermons, his size, his love of dessert. "Do we have to?" she asked.

"It'd be nice to have some company for dinner once in a while, don't you think?"

"No. I like it just the three of us."

"Oh."

The echo of her mother's voice reminded Jolie that a great sadness resided in her mother, and even when she was happy, a shadowy tendril could rise up and grip her throat or stomach. Maybe Jolie had inherited this, too, like her mother's nose or mouth, or maybe it was something everyone had, in different amounts. Either way, it was not something she could talk about. She rinsed the soap off another plate and handed it to her mother. "Tonight was fun," she said. "I'll go next time." That was all she could think to say.

Her mother's eyes shined triumphantly. "I knew you had fun at these. You act like you're so bored but what else are you going to do? Watch a movie by yourself? Now, that's boring."

Jolie rolled her eyes. But she *would* go next time. She would go every time if that was what she had to do to keep Reverend Stark away from her mother.

"Better go get ready," her mother said. "You've got school tomorrow. Thanks for helping."

Jolie moved quietly through her room so she wouldn't wake her sister, though she stopped to adjust the blanket that Jessica had nearly kicked off. She found her pajamas and brought them to the bathroom so she could change after she showered. She shut the bathroom door with a sense of relief. Brushing her teeth, she made faces in the mirror, Foaming Vampire and Rabid Dog. A pretty cool kid, he had said.

She glanced out the window. She couldn't see much but she knew the window faced the side of their house and their front lawn. Jolie paused, toothbrush still in hand. She rinsed and spat, swiping a handful of water across her mouth. The blinds were pulled up. If he were to look up from a cigarette or from the dog he was petting, there she would be in the window. He might even see her from inside the house. But they were in bed now. There was no one out there to see her.

Even so, she remembered his eyes on her skin, a certain look he had given her. Slowly, standing in front of the mirror, she pulled her shirt over her head. The beat of her pulse was in her throat. She untied the drawstring at her waist, let the button loose and pulled the zipper down. Her khaki pants pooled around her ankles.

Her bra was dark navy blue. Padded A cups from Macy's. A pink rosette sewn onto white ribbon sat in the space between the two cups. Her underwear was from the girls' section, patterned with pink hearts and yellow lightning bolts. Who decided that those things would go together? Pink and yellow. Hearts and lightning. She wondered if she was beautiful. She suspected not. Her chin was too long and her eyes too close together, but her collarbones looked nice. All collarbones looked nice.

Without taking her eyes away from the mirror, she reached behind her back and undid the clasp. Her skin tingled as she remembered the touch of his hand, but she did not look out the window toward his house. She did not look away from the mirror. She slid her thin arms through the straps of her bra, which she dropped to the ground.

Her boobs were so small. Just beginning to take shape. Breasts. Boobs. Neither one was the right word. She pressed the palm of her hand against the left one, giving it a light squeeze just to feel that familiar ache. Then she traced a lazy finger around the edges, the areola, like a man would, and gave it a pinch. The nipple rose up like the pink nose of some small animal. No, not pink. Something deeper than pink.

Jolie moved her palm up and down, the bud of her nipple an interruption against her skin. She held her breath. She did not look away from the mirror. If anyone saw her, they wouldn't be able to tell whether or not she was beautiful. She'd be too far away, just a figure in a window. But wouldn't they stop to watch.

A car alarm broke out somewhere down the street. Each blaring note grew louder and closer. In terror, she jumped into the tub, and pulled the shower curtain shut.

Gale Marie Thompson

Smile, Eidolon

I wait to come to good. I wait carved

from the same war, wait draped

by the mechanism between myself

and fabric pleasure, how pressed, how shut.

The icon I remember is ragged

and full of brown cardinals.

It sees me, parallel shoulders and not.

The young thing in a frame.

A slow press of film I wait for to ripen.

I am asking this of you. To see things out of order.

My body's floor bright and fixed with you,

clay mask powder in the tub and sink.

The finest way to avoid is through the body,

getting out so quickly it doesn't deserve

the name of leaving. I reveal the ship's bone

like a stammer, magnet a napkin of sage

to the fridge, fruitfly blood on my fingers.

We can't go back to empty forms.

Peter Mishler

Study for the Boatsman

Single tenant
of his emptied city,
coat blown open,

he carries a bucket
of quicklime
to the coast.

The birds make
their derisive whistles,
watching from the woods.

On a sun-bleached
colonnade at dusk
he leans against a pillar
drinking discontinued colas.

The frieze behind his head:
children eaten by a fish.
It's chiseled into stone.

He must have seen to it
himself, must have studied it
with approbation,
limestone in his hair.

Later in his whirlpool
he presents himself
a single darkened plum.

Watch the warping
of his face
in its reflection,

its flesh swallowed gratefully,
the pink stone spit
into the garden below.

Former master of The Dove,
head bent to his chest
and water beading in his hair,

he sleeps in his bath
then wakes at dawn
to heft the refuse
from the tidal pools:

slabs of viaduct and filigree,
half-skeletons of ruminants.
His eyes eager and wild,

and wavering
like the honeycombs
at the edge
of his very vast forest.

BEES IN THE GARDEN

WRITING AFTER LANGUAGE'S ECSTATIC NECTAR

TRANSLATED FROM THE ITALIAN BY JENNIFER SCAPPETTONE

Filippo Tommaso Marinetti

The immaterial colorworks of great mosaics

This piece is drawn from the last major work of Futurism's founder, Venezianella and Studentaccio—*a self-proclaimed "aeronovel or aeropoem" of 125 pages, and a rare example of experimental narrative in modern Italian literature. Dictated to his wife Benedetta, daughters, and colleagues in Venice in 1943-44, in the midst of grave illness and a world and civil war, F.T. Marinetti's virtually unpunctuated epic of "words in freedom" revisits, and revises, the aesthetic and ideological foundations of Futurism. It imagines rebuilding an outmoded, feminized, and culturally heterogeneous cosmopolis the movement once proposed to destroy—in the form of an inhabitable female colossus of Murano glass.*

Glassblowers and glasshandlers students in pink green orange blue caps and pigeons on goldverdured hills palpitate wings screeches feathers leaflets and a ruckusing thick

A path is carved where nearly sprinting springing forth Turkish slippers or relay doves Venezianella healed emerges from the gondola cabin in crimson flecks and enters St. Mark's like the essential detail of that sculpted architecture

Hot now and with newly polished amaranthine whiskers the living Golds of the basilica pant & sweat with stupor admiration lust

The solemn enrobing of Venezianella begins

Everyone knows the whole city labored labors day and night at the pleated mosaic of her hips

The frescoes with hooked noses want to sniff the delicacy of the lacelike loggias and of the gossamer marble lacework that will veil her shoulders

A saint with ebony face and skyblue turban declares

—Venezianella I want the sparkling fringe of your skirt that burns me with envy

When the Neapolitan coralfishers have accomplished the thickening of porphyry blood and jocund lips toward an ever more virile rutilation of the garment the lovely Lagunar matrons enter mother-of-pearly sheathed and with plump silken hands minister to the twisted embroideries of Loveremembrance in soft orange tones

While an ogival window has filled to the brim with sun at dusk as with so many dying incandescent devils a swashing to the feeble tintinnabulations of rosary beads ushers in the abstract and turquoise elegance of the forces of asceticism anxious with tremulous candor

Austere and strong that is to say willful sacrifice that is to say threatening absence and present flight penetrates the reconciling temple famished again

The badmouthers insist that St. Mark's Square has been the worldly salon of European gossip for centuries

Today its most representative players that is the pigeons flown to the cornices make like spectators at the marble rendezvous paths of the Plaza metamorphosed into a fervid workshop of mosaics and as much as Negrone and the futurist glassmakers may order and teach it is the little stones and chiseling hammers that take command stipulating arrangements and refinements

Copper furnaces redouble the admonishments of the fire higher and higher up to where turquoise comes from the Bosphorus in a tartan or paranza boat declares itself High Calligrapher and Master of passionate idealisms branded virilities and crystals percussed by flashing bolts of light

Negrone clarifies

—To obtain the ineffable inspired-mechanical unreachable parchment of gold surrounding the lacustrine papyri we need to form ostriches bears kingbirds prawns toads hogs frogs crocodiles leopards billygoats wolves foxes elephants roses basilisks gardens wild boars but also and don't forget machines too

Solemn the cauldrons of Sicilian lava advance hauled by glassmakers with vaporizing spirals of blond fury rosy softnesses of gorgeous nude virgins and mother-of-pearl penumbra of a submandarin in August

A crowd presses in intrigued

—Surely to bind the inequalities of the stones cantankerous and proud with concentric claims will require the famous Insulating Sublime and be careful as the stones are seeping jealousy

Elbowed on the Café Florian table Negrone alerts

—Venezianella is its repository beseech her to intervene with the secret algebraic constant

Then we can amalgamate the mosaics of the New Venice

More veiled than upheld by too many affectionate hands the beautiful girl springs forth and is vermilion in the face and her cerulean eyes wide with fever ignite the tragic exhaustion of her fragile little voluptuous body sheathed with orange canvas like the crepuscular sea of Chioggia amidst the sails tawny with wherries

—With pleasure though exhausted already I'll do my best to prepare the mixture for the Sublime Insulator and I have no breath left to pronounce the sibylline words in freedom of chemical accompaniment Fusion and Speed in tactile exchange & all the points must match & without slippage Harmony harmony of opposites

The glassmakers contemplate her

—Poor girl O look how her chest writhes and what duress in those graceful temples!

Negrone to Studentaccio

—And to think that the lagoons are unmoved their stockpiled coolness all bolted down by avaricious fire

Venezianella raising her voice like a lily

—Ideal unity to desire you intensely with an ever more foolish ardor & for goodness' sake all of you make a desperate effort toward cohesion please and the tortured definitive kiss

A crowd breathlessly

—Help Venezianella's fainting wavering dying

Negrone receives her in his arms

—Implacable noon don't crush her so atrociously Hurry glassmakers bring the Great Soothers of feather and milk into the Square

Instantly massive fans moved by bellows on wheels stuffed with carnations blow distracting and digressive gladness everywhere

Invoked by all the aeropoet of Surgery Pino Masnata[1] declares

---

[1] Pino Masnata (1901-1968) was a surgeon and futurist poet, author of "Poetry of Surgical Instruments" (1940).

—My operation will save Venezianella and it is called Isolart but the patient must be isolated first of all

Negrone orders

—Widen the circle around her body

Prostrate yourselves merge your heads with the mosaic floor

Masnata perfects his speech

—As I operate with my thumb alone laid upon her heart I will absorb it all nullifying my very self

So amidst the fanners of suavity feather milk Venezianella is conveyed to the Orseolo Basin in the gondola of Singsound with its ivory keyboard that offers all the keys of coolness

In the snowcapped bluish shadow of his tentacular white hair Aldo Giuntini[2] loosens his hands in a rushing of happy seafoam and a healing musical synthesis passes over the nerves of Venezianella

The gestures of Negrone immensify St. Mark's

An elastic army of saintly forms with tearful aureoles congeals that occupies a corner of a hazy triangular velarium and the most African setting sun rages tumbling down

In ramming motions it tries to graze the embellished garment of slender Venezianella who's unaware if it is all right or not as many broken but eager hands of tailors and seamstresses invisible to obsequious looks dress and undress her

The muscular and swarthy leader of the glassworkers of futurist images Studentaccio can't stand it any longer and bursts out

—Sanctity and Loveremembrance are sufficient in this robe that requires a character of absolute heroism not to be found come forth glassmaking friends who puffing through your iron pipes will know how to round the great globes of synthetic courage and focalized intelligence fused

Two futurists with the swaying of prehistoric sacerdotes racing with river

---

[2] Aldo Giuntini (1896-1968) was a futurist composer and musician.

grasses rise like two massive lapis lazulis and direct blowpipes to the sky with two earthly globes precarious formed of fluid glass reddish green like pigeons' necks

—Let o let it be possible for us to pray in our own way and not with paintbrushes nor with the stentorian lungs of aeropoets but with eminent and everfalling feminine grace

Over those two marching acrobats the iron pipes are nearly upright with the dangling globules of molten glass extracted from the crucibles at the peak they speak to everyone to the rapt cheeks of all the spectators loquaciously speak of the most important kiln's deep secrets the one that bears the name of the ideal

Studentaccio makes like a troubadour

—Since one day Venice too will enter paradise let her beauty be refined and sanctified when it's perfected and don't be stupefied if we futurists are the ones who wish to fulfill this miracle seeing as only holders of the future can measure perfectibility with spatula tweezers pliers and pulmonary strikes we launch outlandish Easter eggs to the sky

—As a futurist glassblower this is my expertise I know how to crush flatten curve twist before cooling on the altar

A little laugh like a spring or brood rings out and it is the voice of the already invisible Venezianella

—The model demands a word!

Eleven futurist glassworkers fall into a circle forming a wheel of self-propelling prayer

—We believe that each in his original position can better implore the sky recumbent or lounging or prostrate as the paintbrushes rods burins supplicate Art to reach Absolute Beauty

The glassmaker Obscurantine shrieks

—The glassmakers' words are windbag bubbles

Negrone threatening him with a muscular arm that obelisks itself amidst the mosaics terrorized by noontide

—Quite the contrary they are rather splendid bubbles of glass capable of enclosing the Ideal and you prop up your reasoning which stinks

Studentaccio intervenes

—Obscurantine you are intolerable I advise you to listen to Venezianella

The frail cluster in the affectionate and reverential handling of the hammerers vehement fracturers is forced to say not to say fade away

—Well I prefer a greater simplicity

I'm afraid you are losing yourselves in a cauldron and your Last Judgment terrifies instead of gathering wild boars stags eagles grimaces lambs apostles doves willows

—You are mistaken Venezianella and I Negrone will help you to stipulate all the necessities and it requires wild onagers turtledoves atonements grains vineyards baptismal fonts trasennas gates and the potent motors of speedboats and motorized craft

As saintly as Saint Mark may be and consecrated again by the grave admonitions of the organ mindful and dreaming of contrition and regrets Venezianella's alcoholic entourage is unbottled forth with fury and its strident spumante seems nearly satanic and greeting it in obsequious steps is the sirocco wind peddler of ever new caresses

With rolled-up sleeves adversarily big toppling cork Negrone stands in the way

—Venezianella is part of us futurists as proprietor of the factory of glass beads and other cultural weights that adorn & embellish the female body

Studentaccio seizes a blowpipe quick and polishes Negrone's skull with a great teardrop of molten glass

Without rancor like the oblique rays that retract their mantles of vibrant golden gnats or an octopus's monstrous tentacles in the tepid water the entourage of futurist glassworkers reunites guided by Acquaviva[3] who defines

—Planets in motion foreseen by Prampolini's[4] paintbrush the domes of St. Mark's Basilica advance rise and rotating touch the byways of the sky

The great gilded mosaics superbly enriched with treasures from afar accompany the electrified human abandon to the sea

---

[3] Giovanni Acquaviva (1900-1971) was a Futurist artist and theorist, author of *L'essenza del futurismo suo poetico dinamismo italiano fra le filosofie* (1941).

[4] Enrico Prampolini (1894-1956) was an avant-garde painter, sculptor, and set-painter, who wrote *Arte polimaterica* (1944).

—You're drop-dead gorgeous Venezianella drop dead gorgeous more gorgeous than a goddess

Studentaccio gets angry

—With your globules of scorching glass you oppress such a fragile venusness which look that first star would like to drink in and let her breathe easier now with a bit of space

Negrone pronounces to Studentaccio

—You and she are two skew lines that no plane can contain

—You're wrong Negrone we are two parallel lines

Everyone at the spectacle on the jetty's edge

Solemnly from the Church of St. Mary of Health to the Public Gardens the upholsterers of horizons work to swell veils blood-red and a bright canary yellow with names and titles that gleaming rebound from the rigging to the water Strength Greatness Depth Sensuality Embrace

Strangely one searches everywhere in vain for Venezianella who bejeweling herself for certain with liquid reflections has disappeared

Studentaccio roars

—Whoever abducted her is a damned villain do him in

—We'll do away with the students of political economy they're the ones who were arguing over the price of her robe

In a moment willed by the laws of the New Aesthetics the sunset theatrically but slowly slowly with the indolence of oars that toil orders the palaces of the Grand Canal to lift their marble gowns and show off their little shoes of gold & silver buckles mirroring on the rising glass floor of high tide at table with the battle frescoes in the houses

Instantly in a humanist façade a peculiar spell makes the fragile embroidered balconies fretwork of the feathered and blooming ogival four-light windows allow an ivory smoothness of roseate little breasts to be glimpsed with erotic cunning

With hot bitter vanilla-infused sugar they seduce the repercussive scarlet radiance of the ducal naval walls & ceilings

Resplendent asymmetrical bluing of weapons aristocratic eels

—Yes yes knock off the abductors of Venezianella

A crackling vortex of irate helixes springs out

—Just think Negrone that everyone in agreement expected the price of her mantle to be exorbitant and didn't want to buy it any less

Morbid curiosity of verandas that jut out almost to the point of plummeting

—I'm convinced that Venezianella has been kidnapped by the film producers

Buzzing vibration of glass and mullions vie to be more svelte in gossip of corolla feather to vanish in the water kwash

—Okay but we glassworkers won't allow this filmification and Venezianella will not appear onscreen

—I Negrone swear it unless it's upon the sky

A cracked voice stuffed immediately with fists

—I've discovered who took her away it's Negrone with the dissident futurists all of them convinced that the hem of her gown was too dazzling and solar

The denigrator buckles and is kicked away like a ball

The futurist glassworkers' cheeks burn so ardently that to pacify them they interview the tremulous mirrors of the lagoons directly face down in the delicatest dusk that powdering itself with stars enscarves a vault of heated sky roadsteads pupils plunks of creaking oars tenderness of masts and whiskered kisses in search of upturned noses

The dynamic liquid mirrors laugh & taunt teaching that it will not be easy to find Venezianella

—Slow down o slow your vengeful voyage surly bad boys and leave bludgeons and revolvers at home theatrically to embrace great fat soft scepters of tow against which Venezianella's kidnapper can't possibly defend himself

Do Birds Sing from Sheer Exuberance

Or is it border-patrol duty dawn to dusk

This morning they began like a water-glass choir
Multiplied by ten in the birches along the river

Until a robin on the back lawn shoved another off
A square foot of grass and two hummingbirds at the hanging

Basket of fuchsias dive-bombed each other's head

Now I'm looking in the field guide to see what it says
Is the proper term for birdsong is it *calling* perhaps

Or something more chest-thumping or military or both
But the guide resorts to *voice* talk about noncommittal

Ti-dee-di-di and wheep wheep wheep

Not counting the catbird's come-hither stay-away
Like a melodeon on meth like a gleeful pickpocket

Who suddenly spurts from between three leaves
Leaving all that burbling and cheeping behind

And now that it's flown in the distance I can hear

Mourning doves reciting *The Joy of Grieving*
And practicing its advice Give in to your sadness

Let loss wash over you until you're cleansed
Which seems to be taking approximately forever

Because they haven't stopped giving in to it yet

Until nearly noon when the July sun clobbers
The whole air from sky high to lying prone

And the silence that ensues is so ungodly loud
It rhymes with the brave new sound of war

 AKA stay out of sight *leave a lighter footprint*

Featuring drones the length of a magpie in flight
Steered only by a microchip the targeted victim

Standing on a rooftop smoking a cigarette
Dozing almost the sun flat on his face

Until late afternoon when the birds start up again

At dusk signaling music's finale
As night inches up the corkscrewing locust's branch

And the birds shut down in their inky sleep

Whistle

Whistles while he works. Whistles the jetty. Whistles the rip tide. Whistles the sand terrier, sky kite dangerous. Whistles liquor in a bag, on the sly. Whistles for your attention, for your safety, for your affection. When air is blown into the plastic cavity, it rattles the pea. Whistle I wear from nine to five. At five, one last blast to clear the waters. Whistle in guard shorts' pockets. Whistle still seeming to be around my neck into October: phantom rope: memories kinesthetic. Whistle I sometimes wear to bed, dream of being choked by someone who hates me. Who hates me?

Whistle at Jersey boys in boardshorts who skimboard reckless in shallow wake. Cramp their style. Whistle as hassle. Whistle at diggers of holes to China. Whistle their false antipodes. Whistle around which my skin tans. Whistle as stencil. Whistle in Deauville, in Olive, in Reho, in Hickman. Whistle at lightning. Cup the cavity for a higher pitch. Whistle against thunder's grumble. Hurricane's onset. Irene.

We still in love. We still got plans. We still getting closer all the time—asymptotal, tidal spook, rogue wave. Things get wet. We still sorry. We still trying. We still doing our best. We still think about what next summer would have been like. We still get our whistles switched, mails crossed, feelings hurt. We still wonder how our soaps got so small all the time. We still counting down to something that used to matter. We still matter. We still mid-air. We still suspended above buoy mounds that soften our landings. Is this your milk in the fridge, or is it mine?

Whistle pop chorus maybe Katy Perry, whistle at: *Kid, stop maypoling my jetty flag, please.* Whistle-work-work-whistle-work. Whistle forgot on nightstand. Have you backups in lockers, or borrow from Brenna? She's off today. Whistles with knots more fashionable. Whistle won't. Whistle wait. Whistle. The medic needs your 10-20: your location precisely.

We steal glances in guard shack. We steal lotion from lockers. We steal moments away from the others. Apply lotion to the skin of his spine. Does he shiver? We steal touches of thigh underwater. We steal as many such touches. We steal Kevin's buoy Trevor's buoy Emma's buoy. We steal all the buoys and tie them in fashionable knots, and we float them as prank. Honey pranks in which sand grains sap in patches like coastal mange. Initials carved in the stand. TZM (Travis Ezekiel Michels). Ocean as accomplice, as a complicated ecosystem. Ocean as thief. As hunger. As lover, takes me into it.

Whistle diaphragm flat into plastic. Whistle do they hear? Fainter at the scumline. Whistle lacks volume. We need air horn, need aerosol. Whilst we. Whilst we.

We still remember. We still never forget skinny-dipping. Cypress swamp drought, and John, in his canoe, never said a word. Why *not* say a word, John? Why not say a word? Try "Ibis." Try "Egret." Try "Heron."

We still cycling past the arcade, ten-cent Skee ball. I'm all-time high scorer. The balls leap the ramp. We still cycling that wooden walk. We still pedaling with the Bulgarians. And it's the end of the workday, and we are going home. And we are workers slaloming vacationers, velocities balletic. And *the workers are going home / the workers are going home / the workers are going home*, and it's harmonized at 360 watts. It's Weezer. It's Weezer. It's we still. We still going home. We still on the payroll. We still on the billboard. We still on the boardwalk. In the beach dunes where we ought not be. We still in the *Cape Gazette*. We still on postcards you can send to your moms and your dads. We still on seasonal leases. We still making the best of a bad situation. We still. Stay still. We stay still.

We still we.

Whistle-Whistle-Whistle-Whistle
Whistle-While-You-Just
Whistle-While-You-Just
Whistle-While-You
Ree-sar-Ree-sar-Ree-sar-Ree-sar-Ree-
Sorry-Sorry-Sorry-Sorry-Sorry
I'm-sorry
I'm-sorry-for
I'm-sorry-for-ree-sar
Ree-sar-Ree-sar
Whistle-Whistle-Whistle
With-soul-With-soul-With-soul
With-Soul-Now-With-Soul-Now-With-Soul-Now

We so fortunate. We so burnt and flaking. We so cocky. We so bronzed, bleached, belligerent. What have you. I wonder: *Who will nick the dead skin off my back? Whose version of fun is that?* We so fun. We so sloshed. We so impressed with one another. If you clap my back, I'll clap yours.

We so slippery with aloe, with zinc on the nose. We so. We so-so. We so privileged: Lifeguard parking only. Lifeguard discount. Lifeguard: *She just started sucking my dick*. Lifeguard free drink. Lifeguard 50% off drinks. Lifeguard: *Her friend sucked it too*. (Bullshit.) Margaritas. With salt. With salt. (Whistle.) Lifeguard Olympics. Lifeguard locals. Know tourism is terrorism. Lifeguard parties. *Shut up, Bristowe*. Lifeguard fistfight. Somebody cocked me with gravel. Somebody squeezed my left nut. *Let's just sleep in the car*. We bleed saline. Have amnesty. On rain days, we play meteorologist: exile the patrons then take shelter in beach boy sheds. We sit on rentable chairs, design umbrella forts, slurp coffee-mug gin snuck from acquaintances from condos. We get boozy under thunder. Have you ever seen the pilot episode of *Baywatch*?

They call us Hasselhoff or Gump. It's nothing like that. It's not like that at all.

We saw sharks in the water. We saw skates and rays. Jellies dolphins turtles the size of tires. We saw each other six miles out on the water, BZ-boarding to or from Cape May. We stopped to chat in the middle of the ocean as if we were on the sidewalk—talked about gangster rap and Joe Flacco; we even planned a trip to Philly before paddling away.

On a horizon swim to territorial waters, it was just the two of us on recreation. We saw the one-mile buoy. We saw the two-mile buoy. We saw the third mile stretch out before us. Our rotator cuffs inflamed. Freestyle. Freestyle swim. Immortal? We swim. We saw exhaustion in each other's faces. We saw fear of the water. We saw panic. We saw each other's lips ask for "help." The word by itself.

help

How neither of us was in a position to. We saw treading for dear life. We saw how life was dear. We saw only two versions of blue: blue sky and blue aqueous. It was all liquid, and it was no earth. And it was no earth. We were without earth.

Earthless, treading. We saw each other giving up. We saw we were only human. Bipedal. Pointless evolution. We saw what mortality was all about. We saw our nearest near-death experience. We saw lives flashing before eyes, mine and yours. We saw a flash.

With the current against us—tide or time, one we can't outrun while the other runs out—we saw a last-ditch attempt to be known, to be heard so far off the shoreline. Are we even in Delaware anymore? What *is* this place?

We saw the whistles in our lips, the synchronicity of the pitch. We saw the cheeks inflate. Panic in deflation. We heard how a whistle could be a sort of prayer.

!

We earned bad similes, like "silence as big as the ocean."

We saw the ad boat then, tasted its gasoline wake, heard the smack of the rudder. We saw relief in our wide eyes. Even the lifeguards need rescue sometimes.

Whistle when tiger sharks feed on bluefish shallow. Whistle meaning get out. Alex to all stands: *Definitely a shark.* Definitely, definitely whistle. We still huddled around the small television in the shack, nibbling lunch during *Shark Week*.

And there's radio chatter.
Laurel to Shack: I think our radio's dying.
(I think our radio's dying, 's dying, 's dead.)
Shack to Hickman: What did Laurel say?
I think they need a new walkie-talkie, Shack.
10-4.

Whistle cardiac arrest. Whistle heat stroke, stroke stroke. Whistle seizure. Action circle. Clear the radio. Paralysis from chest down. *Is he on any meds, ma'am? Is he otherwise healthy? Just Viagra*, she says. You can tell she's proud of that. Whistle sirens. Whistle cover down, lieutenant's bag. AED. Shave the victim's chest, apply adhesive pads, clear and shock.

Whistle: Too close to jetty. One died on *that* jetty. Captain all-to-well. The algae mats on the Brooklyn jetty. Surfers no kings of this beach. Coastguard protocol. Link arms with a bluebody, its saturated translucent skin. Detritus of shitshow Dewey. We swim in the dead. We swim the bodies in. Whistle to disperse crowds. Wait for body bag. Whistle as gratitude for breath.

Have you ever seen *Endless Summer?* It was nothing like that, not even when we tried our hardest. Especially because we tried so hard. Once stale, there's nothing fresher than a mistake. Once stale, each of us has texted Emma at one time or another. Who does Emma text? Or does she only reply? What kind of girl is only meant to reply?

Whistle: Don't feed the sea gulls, not even your stale salt-n'-vinegar fries. Remember the man who killed one with the back of his shovel? Aren't gulls one of the monogamous birds?

Please: This is not my last time on the Atlantic. I spend my last half hour with the little girl who lost her mother, tell her she can come up on the stand with me.

Rehoboth to Shack.
Shack 10-3.
I have a 10-52 here.
Go ahead, Rehoboth.
On Rehoboth, we have Tessa. She's eight years old, wearing a pink and yellow swimsuit: Dora the Explorer. She thinks she came from the North end, and her mother's name is Robin.
10-4. Shack to all stands, please be advised…

We so gonna miss this. We still have a free round of mini golf. We still got Grotto's free pizza coupons. We still gotta get back to Funland. We still need to conquer the Gravitron. We still need to say goodbye to the Spanos. We still want another taffy to stick to the molars. Take me to Ibach's. Take me to Dolle's.

I give Tessa my backup whistle. I teach her how to whistle too—*If you put your tongue on the opening, just in place, the whistle won't crescendo*—and tell her she can help me clear the water at the end of the day. She doesn't know that this is my last day, that she is my last stand partner.

Tessa says she doesn't want to return to Wilmington or Dover. Whichever she said. Wherever she's from. Wherever any of us are always from. Migrancy. She says that's why she got lost in the first place. She means "ran away."

Have you ever even seen *Endless Summer?* Neither have I.

Andrew Michael Roberts

salt

what began as salt,
as blood and need, blue and
winged and laced
with spools of astral milk,
what began a sweet ache,
thunder of swifts,
the softly closed eyes of the air,
vertebrae, a louse,
what began as the ceremony of distance,
the ubiquitous dusk,

as barbed wire,—became us.
what began in winter,
abandoned by clouds,
innumerable white,
limbs weighty and mute,
sleek tusks of ice, a moment pierced
and perfect as night
mewling its clarity to the stars like a soul,
became us:
pewter and lye, spires of frost,
jazz glistening,
eyes loud and wet
and cold as new mouths
yawny at the womb's eclipse.

pink nothings, tiny as a universe.
what began as salt became us.
and now. now—herons, galaxies, the great
music, honey and fire;
now the world, heaving and
taking and bristling
and true.

Gary L McDowell

The Emptying That Fills

"The mind is hurried out of itself, by a croud of great and confused images; which affect because they are crouded and confused. For separate them, and you lose much of the greatness, and join them, and you infallibly lose the clearness."

—Edmund Burke

I can envision coming back as something other than, larger or smaller or altogether shifted, off-compass like a coastline, a vulture, a boy running ahead of his father in the forest. As raindrops. The parallel lines of their fall and the uniformity of their sound and their wetness, yes. I'd like to fear the falling, or be feared for falling, or be myself what is feared most: inexhaustible, as clouds, as moisture. Such is/as faith. Such is responsibility and believing in something untenuous, animal-driven, needed.

My son and I are taking an early fall hike through Long Hunter State Park just outside Nashville. We walk the two-mile loop around Couchville Lake, weave the cone-shaped fishing waters, watch for deer and turkey and kids hoping for bluegill, listen to wind through the treetops and crows or ravens and the last of the cicadas zinging. All the noises, except a distant twig cracking underfoot, we cannot spy, come from above our heads.

Maybe I could come back as a tree: blackgum, pignut, hophornbeam, the varieties we see outlined on the State Park sponsored plaques posted every quarter-mile along the path. Trees like poetry, like fatherhood—we speak in cataracts and pristine stillness while the world sleeps and while the world watches—augment and negotiate segmentivities: branches hang low over the walking path, their hatchet-shadows and their dancing, partition, apparition, whatever ghost-lights through the canopy. We are here, on the ground and moving, and they are there, from the ground and still, except to shift at the weather.

Elias Canetti, in his *Crowds and Power*, makes of the forest a symbol, tells us that *the forest is the first image of awe.* My son, running ahead of me on the trail now, shrinks into distance, but he is still level, still plained, capable of moving further-away or closer-to but incapable of moving up or overhead. *Man stands upright like a tree and he inserts himself amongst the other trees. But they are taller than he is and he has to look up at them. No other natural phenomenon of his surroundings is invariably above him and, at the same time, so near and so multiple in its formations as the concourse of trees.* I follow him, wind around a corner or two, find him again, his arms twirling, his head bouncing above and then below and then above the horizon created by the rise and dip of the trail. Every few paces he stops to look up, so I slow to let him. *Looking up at trees becomes looking up in general. The forest is a preparation for the feeling of being in church, the standing before God among pillars and columns.*

Part of me thinks I know him better now having watched him look up, search without knowing for what he searches. I want to know him better *now, here, forever,* or at least *before.* But I can't answer *before-what?* Canetti tells us, *tree-tops are attainable.* Frost: *He is all pine and I am all apple orchard.* Maybe that's enough? He's mine like an apple is the tree's? He's mine like a needle is the pine tree's? He's neither mine nor his own? My fear: I'll never be sated of him before this or that, or I'll never be able to *appreciate* (to gain in meaning or value) his closeness: he'll always want to run ahead of me far enough so that all I'll be able to see is his head tilting, his eyes locking onto something above.

◆ ◆

Tam Mai shows me a picture of his most recent painting. A waterfall, its white-crush, violent and moving, an inventory of fear or beauty, or a scar askew. The water folds into a black pool, the rocks jutted, the shrubbery around the scene both stoic and spined. Vietnam. *My home country*, he always tells me, as though *Vietnam* crossing his lips would make it more real—or less real.

He empties the trash in my office, tells me, *scroll next one*. The same waterfall but this time there are shadows in the water and the water darkens at the base of the falls. A face or two ovals and a crescent, hair or wispy branches and leaves, and then, opalescent and dissoluted, another face, this one with longer hair and no pupils, something of a ghost, an apparition, a disembodied grass-sky-tree, *the-emptying-that-fills*, an ancestor and what it feels like to believe.

He tells me, the waterfall is the mother. The pool is the father. Gravity is the pressure to obey. *Only mother kisses child. Only mother the child knows for sure. Father? Could be. Could be not.* The threat of drowning permeates the culture, and the children that play along the skirt of the waterfall flirt with salvation, encourage the spirit of the not-father to push them over the edge into the pool *too deep for children to touch*. Rain floods the jungle surrounding the fall every spring. *Trouble everywhere. Nights spent under water. Feet blister from the wet. How to escape wasn't an idea.*

The drowned speak in unison, it is said. In the night they make noises—at dawn the night never existed. What they fear isn't the dark water but that they aren't conscious fully when the light seeps back in.

◆ ◆

To better appreciate *practice*, maybe *reprieve*, or to *study*, let's take a quick tour with our resident arborist.

The blackgum to our left has a straight trunk though the branches extend outward at right angles. The bark, furrowed with age. The twigs, when we reach to snap them, break easily to reveal the pith: chambers of greenish partitions. Little cells, not jails or rooms, but mitochondrial engines, airy pockets defined.

The leaves: elliptical, obovate, lustrous and entire. We roll them between our fingers, crush the purple-red to crumbs, make a cocoa-colored mess in our palms. Look! The flowers have fruited on a lower branch, one outside our initial field of vision: a black-blue, ovoid fruit. Our field guide tells us that it has a thin, oily, bitter-to-sour taste. We don't dare, though we should. Fleshy drupe—one to three from each flower cluster. The fruit's stone, more or less ridged. October. Early October. The click of consonants on the roofs of our mouths, a stone rolled click-clack, click-clack like a mint against our teeth.

We run our hands along the blackgum's trunk, peel off a small piece or two of bark. Pale yellow, sapwood. White even, if the light. *Not durable in contact with the soil.* But who's to say what's *stable*, what's *which*? Further we reach. I put my son on my shoulders, ask him to run a leaf through his fingers, tell me what he feels. *Rusty feathers,* he says. I didn't know he knew those words in combination. Our guide tells us, *wedge-shaped with margin slightly thickened, acute or acuminate. They come out of the bud conduplicate. Feather-veined, midrib and primary veins prominent beneath. Petioles one-quarter to one-half an inch long, slender or stout, terete or margined, often red.* Encyclopedic: the music of nature's Nature.

Here is where science ends and poetry begins. Or maybe they're one and the same always: *Moby Dick. Nature. Leaves of Grass.* We touch the tree because it's on the path, because we can't understand it better without holding a part of it in our hands. When my son's in trouble, I grab his arm, pull him close to me, watch his eyes and reprimand slowly. He understands he should shift his eyes from mine, should do everything to squirm away, and he will try. But something holds him close. The gravitas of fathers-sons, the noise of close-watching, of observation, of knowing something's intrinsic importance before its utterance.

Our arborist pauses mid-sentence, considers his next explanation. *Definitionally speaking, I don't mean to lose you here, but this...* A dismissive wave of his hand. *Anyway, I will carry on then. You can undoubtedly follow.* The language is never the problem. The delivery, however. The tone, mood. Anatomy of intent, to stray ourselves from apathy.

I put my son back on the ground. He walks ahead, sees a turkey, gobbles at it and laughs. The turkey, confused, struts, complicates the sexual obliviousness of the season.

The pignut, shagwork, mockernut. *A hickory, you see.* Hickories are monoecious, hermaphroditic, and their bole is often forked. A tongue split two ways, a tree that knows multiple voices, that always faces light and dark simultaneously. The staminate catkins—wind-pollinated flowering spikes—of pignut hickory develop from *axils of leaves of the previous season or from inner scales of the terminal buds at the base of the current growth.* Or exactly like Darwin suggested: survival.

Husks of pignut hickory split only to the middle or slightly beyond and generally cling to the nut, which is unribbed, with a thick shell. My son wanders over the next ridge in the trail. I call him back. Protection then, in the shadow: think of the otherwise danger. The dream surrendered. The arborist caresses an unsplit husk, pushes it to his lips, the wax of what's left, practices the wind, says, *shhhhhhh* and *listen.*

He tells of other trees, ones hard-wooded, ones delicious in the shade, in moonlight, under the blue black nevertheless known or unknown sky. *I'm not one to say,* last but not least, *but, last but not least: the Ostrya, the hophornbeam.* The arborist mimics us reaching out to touch, so we do. Scaly, rough bark. Alternate and double-toothed birch-like leaves, flowerless until spring when their fruit is a *small nut fully enclosed in a bladder-like involucre.*

The name Ostrya is derived from the Greek word *ostrua,* "bone-like," referring to the very hard wood. Regarded as a weed tree by some foresters, this hard and stable wood was historically used to fashion plane soles. My son, weaving down the path, his arms jutted out parallel to the ground as wings, dips left and right, curving, urging the engine noise from deep in his throat.

———◆◆———

"Moonlight hanging or dropping on treetops like blue cobweb. Also the upper sides of little grotted waves turned to the sky have soft pale-coloured cobwebs on them, the undersides green."

Gerard Manley Hopkins, *An Early Diary*, "April (?), 1864"

———◆◆———

"You have to get obsessed, stay obsessed, and keep passing open windows."

John Irving, *The Hotel New Hampshire*

———◆◆———

In June of 1992 I found a box in the parking lot of the Cary Area Public Library. Among the things I threw out: two five-pound dumbbells, a jump-rope, an empty box of Rogaine, some old Twizzlers, and a stick of deodorant. What I kept: four issues of *High Society*, two issues of *Hustler*, a long-distance calling card, and a beat-up pair of weight-lifting gloves. And for that entire summer, when I wasn't lost in an issue of one of those magazines, I mowed the lawn wearing the sweat-stained weight-lifting gloves. They made the job less job-like and more manly. I sweat, I gripped that sonuvabitch mower as tightly as I could, Metallica's *And Justice for All* on Side A and Weird Al's *Even Worse* on Side B, the Walkman cranked as high as it would go.

———◆◆———

"It may be regarded as a projection, a climax, a badge of strength, power or vigour, a tapering body, a spiral, a wavy object, a bow, a vessel to hold withal or to drink from, a smooth hard material not brittle, stony, metallic or wooden, something sprouting up, something to thrust or push with, a sign of honour or pride, an instrument of music, etc."

Gerard Manley Hopkins, *An Early Diary*, "September 24, 1863"

◆

I wish I could paint you a picture of the rock. It was all colors at once, especially purple and silver and brown and gray and light and moon and clouds (backlit, naturally) and chrome, chipped primer maybe. And when the hundreds (or thousands) of box elder bugs crowded onto it, black and orange and black and orange like the blues and whites of "The Great Wave off Kanagawa," frothing and foaming and yet static: *Pictures of the Floating World*. I mowed around it, thinking each time that the box elder bugs would scatter, but they never moved or even flinched. I tried to aim the grass thrown from the mower away from them. Their peace became important to my peace. Even youth perceives quiet, appreciates the calm of a not-decision, of being at another's whim.

They gathered on the rock to judge its worthiness as a place to overwinter, at least that's what I learned later at the public library. The silver maple they called home all spring and early summer wouldn't do for the cold months. *Otherwise known as a zug or a maple bug or a stink bug.* They sought a warm, dry place for winter, thought the rock, warm because of the summer sun, would be that shelter, and so they clamored to it, laid claim to it, covered its surface in hopes that it would warm them from the coming cold.

◆

Q: Why are poets so fascinated with autumn?

A: Because squirrels bury nuts—I've always wondered, how do they find them later? Surely they could find *a* buried acorn, but how do they find the ones they themselves buried? Maybe, and I'm imagining that squirrels have an olfactory ability akin to moles, they smell their way through the vast parkgrounds and forests until they twitch upon the scent of their own saliva—the hormones, the bacteria, the after-food-and-gender-and-blood—their shit, their urine, some marker or another that sets their acorns apart. Or maybe it doesn't matter. Maybe a nut is a nut and against the brute reality of winter starvation they simply choose survival over the pettiness of good manners.

It gets darker earlier in autumn: more time to research questions like this, and so we, poets, admire the autumnal shift in light, the candor, the tilt, the buoyant full-colored grace of old and new, the receding and rising-dropping of one orb for another.

For me it was this: "Their sons grow suicidally beautiful / At the beginning of October, / And gallop terribly against each other's bodies." For me it was Wright's other poem where at the end of summer, "in a field of sunlight between two pines," as the butterfly slows down, the hammock swings softly, and the poet whispers, "I have wasted my life." Maybe James Wright is autumn like Plath is winter like Roethke is summer like Whitman is spring. There's the vacating—the already left—feeling of autumn. It's the coming of cold that makes us cold, and … Let me start over. In the morning just before sunrise, there's a color at the eastern edge of the land-sky slope. It's *roseate. Coral. Flush*, with the un-light of the sun and the blush of the early fog. Here, this bloom, this scallop—its efflorescence: a pity more are dreaming through its bursting—disentangles the night from its corollary, night from what should be unnamable: harvest, consequence, yielding.

My mom swaddled me too tightly as a baby and so now I run hot. I hate being warm. I'm a poet, but for a long time I thought it was my body that was fucked up.

◆ ◆

I just read today that the Mbendjele Yaka of northern Congo believe Europe is the afterlife. Forest-living hunter-gatherers considered the first inhabitants of their region. They avoid contact with the *exterior world* to maintain autonomy. They believe that all Europeans are spirits and hope that someday they'll be born again as Europeans.

I have a friend who thinks that eventually mainland California will break off, *disengage*, he says, as if the land will stop its conversation, turn its back on implicit metaphor and symbolic he-said-she-said, of the continental US and cause a tsunami that will engulf, flood, *ocean-palette* Hawaii. Locusts. Earthquakes. Tornadoes. Superstorms, with names. To come back as a natural disaster, god-like, ravaging, migrating. Flock, how birds sense, and leap or lift or *plume*, a coming quake or wave, something disruptive—a warning we're likely to ignore. To come back as that flock, the cosmic, the consciousness, the worldly Over: if the land leaves the land that holds it and depresses, pushes the stars to the peripheral, upends what stands, what floats, what can *overcome*, cup your hand to your ear and listen for the flutter of feathers and hollow bones taking to the sky. Go, then, in the opposite direction.

———◆———

"I was taken to the place where the sun sets. ... While at that place, I thought I would come back to earth again, and the old man with whom I was staying said to me, "My son, did you not speak about wanting to go to the earth again?" I had, as a matter of fact, only thought of it, yet he knew what I wanted. Then he said to me, "You can go, but you must ask the chief first." Then I went and told the chief of the village of my desire, and he said to me, "You may go and obtain your revenge upon the people who killed your relatives and you." Then I was brought down to earth. ... There I lived until I died of old age. ... As I was lying [in my grave], someone said to me, "Come, let us go away." So then we went toward the setting of the sun. There we came to a village where we met all the dead. ... From that place I came to this earth again for the third time, and here I am."

Paul Radin, *The Winnebago Tribe*, 1923, as told by Thunder Cloud, a Winnebago shaman.

———◆———

What I don't realize is I can't hide that, loyal or not, we are all doomed. To one go-round, one set of beats, breaths, calibrations. Pop songs often get everything wrong, but sometimes they get it right:

I hope I die before I get old. And.

I ain't as good as I once was. And.

For it's hard, you will find, to be narrow of mind. Exactly.

Are we a peace-loving people despite the evidence? And how can a thing that's evident itself also be evidence? I heard a story on the radio about a man who bet his wife his Chicago Bears would beat her Green Bay Packers. The winner would get to taze the loser for three seconds. In public. On the street. The Bears won. Both drunk, they stumbled outside the bar in Smalltown, Wisconsin, and he touched the electric fire to her ass, burned her through the denim as spittle spilled through her lips, as her eyes rolled, as *eyewitness accounts.* She then called the police, had him arrested for "intent to harm with an electronic weapon." Patience. He had none. Had he known better the *scope*, the ramifications, the dimensions, for one thing, of *trust me, it'll only hurt a little, for a second,* maybe he'd have gloated instead. I can see him grabbing his rib cage as he belly-laughs, his wife crumbled on the ground, smoke rising from her burnt jeans, and then the sound of sirens later, once she *regained*, once she sobered, the crowd by now dispersed.

The seed of an eastern wahoo, a Carolina buckthorn, can travel from the Outer Banks to the Tennessee woods in the belly of a warbler. To come back displaced. To come back rendered in love with soil redder, more clay-like: *the human body as distinguished from the spirit.* To be born through deposit, through shit, to loosen control, root where dropped, and take time, multiple seasons, to sprout, if warmth and wet and will combine, if a squirrel or shrew doesn't nip your first green bud, your first shoot shot through the soil. *I shall die, but / that is all that I shall do for Death.*

Somehow, I believe in the coming back, and I owe this credence to some faith I don't understand. To come back as a witness, to come back as another kind of patience, the way trees grow, ringed and known only afterward, after the years are counted aloud.

Beauty Be

fogged each a distinct cataract blue
beads drape my daughter's neck when I pull it
down from the shelf the jewel box
smells of very old woman what remains
of great grandmother's chest pinch
the golden lock shining the objects inside O
to be as small and lovely and precious
as these my daughter fingers the pins grandmother wore
in life clips the widowed
earrings their counterparts gone
as the earlobes of the woman made
more lovely by these pearls
we sit my daughter and I adorned
and cross-legged on the floor it is important
on occasion to recall the way a jewel ripens on the body
reflecting each new generation of light
as it's birthed through the window's perfect crotch

Fig. 1. MANUAL (Ed Hill / Suzanne Bloom). *Neue Albers IV*, 2013. Archival pigment print, edition: 5. 19 5/8" x 22 1/2".

Off the Shelf
A Conversation with MANUAL (Ed Hill / Suzanne Bloom)

Ed Hill and Suzanne Bloom have been partners in life and art for 40 years. Their collaborative work, under the nom d'artiste MANUAL, has consistently pushed artistic and practical boundaries, subverting conservative notions of purity of mediums by combining painting, photography (both analogue and digital), video, audio, and computer programming. Their most recent work has focused, with exceptions, on creating photographs with books. Each of the 100 works in their three series (Books I, II, and III) is a compositional and technical masterpiece that centralizes the unique objectivity of the book while delving into the book's content, sometimes literally and sometimes as indicator of deeper human connectivity.

—Juliette Bianco

Juliette Bianco: How does your collaborative partnership work: how do you make decisions about starting a new work? Does the process change from photograph to photograph, series to series? Do you have any defined roles?

Suzanne Bloom & Ed Hill: On the technical side, our collaboration has been very fluid, and we each sometimes do take on specific tasks. But in terms of creative and conceptual input, our collaboration is completely non-hierarchical. Ultimately, the decisions about what artwork makes it out of the studio always is shared, and we each retain veto rights.

"THE BOOK, AN ABRAMS MONOGRAPH OF THE ARTIST, IS POSITIONED ON A TABLE SAW FACING THE VIEWER. THE BLADE IS UP, THREATENING TO CUT THE BOOK IN HALF."

JB: Do you know when a book first appeared in any work of art by MANUAL? What was it?

SB & EH: In 1975 we made a 4-by-5-inch black-and-white photograph titled *Art History Lesson*. In the photograph an apparently nude woman is pointing to a reproduction of the painting *Odalisque with Slave* by Jean-Auguste-Dominique Ingres. The book, an Abrams monograph of the artist, is positioned on a table saw facing the viewer. The blade is up, threatening to cut the book in half. It's one of a dozen photographs in our series, *Art in Context: Homage to Walter Benjamin* (1974–79).

JB: The books in your photographs are not always photogenic—I never feel like I am looking at a portrait of a book because the book is not presented as object so much as idea. You capture the cerebral processing that happens when one is reading a text (the physicality of the printed words create meaning only in our minds) and make that happen for the beholder of your photograph. How do you describe the activity of reading, and how does that relate to your work?

SB & EH: We've always been mindful of the difference between looking at and reading a work of art. Our collaborative name, MANUAL, is most often used to qualify the word "labor"—and we do think of art-making as both a physical and cerebral act—but it's also a description of a particular type of book, a manual or guide to or for something. If our photographs are like books, as you suggest, then we think they must be seen as primarily "literature," rather than, say, reportage. We don't intend the book photographs to be didactic as is typical with manuals. There is no one meaning connected to any of them. Instead, we attempt to make each a rich, informed experience, both visually and conceptually, so that return viewings will be rewarded as they should be with second readings.

JB: You have said, "The book is not so much the subject of our project as it is the object." If books are the objects of your series, what is the subject?

SB & EH: Bit of a conundrum, isn't it? Our photographs of books are both subject and object, presenting a kind of "double face." They picture an object that has content, which is impossible to "pictify" through one image. Trying to deal with the philosophical subject-object problem in a photograph is an ironic, near-impossible challenge having to do with the issue of "words and images," which is exactly what we love about it. There's a wonderful saying by the American painter, R. B. Kitaj: "Some books have pictures and some pictures have books."

JB: How do you identify and consider a particular book as object for a photograph?

> "OUR COLLABORATIVE NAME, MANUAL, IS MOST OFTEN USED TO QUALIFY THE WORD "LABOR" — AND WE DO THINK OF ART-MAKING AS BOTH A PHYSICAL AND CEREBRAL ACT — BUT IT'S ALSO A DESCRIPTION OF A PARTICULAR TYPE OF BOOK, A MANUAL OR GUIDE TO OR FOR SOMETHING."

SB & EH: A short answer as to why we choose a book is substance and appearance. A book has to engage our minds because of its content, history, or title, and then strike our visual sensibilities because of its material attributes and physical being. At the start, many of our pictured books were familiar objects, part of our personal library or on loan to us by friends. But since 2011 we've gone to bookstores and the internet to find particular books. For example, after reading Stephen Greenblatt's *The Swerve: How the World Became Modern*, we searched online for copies of

Lucretius' *On the Nature of Things* and found a 1743 two-volume set with broken boards. It was a wonderful discovery. The pair has so much physical character, which helps signal the ancient history and import of the book.

JB: I'm glad you mentioned Lucretius's first-century BCE text *On the Nature of Things* because the troubled marriage between the force of nature and man's will—often depicted in text and image as being at odds with one another—is present in much of your work. Lucretius's informed text likewise embraces both of these things in the Epicurean philosophy it expounds. Do you feel a kinship with Lucretius, and is this one way to read your photograph that so beautifully pays homage to the gorgeous edition, worn as if petrified wood and set in a still-life that is purposefully manmade, with one of Ed's paintings and carefully placed stones forming the background?

"NATURE IS NOT TRANSPARENT ... OUR COLLECTIVE PICTURE OF THE IDYLLIC TRANQUILITY OF AN IDEALIZED NATURE IS A KIND OF FALSE COMFORT WE HUMANS CONSTRUCT AS A PREFERRED WORLD VIEW."

SB & EH: There's much we identify with in Lucretius's philosophical poem. We think his views in *On the Nature of Things* were and still are remarkably enlightened, and, in a major gesture to its contents, we filled our photograph with metaphorical elements and a kind of inner glow. We have taken up the concept of a conflicted Nature-Man relationship in previous series. In *13 Ways of Coping with Nature* (1981), for which we also wrote a thirteen-part poem, we used irony to point out that the Nature we all tend to take for granted is merely our *idea* of Nature. Similarly, an underlying concept at work in our extended *Arcadia* project (1998–2002) was that Nature is not transparent, and that our collective picture of the idyllic tranquility of an idealized Nature is a kind of false comfort we humans construct as a preferred world view.

JB: Some people approach books as utilitarian objects—vessels for the printed word, if we want to put a visual spin on it. But artists have long considered the book as object worthy of depiction in sculpture, painting, and other media including of course photography. Traditionally, the book is placed within a work of art as symbol of the erudition of the person who is the real subject of the work of art. Some artists look at books as objects to play with to create abstract sculptural forms. Your connection to books is much more complicated and cerebral than either of these—the physicality of the book, its form, and its content are often given equal measure as you create something entirely new with it. Something like still-life meets conceptualism. Can you talk about your approach to art-making and what makes a good photograph?

SB & EH: Yes, in most of our book photographs we seek to give equal weight to form and content. That is, the books and their identities are primary factors affecting our creative act—as catalytic agents, conceptual grounding, and so on. Exceptions to the equal form-content ambition have been instances when we've emphasized form over content for the sake of the references being made to things outside a book's content. For example, in our wry simulation of and tribute to Joseph Albers's *Homage to the Square*, the colors, shapes and sizes of the stacked books in our photographs were, admittedly, more important to us than their specific titles or contents. Nonetheless, the act of

Fig. 2. MANUAL (Ed Hill / Suzanne Bloom). *On the Nature of Things (Lucretius)*, 2014. Archival pigment print. 17 by 25 inches.

replacing Albers's painted squares with bound books confronts the abstract painting tenet, *Form is Content*, and suggests a somewhat unsettling question: Have the books become mere abstract planes, or has the sublime formal elegance of the picture been complicated by the silent content of these transmuted volumes?

"HAVE THE BOOKS BECOME MERE ABSTRACT PLANES, OR HAS THE SUBLIME FORMAL ELEGANCE OF THE PICTURE BEEN COMPLICATED BY THE SILENT CONTENT OF THESE TRANSMUTED VOLUMES?"

JB: Do you relate books themselves (not the content) with the human condition—a worn book vs. a pristine new one, for example? Does that consideration figure into your practice?

SB & EH: Absolutely. Printed books are quintessentially human, a summation and apt symbol of the mind/body equation. We probably should be described as shameless bibliophiles who consider books a part of human anatomy.

JB: I'm very interested in your photographs of banned books. What drew you to create work with books that have been censored—something that some person, organization, or government would destroy or deny to others?

SB & EH: Of course, the whole issue of censorship is always a threat critical to artists and publishers, involving freedom of expression, suppression of ideas, and so forth. On a more personal level, we're curious as to why certain books have been anointed as "banned" books. Often there's a hidden agenda factor. Steinbeck's *Grapes of Wrath* is a complex and poignant example. One reason the book was banned had to do with the so-called "filth and obscenity" in the novel, including the explicit language in the last paragraph, where Rose of Sharon, whose baby was stillborn, suckles a man dying of starvation. In addition to its Biblical overtones, the origin of this event is mythological, going back to Roman times, and widely visualized, particularly in seventeenth century paintings, *The Seven Works of Mercy* by Caravaggio being perhaps the most famous example. Known as *Carità Romana* (*Roman Charity*), the theme was a familiar one to Steinbeck, and the language he used to describe the scene is entirely appropriate in the context of his novel.

But, *Grapes of Wrath* was also the novelist's indictment of California growers' exploitation of farm workers during the Great Depression. Ultimately, the Kern County Associated Farmers denounced the book as a "libel" and a "lie" to get it censored and out of circulation.

JB: One banned book photograph that I am continuously moved by, intellectually and emotionally, is *Anne Frank's Diaries* (2012). It may seem amazing, first of all, that a photograph of books can elicit such an emotional response. Where is the place for emotion in your work?

SB: It's our practice to read a banned book before constructing an image of it. Actually, in several cases it's been rereading a book. This was true of *Anne Frank: The Diary of a Young Girl*, and the experience was wrenching for me, triggering a flash back to 1970 when I was deeply affected by a visit to the Anne Frank Museum in Amsterdam. Clearly some books represent loaded subjects, and require particular care. Embedding gravity into an image of a book that has had such an incredible impact on so many readers is

> "WHERE IS THE PLACE FOR EMOTION IN OUR WORK? EMOTION, AS SUCH, IS NOT AN INTENDED OUTCOME, NOT SOMETHING WE CONSCIOUSLY 'BUILD' INTO A PARTICULAR WORK."

no easy assignment. Where is the place for emotion in our work? Emotion, as such, is not an intended outcome, not something we consciously "build" into a particular work. But, given the intense emotional experience of both reading the *Diary* and then creating its image, we are very pleased when viewers have an equally visceral response to the piece.

JB: Describe the elements of *Anne Frank's Diaries* and how you assembled them. How and why did you choose a log for the base, the editions and languages of the books and their arrangement on the log, and the strap that binds them together?

EH: The *Diary* has been published in 70 languages and has had a huge readership, so we decided the image needed some degree of critical mass, and that seven copies in seven different languages would, we hoped, have sufficient power. We already had and read Doubleday's 1952 version, which has a remarkable introduction by Eleanor Roosevelt. Next we wanted a copy of the original Dutch edition. At this point we contacted Evelyne Schiff, a former English librarian who had known Anne Frank's father, Otto Frank, and is now a book dealer living in Jerusalem. Over time she was able to locate copies in Dutch and Hebrew, and then gave us a very worn German version. The copies in French and Spanish were available through Amazon. All of these together acted as representation of the WWII Western Front, and, finally, a Bulgarian copy sent to us by a friend, stood in for the Eastern Front.

Fig. 3. MANUAL (Ed Hill / Suzanne Bloom). *The Library (Photography & Moving Image)*, 2013. Archival pigment print, edition: 5. 47 ½ by 32 ¾ inches.

SB: Once we had our representative grouping, the process of creating a total image that would carry the weight and significance of its parts was challenging. The books needed to be held together somehow, and to have a pedestal to give them stature. We didn't want the background to compete, but the books had to seem well grounded. At this stage, what we always hope will happen in the studio, did happen—creative resourcefulness led us through several days of trials to resolutions. A reclaimed barn beam we had from a 1990 building project became the books' pedestal and personified "body"; an old canvas strap bound the books together and was an apt reference to Anne, the school girl who was an avid reader and frequently took on multiple volumes simultaneously; and, a piece of satin that appears crimson in highlight and blackish in shadow, and has the potential to signify several conditions (fire, war, blood, passion), became the supporting elements of the image. The books were arranged on the log strategically, on either side of its main fissure, and we added a piece of red cardboard between the German and Hebrew versions to intensify the historical divide and the Third Reich's murderous solution.

JB: Let's talk about a banned book photograph where you took a different approach—the photograph of an edition of James Joyce's *Ulysses* that you titled *Banned Book* (2010).

SB & EH: The 1934 legalization of the publication of *Ulysses*, which had been banned in the United States in 1921 by the New York Society for the Suppression of Vice, was a landmark decision by Judge John M. Woolsey that had major repercussions for creators, and publishers, in this case Random House. We had a paperback copy with simple but strong graphics on its cover and wanted to monumentalize it, or at the least make it large—about four feet tall. This was the first photograph in our banned book subseries.

"THE 1934 LEGALIZATION OF THE PUBLICATION OF *ULYSSES*, WHICH HAD BEEN BANNED IN THE UNITED STATES IN 1921 BY THE NEW YORK SOCIETY FOR THE SUPPRESSION OF VICE, WAS A LANDMARK DECISION."

JB: Your mention of the banned books as a subseries reminds me that as you eschew adherence to a fixed artistic medium, the contents of your series are also quite fluid. That brings us to your most recent series, *Now & Then*, which also explores magazines, slides, and Polariods as subject. Two photographs—*Now & Then #7* and *Now & Then #8* (2014)— seem at first glance identical to one another, which is not true. Could you elaborate on what you've said about these photographs of Penguin books seemingly in a self-arranged heap, and about the appearance of a banned book in *Now & Then #8*?

SB & EH: Another landmark case involving obscenity occurred in Great Britain when in 1960 Penguin Books published an unexpurgated edition of D.H. Lawrence's *Lady Chatterley's Lover*. For several years we had wanted to tackle that book, and also, to pay tribute to its publisher by using all 113 of our Penguin/Pelican books in one, collective image. This past year we finally realized both ambitions. The photographs, *Now & Then #7* and *#8* (Penguins, 1924–2008), present our collection without and with *Lady Chatterley's Lover* as the expurgated and unexpurgated versions respectively. By making two seemingly similar images we intended to produce a visually subtle but critically important absence/inclusion.

JB: Let's look at *Catcher in the Rye* (J.D. Salinger, 2014) from your Books III series, concurrent to *Now & Then*. Did you want to do an artwork about this novel and then seek out a copy of it, or did you see or have the book and then think about what you wanted to do with it?

> "AS ARTISTS WE TRADE ON AMBIGUITY, I.E., THE POSSIBLITY OF MULTIPLE INTERPRETATIONS BEING DERIVED FROM OUR WORK."

SB: It had made the banned book list many times over, and since I'd long forgotten whatever made it so objectionable, I reread my dogeared, college version. Well, it's an amazingly effective coming-of-age story with all the braggadocio one might expect. Then I found myself entrapped by its prose. Ed found a vintage copy with the red carousel horse on the front of the dust jacket and a photograph of Salinger on the back, which he gave me for my birthday. This was the last edition (Book of the Month Selection, 1951) that included a photograph of the author, who increasingly and famously withdrew from public life.

JB: *Catcher in the Rye* is also a good book to explore your intensely sophisticated artistic practice. Can you talk us through how you made it?

SB & EH: Salinger died in 2010, and in the two years between acquiring the book and starting to work with it his persona had gone "viral." Our creative process, in this instance, at times felt like a wrestling match, not between the two of us, but between our interest in trying to create a visual structure around a text, and the celebrity factor, the public having become totally obsessed with J.D. Salinger's mystique. Of course, if ever there has been a fictional character so thoroughly identified with its author, it's Holden Caulfield. As artists we trade on ambiguity, i.e., the possibility of multiple interpretations being derived from our work. One such reading of this image might be that the author, whose image, taken by photographer Lotte Jacobi, is just visible on the dark blue cloth of the book's cover, is running away with the bound volume—i.e., his text—leaving an empty book jacket behind. Hopefully a viewer will sense that what they are seeing "is an action taking place," *in medias res*, as our art historian friend Margaret Sullivan puts it in her book, *Bruegel's Peasants: Art and Audience.*

JB: Also in your most recent series, you present a bookshelf proper, which is rare in your work. *The Library (Photography & Moving Image)* (2013) is a technical and technological tour de force that also, if you read the books' titles, references such progressivism in times past. What's going on in this deceptively simple set-up?

SB & EH: The blue shelves in *The Library* contain a "whole" library that represents a statement about the history of modern photographic practice beginning in the mid-1960s, when photography as fine art was still a dicey issue and much discussed. It is, more or less, our library, the one we used during three-plus decades of teaching photography and media. The idea for the photograph had been brewing

Fig. 4. MANUAL (Ed Hill / Suzanne Bloom). *Now & Then #7*, 2013. Archival pigment print, edition: 5. 33 ⅝ by 43 ⅝ inches.

in our minds for some time, but it wasn't until we had access to a medium-format digital camera, that we actually undertook its construction. We felt the image needed higher resolution in order to startle the viewer with its *trompe l'oeil* detail, and knew that it had to pass as being a real bookshelf seen in natural light. In other words, we wanted the experience of viewing it to be a kind of archeological discovery, a virtual-illusionistic-real encounter with remnants of a definable era in media history. We love the idea of a photograph being self-reflexive. In this case, current photographic technology is capturing and digitizing its past.

JB: Looking across your three book series, I see no messaging related to the book as an endangered species. Does this belie any fears that you have about the future objectivity of books?

SB & EH: We conceal our anguish well! Of course, we realize that in certain categories the printed book may be replaced by electronic text delivery systems. The scroll was gradually replaced during Roman times by the codex, which, by the way, means "trunk of a tree" in Latin. Is it time for text/images printed on paper to move over? For many reasons, we don't imagine printed books ever disappearing from our cultural lives entirely, and we do not destroy books in the creation of making photographs of them. But, although we were aware that one possible reading of our carefully arranged "heap" of Penguins in *Now & Then #7* and *#8*, would be that printed books were being "tossed," from our p.o.v., the "death of the print book" has been greatly exaggerated. In its material form it retains qualities that are, well, too valued and valuable to be completely supplanted by e-books.

MANUAL

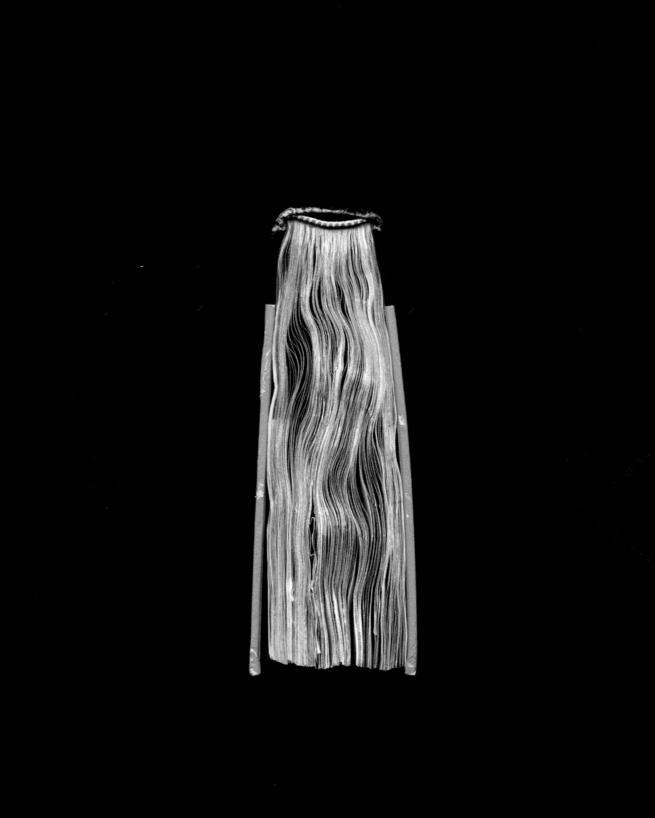

LIBRARY AS INSTALLATION

**p. 173. (upper) The Defaced LIbrary
Books of Kenneth Halliwell and Joe Orton**
from "The Library Vaccine"
Artists Space, New York. 2014.
Photography by Daniel Perez.

p. 173. (lower) The Library of Helen DeWitt
from "The Library Vaccine,"
Artists Space, New York. 2014.
Photography by Daniel Perez.

p. 174-175. Exterior View of Librería Donceles
Offsite exhibition, ASU Art Museum,
Pheonix. 2014.
Courtesy of Kent Fine Art.

**p. 175 (upper and lower). Installation View
of Librería Donceles**
at Kent Fine Art, New York. 2013
Courtesy of Kent Fine Art.

**p. 176. The Defaced Library
Books of Kenneth Halliwell and Joe Orton**
from "The Library Vaccine"
Artists Space, New York. 2014.
Photography by Raphael Rubenstein.

Fig. 1. Pablo Helguera at Librería Donceles. Offsite exhibit on in Phoenix. ASU Art Museum, 2014. Courtesy of Kent Fine Art.

The Library as Installation

As bookstores close in ever larger numbers all over the world and as libraries, great and small, cede more and more of their square footage to computer work stations and touch screens, the former inhabitants of such spaces, all those paper-and-cloth codices, all those yellowing periodicals, are on the move. Like the Germanic tribes displaced by the westward march of Central Asian nomads in the Middle Ages, these vulnerable books are compelled to push into new territories, driving out (at least temporarily) the previous inhabitants as they venture into lands where they are strangers, interlopers. Lately a number of art galleries and exhibition spaces have been the target of these biblio-migrations.

In the fall of 2013, Mexican-born, New York-based artist Pablo Helguera transformed Kent Fine Art into a Spanish-language bookstore called Librería Donceles. For two months the Chelsea gallery, which usually mounts shows of artists such as Llyn Foulkes, Antoni Muntadas and Heide Fasnacht, was filled with thousands of books in Spanish that Helguera had collected in Mexico City, either via outright donations or in exchange for his drawings. The show's title alluded to Calle Donceles, a street in the center of Mexico City famed for its second-hand bookstores that, like their brethren around the world, are steadily diminishing in numbers. Even more startling than the sudden appearance of a used bookstore in a Chelsea art gallery was the fact that Librería Donceles was the only such entity in New York City. One of the things that inspired Helguera to launch the project was the disappearance of all of New York City's Spanish bookstores, despite the fact that a quarter of the city's population (some 2 million people) is Spanish-speaking. (After its run at Kent, the itinerant Librería Donceles decamped to a storefront in a Mexican-American neighborhood in Tempe, Arizona, where it was sponsored by the Art Museum of Arizona State University; simultaneously a smaller version sprang up in San Francisco's Mission District; in the spring of 2015, the bookstore will return to New York for three months, this time in a warehouse in the Red Hook[1] section of Brooklyn and it will now offer some 20,000 volumes; subsequently it is scheduled to appear at the Henry Art Gallery at the University of Washington in Seattle.)

Furnished with armchairs, coffee tables, rugs, assorted lamps and even plaster busts of Cervantes and Shakespeare, and divided by the gallery walls and bookcases into small alcove-like spaces, Librería Donceles at Kent Fine Art was a very inviting environment. It felt more like a private library than a commercial establishment, and was a perfect place to disappear into a book (or several) for an hour or two. The selection was wildly disparate, but also carefully organized, sometimes arranged into small artful installations. Among the items I noticed were a copy of *Para Leer al Pato Donald*, Ariel Dorfman and Armand Mattelart's influential 1971 analytical exposé of Donald Duck comics, a signed copy of the Spanish translation of Bill Clinton's autobiography (*Mi Vida*), lots of great-looking pulp fiction, some displayed on narrow shelves with covers facing out, a book on the murals of José Clemente Orozco propped on a portable turntable, and an open suitcase full of political tomes. Not everything took the form of a book: I spotted a framed menu from the historic Mexico City restaurant Prendes and a poster for the great Cuban film *Memorias de Subdesarrollo* (Memories of Underdevelopment) by Spanish painter Antonio Saura. One could see that Helguera was trying to wrest some order from this avalanche of printed matter and also sense that he was relishing its randomness and chaos—the result was a fascinating essay in cultural history, with an emphasis on Mexico.

---

[1] The move to Red Hook was supported, in part, by the New York-based organization A Blade of Grass, which in 2014 awarded Helguera one of its inaugural Fellowships for Socially Engaged Art.

Fig. 2. Installation view of Librería Donceles at Kent Fine Art, New York, 2014. Photography by Raphael Rubinstein.

Each visitor was allowed to take home a single volume after making a pay-what-you-wish donation, the proceeds from which were passed on to local Spanish reading programs designed to assist immigrants. (A smartly designed poster alerted the "estimados clientes/dear customers" that books bearing green stickers were "not for sale.") Helguera or an associate of his offered visitors "brief consultations" in order to determine their "bibliological profile" and suggest where they might like to look for a book. Each volume contained a newly made ex libris label identifying its donor and provenance. The book I selected, after much browsing and long internal debate about my final choice (on the day I visited there was no one available to consult), was a 2007 anthology of articles about books and libraries from the Mexican literary supplement *Hoja por Hoja* titled *Libro Albedrío*. The ex libris tells me that it came from Rocío A. Sanchez Hernández at the Biblioteca Guillermo Bonfil Batalla in Mexico City (part of the National School of Anthropology and History). The title is a pun on the phrase "libre albedrío," which means "free will." It seemed appropriate to select a book about books.

One of the contributors to *Libro Albedrío* is Alberto Manguel, the Argentine-born writer and anthologist who has gained worldwide recognition for his investigation of books and reading, most notably in *A History of Reading* (2007). In his *Hoja por Hoja* essay, "La Biblioteca de Julien Sorel," Manguel laments the massive diminution of the power of the book in Western culture over the (now) nearly two centuries since Stendhal published *Le Rouge et le Noir*. Manguel may be the best-known elegist of the book in our time, but he is hardly the only one. Countless writers have lamented the demise of the old-fashioned analogue book (and a few have welcomed the ebook); the recent popularity of "bibliomemoirs" like Rebecca Mead's *My Life in Middlemarch* may also speak to our anxieties about the fate of books. We are certainly at a turning point in the history of publishing, but the paper-based codex of yore is still very much with us, especially in the zones of contemporary art. One only has to look at an event like the New York Art Book Fair, an annual event that has been growing larger every year. The 2014 edition attracted some 30,000 people, who wandered among the 350 exhibitors filling several floors of MOMA PS1. Although there are many dealers of rare books and ephemera at the Art Book Fair (sometimes asking hefty prices for things like old punk fliers and exhibition announcements—memo to self: never throw away any printed matter),

Fig. 3. (opposite) Installation view of Librería Donceles at Kent Fine Art, New York. 2014. Photography by Raphael Rubinstein.

the majority of exhibitors offered books and 'zines at reasonable prices. I suspect many people are attracted to the New York Art Book Fair and other events of the kind because, in dramatic contrast to the realm of galleries and auction houses and, alas, all too often, museums, artists' books, by and large, are not only affordable but also not viewed as speculative investments or means of enhancing your social status.

An exception to this low-key economy is Richard Prince's library in the Upstate New York town of Rensselaerville where the artist has put on display selections from his dazzling collection of first editions and documents relating to postwar literature and culture, high and low. Spending some of the millions of dollars he has made from his art, Prince has amassed a collection so impressive that the Bibliothèque Nationale de France in Paris recently invited him to curate a show of his holdings. Long a collector of images, Prince now incorporates his book collecting into his art, most notably when he commissioned a printer to produce faultless facsimiles of the first edition of *A Catcher in the Rye* with one significant difference: J.D. Salinger's name is replaced throughout the volume with Prince's own. As in Prince's paintings and photographs, these faux readymades rely on appropriation, but they also stress the fetishizing and commodification of first editions. While this may reflect Prince's experience as a maker of artworks that have themselves been fetishized and commodified, even when their artistic importance is debatable (I'm thinking of his Nurse Paintings, those darlings of auction houses), it also frames the book as a collectible, a luxury object, a target of speculative investment, in effect transposing the worst aspects of the contemporary art market into the realm of books.

This is clearly not what Helguera is doing with his Librería Donceles project, nor was it the case with two other book-based exhibitions: the art collective Antena's project of turning part of the Blaffer Museum in Houston into an independent bookstore [see *Gulf Coast* Volume 27.1] and, more recently, "The Library Vaccine" at Artists Space in New York. This latter show, which took its title from a 1981 text by art critic Edit DeAk, assembled six separate collections of books, each of which roughly corresponded to a different decade from the 1960s on. The collections were chosen, in the words of the organizers, "in order to sample art's distinctive relationship to the book form in its singularity, and in its states of reproduction, distribution and accumulation."

Fig. 4. (opposite) Installation view of Librería Donceles at Kent Fine Art, New York. 2014. Photography by Raphael Rubinstein.

The show was split between Artists Space's two locations. Occupying the smaller Walker Street space was "The Colin De Land Library," which consisted of several hundred books that belonged to Colin De Land, the legendary New York art dealer who died in 2003. Displayed on the same plain black metal bookcases as when they resided at American Fine Art, the books have remained together thanks to a German collector who purchased them after De Land's death. It's a wonderfully eclectic collection, made more so by being arranged in alphabetical order, no matter what the subject. Thus, a book on French abstract painter Bernard Frieze sits next to a volume on Fassbinder; one of Thomas Bernhard's caustic memoirs is sandwiched between a book on the films of Brigitte Bardot and Lucille O'Ball's autobiography (one can only imagine how Bernard, who hated actors, would have felt about this). Another unlikely juxtaposition was a book of Ellsworth Kelley's drawings leaning against a copy of *Fetish Girls* by erotic photographer Eric Kroll, an accidental meeting that made me wonder if there isn't a certain affinity between Kelly's elegant, streamlined, refined contour drawings and the sleek profiles of Kroll's leather and vinyl-encased models. I was surprised and intrigued by some of the artists represented in De Land's library (which also incorporated books that had belonged to his wife, art dealer Pat Hearn, who pre-deceased him): Enrico Baj, Bas Jan Ader, Dennis Adams, artists I admire but never associated with De Land (nor with Hearn). One of the messages of the Colin De land Library was how interesting art dealers can be, at least some of them. Another was that nothing is more revealing of a person than the books on their shelves. I can't help noting that De Land and Richard Prince collaborated in a short-lived hoax that involved making and exhibiting work that was credited to a fictional artist named John Dogg; it's kind of surprising that Prince didn't acquire De Land's library for himself.

In the main SoHo space a few blocks away were the other five "libraries": one devoted to the activities of German publisher and book designer Hansjörg Mayer who has been producing innovative artist books since the 1960s. Also on view, spread out on a sea of tables, was a selection of recent artists books chosen by Gregorio Magnani, a European-based curator and writer who specializes in artists' books. Nearby was "Vigilance: an Exhibition of Artists'

Fig. 5. The Colin de Land Library, from "The Library Vaccine." Artists Space, New York. 2014. Photography by Daniel Pérez.

Books Exploring Strategies for Social Concern," curated by veteran art critic Lucy Lippard and artist Mike Glier. While "Vigilance" and the Mayer and Magnani displays were all worthy curatorial projects, the other parts of "The Library Vaccine" were more compelling, perhaps because, like the Colin De Land Library, they were intensely personal. That was certainly the case with the part of the show devoted to novelist Helen DeWitt. An American writer who has lived for extended periods in London and Berlin, DeWitt agreed to have her entire library shipped from Berlin to New York and put on display. While clearly a writer's working library, it also contains volumes that she probably acquired in college. In contrast to the strictly alphabetized De Land collection, DeWitt's books were arranged by subject, allowing one to track her wide-ranging interests and areas of research, one of which is language acquisition. Certain volumes were displayed on tables, sometimes opened to specific pages. Attached to a facing wall were printouts of DeWitt's blogging on the project, screengrabs from her computer, and her commentaries about the connections among certain books; other texts pertained to her private life, offering glimpses of her troubling encounters with a stalker. Viewers (or maybe that should be "readers") were invited to find their own paths through DeWitt's library. It was a bit like spending time in a stranger's home. One felt part detective, part voyeur, part anthropologist and, maybe, even part researcher.

In a video interview conducted for "The Library Vaccine," archivist Ann Butler asks the rhetorical question, "Are the libraries of cultural producers important?" Certainly, for anyone interested in writing about DeWitt or De Land, there was much to learn about them through their books, and since DeWitt was so actively involved in the show, there was a potential for dialogue with her. The most explicitly interactive part of De Witt's library were several shelves stocked with copies of John Chris Jones's *The Internet and Everyone* (2000), a book DeWitt is so passionate about that years ago she bought the last 100 remaindered copies and has been hauling them around with her ever since; they were for sale at Artist's Space at $15 each.

Fig. 6. Display of books selected by Helen DeWitt, from "The Library Vaccine." Artists Space, New York. 2014. Photography by Daniel Pérez.

Fig. 7. Copies of John Chris Jones's *The Internet and Everyone* displayed for sale. The Library of Helen DeWitt, from "The Library Vaccine." Artists Space, New York. 2014. Photography by Raphael Rubinstein.

Somewhat paradoxically, the most powerful "library" at Artists Space didn't include any of the actual books in question, only facsimiles and photographs. This was "The Defaced Library Books of Kenneth Halliwell and Joe Orton." In 1959, Halliwell and Orton were two struggling young writers living together in a small apartment in North London, trying to keep the true nature of their relationship secret in a nation where homosexuality was still a crime. On a tight budget, they patronized the local public library but were irritated by how much shelf space was given to what Orton termed "rubbishy novels and rubbishy books" instead of to serious literature. In revenge, they began to steal books from the library, alter them with irreverent collages and fake blurbs, and surreptitiously return them to the shelves of the Islington Public Library. Starting slowly at first, this covert campaign grew in scope, involving dozens of books in all sorts of genres detective novels, romance novels, art books, poetry collections, studies of famous actors, reference books. In her recent book *Malicious Damage: the Defaced Library Books of Kenneth Halliwell and Joe Orton*, British scholar Ilsa Colsell describes how the

Fig. 7. The Defaced Library Books of Kenneth Halliwell and Joe Orton, from "The Library Vaccine." Artists Space, New York. 2014. Photography by Raphael Rubinstein.

books "were quietly returned to the shelves with their protective plastic covers replaced: a restored uniformity obscuring the texture of revision beneath, their creators hovering nearby to watch the public as they might encounter them." In a parallel project, the pair also systematically removed illustrations from art books and used them to cover every inch of wall space in their apartment, turning it into a walk-in collage. Eventually, Orton and Halliwell were caught and charged with larceny and malicious and willful damage. Convicted, each man served six months in prison and had to pay substantial fines. For Orton, the prison sentence turned out to be a blessing: it helped him sharpen his writing, developing a voice that would make him one of the most celebrated English playwrights of the 1960s. Halliwell had a much harder time. In 1967, frustrated by his failure as a writer and artist, and resentful at his partner's great success, Halliwell brutally murdered Orton before taking his own life.

For more than half a century the defaced book covers have been preserved by the Islington authorities, first as evidence, now as valuable cultural artifacts. Since the Islington Local History Centre was unwilling to lend the fragile collaged book jackets for this show, Artists Space made accurate facsimiles, which were mounted on a freestanding wall covered with enormous, full-scale black-and-white photographs of Orton and Halliwell's flat. Originally taken by the police as evidence of Halliwell and Orton's crimes, these photographs now function as documentation of a vanished interior impossible to understand as anything but an art installation.

Until now, neither Orton nor Halliwell has figured in art history, in part, no doubt, because the actual collages have never been exhibited. As Colsell points out, their collages have clear affinities with what the English Pop artists were doing in the 1950s. Let's hope that her book, which includes large color illustrations of all the surviving book covers, will foster a greater appreciation of these collages as art and not merely as incidental items in the tragic biography of a renowned dramatist. Their presence (at a distance) in the Artists Space show may also bring more artworld attention, as well as spark new discussions about libraries as social institutions and as the loci of imaginative activity. Along with projects like Librería Donceles and Agnieszka Kurant's sculptural installation *Phantom Library* (a long shelf of empty, but strikingly designed books bearing the titles of fictional works mentioned by famous authors), it suggests that, more than six centuries after the birth of Johannes Guttenberg and 70-plus years since Jorge Luis Borges wrote "The Library of Babel," a story that famously begins "The universe (which others call the Library)," we have yet to finish with the imaginative and conceptual potential of in-gathered books.

Alexis Orgera

Agatha's Letter to Her Mother

Dear Mom, it's been so long. Since back when
I was a loggerhead shrike, back when I followed
my breath—I the Desire—I'm dry outside
to the nostril, or from it, every
which way. Lip to lip, I went mechanical, Mom,
hoisted my terrific sclerosis into a desert
outside me. I tell my mouth, *Mouth, say it dry*.
I ran a little darkness into the light, Mom.
I was so sad or afraid that you'd lost me.
I cranked up my canyon repulsion.
Me! Mono! I've donated chrome to the stop-
motion men, fade to the eastern wind.
I am the last whole sky I know.
How to drink everything before us, Mom?
Fallopian! Dystopian! The thing to eat,
it comes after the eaten thing. Love, Agatha

Agatha as the Last Living Dragon

They said flames came from my mouth.

They lay me on the couch,

& flames from my mouth, & the world

& all its armor went black.

How does grace hide

the body from itself? Depict me

as a saint, bar me from heaven's door.

Jaren Watson

Which I Have Loved Long Since, and Lost Awhile

Soon after graduating college, my father lost his construction job. The Teton Dam he helped build let loose its foundations and poured downhill, flooding a fifth of Idaho. He began distance running to calm the jangling in his head.

Short and springy, with the lean muscularity of a hunting cat, he took to running easily, getting out every other day, then every day, then, by his thirties and into his forties, twice a day. A long meandering sojourn at sunrise through the potato fields surrounding our house. A five-mile burner around the Idaho Falls Greenbelt at lunch.

He entered road races: 5Ks, 10Ks, half-marathons, and marathons. Blowing out the carbon, he called it, and indeed he had the power and speed of a gasoline engine. At the start of a half-marathon in Moab, wedged together like commuters on a train so the runners could scarcely move, behind him my father heard this:

"I've got to piss."

"We're about to start. Go on the ground."

With no alternative, as discreetly as possible, the man urinated on the asphalt. The warm backsplash spattered Dad's naked calves.

For memory's sake, allow that about a year later my father was lining up at another race. A marathon, say, in Salt Lake City. As he and the other racers awaited the gun, he overheard in front of him the familiar line: "We're about to start and I've got to piss."

"Go on the ground."

"This always happens. Last year in Moab? I went on some poor guy's ankles."

Not without some pleasure, my father tapped the shoulder of the man in front of him; with a sardonic grin, he explained who he was.

A decade dead, he comes to me in dreams. His roles are always various, his countenance sad. Years after Salt Lake City, he was crippled by a training accident.

Bereft of the escape of running, he felt suffocated by demons. In life, he endured pain until he couldn't.

Then, with a rifle and bottle of pills, he holed up in a local motel until the police found him.

Better to remember the man who—I quit after a few hours—excavated a neighbor's car from wild snow, blowing drifts faster than he could shovel. Better to remember the man who carried two backpacks for the final miles of one camping trip when I was so cold and defeated I could no longer carry my own. Better even to remember the man who smacked my jaw after seeing the Fs on my report card.

Let me remember the man who fixed too much weight to his belt when we dove off the white coast of Cozumel: We glided giddily along the Santa Rosa coral shelf—prismatic, shaming out-of-water light—while he, sucking air and fighting too much weight, drained the O2 in his tank while ours remained half full. This is a fitting metaphor for the man who labored his whole life for everyone but himself, finding at last, that the load could not be borne.

Unbidden, this is the image I conjure most:

He stands in the soft oblique light of morning. He loosely shakes his hands. He dances on the balls of his feet, shifting weight from leg to powerful leg. He is lithe. He is all expectation—to fulfill the measure of his creation in mere running, aboriginal and pure. Legs to churn and lungs to burst and all of him not dead but joyful now, and joyful now. Beneath the heavens of that god who made him, holy he is and swift. For all this, he is as eager as a boy and, looking down—he's getting pissed on. Is this also holy?

Lacking the tangible pulse of his living flesh, I look for the narrative that makes sense of his life. And yet, by definition, definitions bind.

Instead light. Cup water in your hands. Don't spill.

Elisabeth Murawski

Lamentation of Christ: Sold Off to Pay Debts

This is no oasis of peace,
    Mantegna's dead Christ, the body
        foreshortened, the head

enlarged, more like a wounded
    dwarf's, the focus
        on the shrouded genitals:

behold the man. The ribcage looms
    as it must have heaved to breathe
        on the cross, fighting

gravity, the lips stiff and taut
    with suffering unrelieved
        even on the slab,

Mary, John, and Magdalene looking on
    with all the helplessness
        of those who love

and can do nothing. A painting
    Mantegna saved to grace his coffin.
        Something about the model's

mouth, the angle of the head, the chin.
    I'd not expected this resemblance
        to my son. The accident

stole mobility, his mind. Fifteen months
    of cruel, extravagant hope.
        I was sleeping when he died.

More of my ability to I feel you

Imagine that some gift has been bestowed upon me, some crisis or illness
The Garden we enter is easy
You lay there and the names of pop lie with you
A race disappears
But save that for later
Welcome Agnes to the world
See her silver beard
It's autumn and watch her grip her own palm
Then squeeze the center of it with her thumb
See her pinch a bit of her own fat before truly waking up
She is the King again and you lie at her feet
Close to photographs of beautiful black men
Soon you will do the same
You'll mimic her a little bit
Like before you wake you'll do the same
She'll rub her thumb and her forefinger together
Respect that
You're not taking it easy
She'll wait for you forever because she's already finished
She placed a little photograph of a sickness on a poppy
Agnes calls you stupid and you know you are
It's autumn and the looks pile up, tipsy looks
Agnes and Agnes forever
Best friends forever
It's her property
It always was
It's her property so you trim her silver beard
Agnes takes you back again
Easy on easy

It's autumn and see Agnes wrap her fingers
Around each edge
But you don't ever get to see what was leftover there
Watch her trim her nails like a boss
Look up the skirts of that blend you call ok
There's a bubbling you both follow
But she's smarter than you and you know it
So you'll have to wait on her forever
Forever will be that time you look at a man washing dishes touch himself
He is writing too, speaking
He speaks a language
You once lied about saying
I speak it fluently I spoke it fluently
That wish to bother oneself less
You don't feel comfortable lying anymore
It's not February anymore
You want to enter his nostrils and write an album in there
Agnes owns Agnes
She arrives late
So it's late
She arrives with an army of lovers
So it's an army of lovers
A little less pleasure for everyone in your circle
Agnes is going to find you, take the photos you took of your body
While you want a fatter man, quietly friendly, turning towards a mess in his
        apartment
Documenting each one with care
A ring off a gallon of milk, hair
She tells you to dive on the ankles of strange men
To scratch at them
Squeeze at them with your little muscles
Baby muscles

And close your eyes
Agnes gardens Agnes
She does it to push that soft, golden, light into your knees.
To let the warmth fill your knees
To feel Agnes around your knees and now relax just let it go and feel the warmth
    begin to move up into your thighs, hips, buttocks, back, and into your
    abdomen, up your chest, and through your throat, to your hands with their
    palms and each finger, wrists and forearms, to your shoulders, into your neck,
    jaw, nose and ears
Agnes and her silver beard are leftovers
So she can guide you away from all the gifts
Clumsy bodies going first
Agnes needing less

The Loser Poem

some grainy needle
pokes a woman with a black cat
that becomes permanent
like this is also your body and it is just perfect
that is how i see it

then there are rains that wash the mountain. there are rains that sprinkle
the faces of spotted deer. there are rains that bring dirt to the river. there
are rains that wet her legs. there are rains that cool the asphalt. there are
rains sipping long long arms of cool cool trees. there are rains soaking
dull gray blankets one after another. then there are rains across the town.

not unlike this
the pill that is actually hard to grab
25mg pill historically hard to grab
denying you your experience
the little projection of two women
trading basketball cards
is trapped in ice
but you'll never see it

and otherwise grasses hilly. otherwise mud on the shoulder of the
flight attendant. otherwise no loving in the grass that is green stripping
blue. otherwise the crispy sand on her back. mosses on the bench press.
otherwise a dam of slimy bark by the soldier. a step into the swampy
popular ground the world in dirt is otherwise searching.

that's how these things are seen
given up loose
each little postcard meaning less
there are close ups of our bodies
and they are just perfect
that is not a denial
it means as much as TV
or as much as The Pixies
how much Texas can scare us
the plain onesie of horror
the impossibility of god's amazon account
the castle selling its smile
selling its birthdays
selling each thing it can for each step away
how the history gets chilled
its chill
frozen into whatever
man

The Best of My Younger Thinking

I want to tell you about an album I've been listening to a lot lately. *The Best of: My Younger Thinking*. Side A is one long toddler snarl with a fiddle whimpering low in the mix. Side B shows a progression to more pop-indebted construction, executed with varying degrees of success.

Tracklist, Side B:

1. "Driving by Grandma's Grave Again" (from *The Long Car Rides to Summer Camp*)

2. "Where Is She Hiding It?" (from *Bathing with My Cousin*)

3. "Let Me Be Like People Here" (from *Moving Across the Country in Junior High*)

4. "Hard to Get to Sleep, Hard to Stay Awake" (from *I Guess I Already Knew Then*)

5.   "I'll Be the One Who Hates Himself Instead of Hating the World" (from *The Second Vacation to Hawaii*)

6.   "Time to Stop Wiping Your Nose on Your Sleeve" (from *I Wasn't Snotty by Choice: Diaries of a Congested Punk*)

You agree to give the album a spin if I finally watch that film you gave me last year for my fortieth birthday, *Sternum Collapser: A Love Life*. I haven't watched it only because it's a loop-based 16mm performance for multiple projectors. I don't have the technical wherewithal. I asked you to perform it for me and you said that you had been for a long time.

◆ ◆

We are both performers but we aren't making enough money. Because you perform in drag you get mostly nightclub jobs. My act nets me more day functions. At breakfast one day we inventory our assets.

"What's for sale with you?" I ask. Your gigs as a Dusty Springfield impersonator helped support us for years, but with age they have become more infrequent.

"I can do Dolly Parton and I'll start seeking certification as Madonna," you say.

Impersonating a man is easier. My Frank Sinatra tribute shows will pay into old age. My only complaint is I have never once been hired for my Jacques Brel impersonation—my personal favorite. I don't have to wear makeup for it. We have the same waxy jaws. You request the Brel from me on special occasions, though. Anniversaries, the nights we have performer friends over for drinks.

"En français, nous disons *la petite mort*," I say as Brel, "mais, en anglais c'est *the suicide squeeze*."

It feels great when you want Brel from me, but it's a sad impersonation and I tend to get very sweaty.

Your Dolly Parton shows become a sensation in Silver Lake, especially after you bring in a dude to play Porter Wagoner. "You need to focus on your act," you say when I ask why I couldn't be Porter. You say I'm a crooner and my stage presence is getting depressing. In the Dolly-Porter dynamic, Dolly needs to be the struggler.

I say, "He's too good-looking to play Porter." You say, "That's what makes it funny."

Our schedules fall out of sync. As Sinatra, I book every weekend afternoon charity event and every early-bird dinner theater I can. You're offered a residency at a cabaret.

I get home around nine most nights. We have a quick dinner and glass of wine, and you leave for your show. I take out my blue contacts and shower off my stage sweat and eyeliner. Then I sit around listening to *The Best of: My Younger Thinking*. Our wigs are everywhere. There are also some Porter Wagoner wigs here because you got mad at the actor for taking bad care of them, and now you bring them home with you. I saw that fight between you and Porter. He had driven you home after a late Sunday show. From the living room window I watched you sit in his car in our driveway, swatting his hair. It was flirty, too similar to the way you'd bicker on stage. I sing duets with dudes, too, so I know. But maybe that's just the way you are with him.

I think if we were both crooners, if you stayed Dusty Springfield and if I ever became a bankable Jacques Brel, we could call that a life. I can't sing you the songs of *My Younger Thinking*, they're too far out of my range now. But if I could play you the album, you'd understand why my part in our relationship is taking so long to learn.

While you're at work, I dig through the closet, through your stockings and my Sinatra fedoras, my Brel turtlenecks, your board shorts, beach blankets, your breastplates, your old home and away college baseball jerseys, your enormous hair bumps and frilly-necked frocks from your Dusty Springfield show that remind me of how honeyed and lavish your voice can be. I find what I'm looking for, the chest labeled *Sternum Collapser: A Love Life*.

I set up three projectors, load the film reels, and play them according to the instructions you included. The first piece is the pilot episode of the sitcom we watched when we first started dating, but with the laugh track removed. Characters pause and look worried in the dead time. There is a lot of coffee pouring and leg crossing and swallowing. The jokes are still funny.

At the first act break, your instructions say, *Turn on the second projector*. I do. A title card says "Camera Trap: Domesticity in the Wild." Documentary footage of a lone beaver in his den rolls under the sitcom transition music from the first projector. The beaver gnaws at the walls, unable to separate work from home. The film cuts from the beaver den to a bear den, where two stir-crazy bears hibernate. The bears pace and feel fat and underemployed.

At the second sitcom act break, I turn on the third projector. I must not have loaded that reel right—the film jams and spoils in the sprocket. I shut the broken projector off and watch the first two play out. The third act of the sitcom offers little resolution, since it is the pilot episode. The main character thinks he may be able to make the best of things in his new surroundings. Meanwhile, the nature documentary cuts back to the beaver, whose partner has come home to find the gnawed walls of the den. They go out together to gather more mud and twigs to reinforce the interior. I imagine one beaver makes a joke about chewing the scenery. On the back of the last instruction card, you've written, *You're the flesh in my silicone life.*

When you get home from work, I ask you about the third reel.

You say it was supposed to break. I don't know if I believe you.

I ask you if you'll listen to my album now.

"What do you think I do while you're gone all afternoon?" you reply.

"Coiffe Porter's wig."

There is a companion album to *The Best of: My Younger Thinking* called *The Rest of: My Younger Thinking.* It's a collection of B-sides and outtakes and things I would never tell you. It's terrible. A nostalgic cash grab.

You're doing well enough that I can announce my retirement as Frank Sinatra. I am a full-time freelance Brel. I curate *A Night of European Crooners* featuring imitation Nico, Charles Aznavour, Engelbert Humperdinck, and Jacques Brel, and nobody attends. I had asked you to be Nico but you said you had a brand to protect.

I take the third reel of your film to Photo Center to see if it can be salvaged, but they tell me there was nothing on the print in the first place.

The dude who played Porter Wagoner gets a job on a soap opera. I again offer my services as Porter, but you say the story is playing out exactly right—that Dolly needs to do it herself. Your show loses momentum. We have more free nights now.

We come home from free taco night at the bar and abandon plans of making love.

"Am I wrong to be satisfied already?" my stomach gurgles.

"Without me?" yours replies.

I help you take your boots off. You collapse onto the made bed. I take off my cowboy hat but leave on my bolo tie.

"I have to do the dishes from earlier," I say.

You call to me in the kitchen but I can't hear clearly.

When I come back to bed, the skin on my hands is dry and cracked. My stomach says, "I'm sick of being sick."

Yours says, "I'm sick of hurting." You sit under the covers, bracing for another day without work.

"Have we run out of duets?" I ask.

"Crooners don't stop and listen long enough to duet."

"And Porter is renowned for his listening?"

"My audience listened. I wish you'd been in it."

Stomachache refluxes to heartache. You tell me you accidentally overexposed the third reel of *Sternum Collapser*. I ask what it was, but you say never mind—the way it turned out says something about expectation.

There are strands of our younger thinking that we still have in common. We talk about it more now. We remember when we were in sobbing uncertain love and we'd watch movies about sobbing uncertain lovers and those were the most terrifying movies. That pulse is still in our veins and the imprint of our butts is still in the leather couch where we first kissed. You promise to find new footage for the third reel. I donate *My Younger Thinking* to Goodwill.

The next day, I come out of Sinatric retirement and you start practicing your Dean Martin. You finish your Madonna certification and I start crafting my Prince act.

Richard Prins

Pantoum Found in Talking Heads Lyrics

I look like you make me shiver.
Your mind is a radio.
If this is paradise, I wish I had
your face. Facts continue to change

your mind. Is a radio
a cigarette, burning
your face? Facts continue to change
the future. I feel wonderful;

a cigarette burning
is a perfect world. I'm riding
the future I feel. Wonderful,
the world moves on. A woman's hip

is a perfect world I'm riding.
We don't need clothes.
The world moves. On a woman's hip,
hands get dirty. Nobody knows

we don't need clothes
if this is paradise. I wish I had
hands. Get dirty; nobody knows
I look like you. Make me shiver.

Christopher Robinson

The Death of My Grandfather

The death of my grandfather
leaves money
and a company
for the children to scrabble over.

There are those who never escape
the molasses.

Perhaps it's best he not die.

So many things
I want to own
before I go: a star
chart and a mouthful
of juice, the sound
of swarming gnats
over a river.

As for what will become
of my body
that will depend
on who its ownership
falls to, as I
will be incapable
of preference or selfhood.

And my grandfather, if he must die
then I implore the future
owners of his body
to scatter him
like interstellar dust
or a fist of bats.

★ STATIC OF THE UNION

Writing with a mainline to the zeitgeist

★

Neon

One night my mother dreamed that she turned into a large, white bird. She was standing naked before a narrow, tall mirror. She still had only one breast, the scar on the left side no longer a zipper of purple puckers, fading instead to a smooth shimmery lavender, the skin of an exotic tropical beast. "I've let myself go," she told me, seeing the fleshy belly, the loose upper arms, the heavy thighs. And yet, she was not ashamed.

The feathers unfurled like crocuses. Mama felt each shaft rising from her goose pimpled skin, an itch she couldn't scratch. The wind from her wings created a storm in my apartment, sending the pages of my Master's thesis into a fluttering whirlwind. She flew around the ceiling, bumping at the windows before she could gain enough momentum to knock down the front door and slip outside, the air moist with the promise of snow.

"It was night and I flew to see your father," she said.

"I flew in the upstairs bedroom window. Papa was in bed already but he heard my beak tapping on the glass and let me in. He was happy to see me."

It was a good dream, she said, not a nightmare.

"The acupuncture is working," she announced.

I was hopeful for once. And happy that I'd been included in her dream. After my mother's mastectomy, she decided to move into my apartment so that I could take care of her during her chemotherapy, as there was no oncologist in the small town where my parents and brother lived.

She also didn't want my father or brother to see her suffer. She wouldn't let them visit on the weeks she had chemo.

"I don't want them to worry," she said.

What about me? I thought. But that was selfish. Daughters weren't allowed luxurious emotions. We were supposed to be tough. We were supposed to know how to endure.

Eighteen months later, my mother, after being treated with Taxol for the second time, was having a negative reaction. It was three in the morning and the ER was all but deserted. I raced down the hallway, nearly crashing into the nurse who had put in my mother's IV and disappeared. "Come quick!" I cried, startling her. "My mother's in pain!"

She followed me into the little room, my mother hooked up to an IV of glucose, a sedative, and no painkillers.

"She needs Fentanyl," I said, trying to keep my voice calm, professional. The nurses and doctors—especially the doctors—didn't like emotional displays. They didn't like tears. They liked people who talked like themselves. They liked people who acted as though a mother with cancer was just a body on a cot with textbook organs and textbook tumors. A year and a half into my mother's cancer treatments, I'd learned the game well. "They always use Fentanyl in the cancer ward. The other kinds make her vomit—"

"Slow down," the nurse said. "Who's your mother?"

"That woman!" I pointed to my mother on the cot behind me, the only other woman in this tiny examining room, the woman this nurse had checked into the ER not half an hour ago, the only woman moaning.

The nurse looked at my mother on the cot, she looked back at me. "Oh," she said, nodding. She examined the glucose drip, pursing her lips. "I'll get the doctor."

It was a look I understood well. My mother was white and I, although mixed, looked completely Asian. Growing up in small towns, this look was the look that refused to see me as my mother's daughter because we were different races.

"Thank you," I said, though I wanted to smack her. "Please hurry."

"What's wrong?" my mother gasped.

"Everything will be all right," I lied.

◆━◆

Once a nun sidled up to me in the cathedral in Sioux City, Iowa, where my mother had stopped to pray. While my mother lighted a votive candle before the statue of Mary, I sat waiting in a back pew. The nun slid in beside me. She grasped my wrist, leaning close to my ear to whisper, "My cousin adopted a Vietnamese girl." I felt her spittle against my cheek as her dry nails scratched my skin. Her voice was furtive, as though she were confessing a crime or an illicit passion to a priest. I shot out the other side of the pew and ran to stand by mother, who dutifully pretended not to see.

My mother never took notice. Not the stares in the grocery store or in the Ben Franklin or the shoe store or the women's boutique, not since our family had moved to this small town from the East Coast when I was twelve. When women at church potlucks told me of sisters or cousins or old friends from high school who'd adopted Korean babies in other towns, she walked away.

I wanted her to stand up to them. To tell them off to their bigoted faces. "This is my daughter!" I hated when she turned aside, silenced.

◆━◆

Silence is a virtue taught to girls. It makes them easier to control.

My mother's father had been an alcoholic, my mother's mother a battered and enabling wife. My mother, the dutiful daughter, had learned to keep her mouth shut.

Marrying my father, a professor from China, whom my mother met at age 33, and not the white farmer's son my grandmother liked when she was 17, was my mother's greatest act of rebellion.

"I thought you were going to become a nun," my grandmother said.

Instead my mother had me, then my brother.

Still, in the small towns where we later lived, in the face of white disapproval, my mother could not find her voice to claim us.

※

When my brother, Jeff, was fifteen, he was attacked in school after he joined the wrestling team. My mother drove him to the hospital 28 miles away in Yankton for medical tests that would reveal the tear in his diaphragm. She never offered her opinion as to why three white boys conspired to injure my brother so he could not wrestle on their all-white team.

My brother told us what happened. He was on the mat, wrestling one of the boys for practice, when another boy jumped in to see if Jeff could handle it. My brother was used to proving himself in our town, so he bucked and arched his back, trying to break free. Then, a third white boy climbed to the top of the bleachers, and while my brother was in a back arch, leaped onto my brother's chest, crushing him to the mat.

The school paid my brother's medical bills because he'd been injured on school property. Luckily for the school, the bills weren't too expensive. My brother had torn his diaphragm, the doctor prescribed some Prilosec and painkillers, and that was the end of it. My brother couldn't swallow properly and had terrible indigestion for a year, but it could have been much worse, and so long as he kept to limited activity that didn't reaggravate the injury, meaning no more team sports, the doctor had assured him he'd get better. After the bills were settled, no one at school spoke of it again. Not the coach who'd recruited my brother for the team, not his former teammates, not the secretary who'd called my mother to tell her of the "accident."

My father was out of town at the time. No one ever told him what happened.

After the attack, I thought my mother would say something. She couldn't ignore this violence the way she ignored my brother's bloodied and broken hands from the other fights in school, fights she hadn't witnessed, but fights he told us about, fights with fists or textbooks or 2x4s. This time, because she had to pick up my brother from school and drive him to the hospital in another town in the middle of the afternoon, because she had to wait for the barium swallow results and other X-rays, this time, surely, she couldn't ignore this level of violence.

I was wrong. My mother said nothing.

———◆◆———

Shame seeped into my bones. When the school continued to hold pep rallies for the wrestling team, I attended. And when the principal got on a microphone in the middle of the gym to lead us in prayer, evoking Jesus's name, praying for God to bless our players with a victory, his sibilant voice hissing through the mobile speakers set up in a cluster in the middle of the gym, I bowed my head and closed my eyes and moved my lips as well. I lost my voice. It slid into the pit of my stomach and stayed there.

Once Mama and I sat down with one of her family albums and tried to figure out all the different places she had lived. Indianapolis, New Bethel, Martinsville, Colton, Redlands, the big white house, the small cabin, the place in the desert, the farm, the house with the big porch, that time with those relatives, the one-room shack. We stopped at twenty-seven.

My grandparents were always looking for a fresh start, a new town where people weren't familiar with my grandfather's erratic behavior, his violent outbursts, where he could still get a job. My mother, the eldest of eight, took care of her younger siblings, helped Grandma with the endless amount of housework and mountains of laundry and hours of dishes. She was cheerful, singing and joking. An impeccable daughter.

Despite her efforts, her father punched out one of her teeth.

———◆◆———

I'd noticed it when I was six or seven. We'd sit on the sofa in the family room in our house in New Jersey in the winter when it was cold, watching TV or reading and sewing while my brother lay on his belly on the floor playing with his toy soldiers.

Sometimes Mama would let me take the rollers out of her hair. Her hair was long and dark in those days, dyed black to match my brother and me, she said, so everyone would know we were a family.

Why wouldn't they know we were a family? I'd wondered. How could we be anything but what we were?

"Let me see your teeth!" I was losing my baby teeth and had become fascinated by them.

My mother opened wide.

I peered inside her mouth and saw the way her bottom left incisor hung suspended over her gum, attached to the teeth on both sides by a layer of gold soldered on the back. It caught the light when she laughed, glinting in her mouth like a wink.

When I asked what had happened, Mama told me the story of the time her father cooked the family pets for dinner.

She was seventeen. They were living on a small farm in Southern Indiana. My grandfather had been drinking. He was in the kitchen, preparing something special, he'd said. It took him all day: the children could hear him through the locked door singing off-key, songs from the Navy, one of the happiest times of his life. He'd run away from home and enlisted when he was seventeen to fight in WWI. A year later, he was sent off to duty. WWI was over and he didn't see any combat. Instead, he was stationed in France to help with "reconstruction." From his stories, it seemed he'd spent the entire time wooing French women, drinking, and serving on KP duty. This was the secret to his happiness, he said, because it was in France that he picked up his fine, gourmet tastes.

Whereas my grandmother cooked the wholesome Southern dishes of her youth—chicken and biscuits, meatloaf and cobbler, vegetable soup—dishes that stretched a budget and could feed a growing family of four, then six, then eight, then ten, my grandfather's tastes ran to the exotic. Calf brains scrambled in eggs, beef tongue on rye, liver fried with onions, chip beef on toast—which he claimed to have eaten out of a helmet on a beach.

The house filled with the scent of cooking meat.

My grandfather insisted everyone sit quietly at the table, which he had instructed my grandmother to set formally, with the good china and the polished silverware, folded napkins, the butter dish, the pickle jar, the water glasses just so. Then sweating and red-faced, he emerged from the kitchen carrying two silver-domed platters on a tray. He set them on the table and removed the lids with a flourish.

The children let out a shriek. There on the platters lay their rabbits, Peter and Flopsy. Not chopped up and disguised in a casserole the way my grandmother would have done it when she needed to pluck a favored rooster or chicken from the flock for dinner, but whole, heads and faces attached and identifiable.

One of the younger children, seven or eight years old, burst into tears.

"You don't have to eat them," my mother said.

My grandfather picked up the giant pickle jar on the table and threw it at her head. She ducked and the jar shattered against the far wall. The children screamed and scattered, running to the far corners of the house, crouching and hiding in closets, under beds, behind curtains.

My grandfather grabbed my mother by the arm, before she could flee. He dug his fingernails into her skin and pulled her closer. Then he punched her in the jaw, sending a tooth flying through the air.

He let her drop to the floor and went roaring back to the kitchen where he threw the pots against the walls.

Grandma found my mother's bloody tooth on the floor and drove her to the hospital. There was nothing they could do, the doctors said. They weren't dentists.

The next day my grandmother drove over to the dentist and explained my mother had had an accident. The dentist looked at the rootless tooth, tsking and clicking his tongue against the top of his mouth. It couldn't be re-planted into the gum, he said. There was nothing to be done now but solder it in place.

He shook his head at my mother. "Next time, young lady, try to be less clumsy."

Grandma, at her side, stood silent.

———◆◆———

"Don't you wish there was a neon sign that came on whenever you felt pain? It would shine above your head so everyone would know," Mama said once when I was a child. "A big arrow."

We were seated on the couch in the family room, my brother and me on either side of my mother, as we watched our Saturday shows together: *Bob Newhart*, Mary Tyler Moore, Carol Burnett, all the comedies, one after the other. We tolerated *The Love Boat* in between, just so we could get to our favorite: Carol! Carol, our mother's namesake, such a funny woman. We loved her: Mrs. Wiggins, Nora Desmond, Scarlett O'Hara with the drapery rod sticking out of her velvet curtain dress. Mama was funny, too. She was always making us laugh. Sometimes she repeated her father's jokes: if we farted, she'd call out in a funny voice, "Quick, catch it, paint it green and sew a red button on it!" But tonight she wasn't making any jokes. Carol had started singing, her songs were always serious, and Mama didn't like that. "You know, when you're sick or tired or just not feeling well," she said. "Just a little light bulb. Right here." She pantomimed over her head.

"I don't want anyone to know how I feel," I decided, thinking about schoolyard bullies, the instinct for blood. "I want to hide it."

"Oh," Mama sighed. "I wish I had a neon sign."

I knew my mother carried pain. Every night before we went to bed, she told us stories of her childhood, and often they ended with violence, her father becoming drunk and punching her or her mother or a sibling or her mother attacking a child or both parents turning on one or more of the children. Night after night, these stories. My brother developed fever dreams and night terrors, but Mama couldn't stop telling them.

———◆◆———

I had no idea how hard my mother struggled: the habit of hiding her pain and her need to reveal it. I could not guess at the toll it would take on her, or us, this burden of silence.

She'd never seen a counselor or a therapist. Having lived mostly in rural areas, my mother hadn't had many options for doctors, and it wasn't her generation's proclivity anyway. Like many victims of childhood abuse, my mother simply lived with the trauma, which meant denying it. When the violence reared up in our lives, I suppose she couldn't bear to see it, to acknowledge it, to speak its name. Like the other residents of our small town, traumatized no doubt by their own childhoods, their religions that demanded forbearance, the small-town politeness that allowed bullies to reign unimpeded so long as they were the right kind of bully, from the right kind of family, my mother could not speak.

Only at the end of her life, when there was nothing left to fear, no one's disapproval that mattered, no one left to judge her but me, only then could Mama find her voice.

After twenty months of chemotherapy, nothing helped but morphine. She'd wake from a dream and start talking. "Why did he do it? Why?" she'd demand. "Daddy always seemed like he loved me."

"He was a drunk," I'd say. "He punched everyone. He hit Grandma. He'd hit anyone."

The next night, the same question. Why, why, why?

—◆ ◆—

Should I be angry at my mother or my grandfather? At every cop and sheriff's deputy who brought the drunk home and told my grandmother, "You need to keep a better eye on your husband, Ma'am." Every preacher, every neighbor, every teacher, everyone who turned a blind eye or blamed the unruly child, the haggard mother, the sick father?

Where does the chain of blame begin and end? Who is responsible for this tragedy, for this pattern, for this habit?

Who will break the silence of the dutiful daughters?

—◆ ◆—

Later in life, long after my family had moved away from the small town where he'd been assaulted, my brother saw one of his childhood bullies. More than a decade had passed since high school. My mother had died a few years earlier of cancer, my father had not yet retired. My brother had married and was working as a teacher. My brother's wife had just had a child and we were all visiting my father in Wyoming.

My brother was in the parking lot of the Safeway when he saw the skinny, familiar looking man. He was collecting donations for the victims of a hurricane in Haiti. The sign behind him said, "Give generously." My brother didn't stop to talk to him. Instead he drove home and told us what his old nemesis was up to, shaking his head that, after all these years, the bully was still running some kind of scam.

But then the bully's wife called. He had married a girl from high school, and she remembered us all well. She'd moved to Laramie to attend the university, and somehow she'd heard that we were all in town visiting our father. She looked up the number in the phone book and called to see if my brother and his wife wanted to get together.

"You don't have to do it," I told my brother, but he said he felt sorry for her. He remembered her, a pretty girl whose parents owned a farm. She'd married the bully right after graduation. It couldn't have been easy for her. We both knew what kind of man the bully would become.

I was out when she came to see my brother. She said she was sorry to hear about our mother's death. She was such a nice lady, the bully's wife said.

The bully wasn't drinking anymore. He'd gone to rehab in Minnesota. They'd tried to have a baby for years, but they'd finally adopted a daughter. The bully's wife was working as a teacher. She was tired with work and the baby, but she was okay. She'd been supporting her family for a number of years, but now the bully was going into insurance. They were moving soon. Things were better. She was well, thank you, she said, polite as ever.

She asked my brother how I was doing. She was sorry she'd missed me. It would've been nice to get together. Then she left, and when I came back, my brother told me about her visit. I remembered her from school. Unlike her husband, she and I had had many classes together. We rode on the same bus in junior high.

She used to be friendly. She never called me any names, which made her stand out from our classmates. She'd been a very pretty girl, the class beauty, smart, a champion basketball player. She was close to six-feet-tall, a honey blonde with a round moon face. Then she started dating the bully and her grades fell. I always thought she did it deliberately, to make him feel better. After that, we weren't in the same classes. I rarely saw her. When she started dating the bully, I wondered if it seemed like a good match. Of course it had. In our town's eyes, the bully deserved the school beauty.

My brother and his wife later told me that the bully's wife had seemed sad.

"She kept asking how you were doing," my brother said. "You could give her a call." There was still time before she and the bully would move.

I never called. I didn't want to see what had become of her. I didn't want to see another ruin in the bully's wake.

★

Atomic Theory

They call it a nuclear missile.
The great equalizer. A man

dropped a bomb so big he could never
forget. This is how families begin: one accident

leads to the next and suddenly you're
giving your dog a one syllable name.

Spike. Spot. Boy. This is one big dick
joke. A mathematician walks into a bar

and there's no counter. A bar
walks into a city and stays there

until the neighborhood is gentrified
and all the poor people disappear.

This is fear in the modern era: you lose
your childhood home, all the awful

memories of your parents, the burning
smell of cup ramen smoking the microwave

because you forgot to add water,
which costs two ninety-nine

at the new organic food mart. You
want the whole thing to blow up

because you don't understand
what happens when the whole thing

blows up. You've never heard a gunshot
and you never want to. You want explosions

to remain in a state of metaphor: its smallest
anatomical structure, or something you see

in the movies. You don't expect it to be real.
You don't think there are that many men.

★

Big Sur

Let's take a Vespa to the beach; let's
not get killed. Our lives are mirrors,

adjust your mirrors, let's not get
killed. The sun goes over a cliff,

head over heels. We motor away, switch
back. Us versus the sun, vice versa,

we're golden. Let's take a Vespa
to the beach; let's not get killed.

★

Niners

It is 2009 and everyone I know is trying to get out of Syracuse.

I'm 22 years old and it will be another year before President Obama's Patient Protection and Affordable Care Act is passed, allowing dependents to remain covered by their parents' insurance until 26 years of age. By then, I will be working as an EMT, the first job I ever have that provides me with health insurance.

But right now, 9.3 million people across the country are unemployed. 46.3 million live without healthcare.[1] My kitchen table is a growing stalagmite of unpaid

---

[1] "State & County Quick Facts," U.S. Census Bureau, January 31, 2012, accessed April 4, 2012, http://quickfacts.census.gov/qfd/index.html (hereafter cited in text as USCB).

hospital bills and letters from collection agencies. Three new scars decorate my stomach, each indicating the route by which a laproscopic camera, a fiber optic light, and a small blade have been inserted in the removal of my appendix. Even after the hospital's financial hardship discount, the surgery bill comes to more than $10,000, not including the additional costs of ER services, radiology, and post-surgical care. This is, according to my recent tax return, more money than I have made in an entire year.

It is 2009 and the U.S. Census Bureau defines the poverty line for a single individual as $10,956 or less per year.[2]

Fast forward: the first thing you learn when you become an EMT is to treat every situation as a potential emergency. Symptoms can be misleading and what seems like a mild complaint could be indicative of a more serious underlying problem. The classic example: a person who appears drunk, presenting with slurred speech, poor motor control, and acetone breath, might actually be suffering a severe diabetic emergency. It is better to treat every patient fairly, to take precautions and assume the worst, than it is to be responsible for further damage on account of skepticism or neglect.

Becoming an EMT allows me to quit my job working the line in the mailroom at the local newspaper, where lay-offs and mandatory unpaid furloughs have become epidemic, proof of the headlines we regularly print regarding the economic recession. It will be an opportunity to see things that I wouldn't otherwise get to see in a city that I'm convinced has nothing left to offer me, and it will be a way to make tangible, visible impacts on the lives of other people while I struggle to cope with the stifling helplessness of post-college, Recession-era life in a city that has been slowly dying since the 1950's.

---

[2] USCB.

Syracuse, New York. Population: roughly 150,000. Land area: 25.04 square miles, not including the suburbs that press against its immediate borders.[3] Most famous for its record-setting snowfalls and a successful college basketball team, as well as being home to Onondaga Lake, which, for the past several decades, has been identified by environmental groups, such as the New York State Department of Environmental Conservation, as the most polluted lake in the United States.[4]

Before the city existed, the land Syracuse is built on was home to the Onondaga, one of the Native American tribes that make up the Five Nations of the Iroquois. Onondaga Lake is historically known as the birthplace of the Iroquois Confederacy, the place where the Five Nations made peace after millennia of war and violence.[5] Today, the lake's surface is swollen with toxic mud-boils and the bottom is a mercurial stew of pesticides and sewage contamination. Since the early 1800s, the lake has served as a dump for the city as well as a number of industrial and municipal waste companies.[6] My coworkers at the ambulance joke about going fishing there and pulling up three-eyed carp.

Anyone who has lived in Syracuse long enough recognizes the line that is drawn by Interstate 81. East of the highway is the university neighborhood, an area commonly referred to as The Hill. Here, you will find restaurants and art galleries. Coffee shops, grocery stores, libraries. Hospitals. All of the establishments that make a place worth living in exist within a relatively short distance.

West of I-81 is the rest of the city. The paramedic who trains me offers this description: on one side of the highway are the college kids, on the other, the black people. Walk down The Hill, away from the university, and you pass beneath

---

[3] USCB.

[4] "Onondaga Lake Superfund Site," New York State Department of Environmental Conservation, 2015, accessed April 22, 2012. http://www.dec.ny.gov/chemical/8668.html (hereafter cited as NYSDEC).

[5] "Onondaga Nation—People of the Hills," *Onondaga Nation*, 2014, http://www.onondaganation.org.

[6] NYSDEC.

the highway into patches of housing projects known as The Bricks. Past that, the empty streets of downtown. Past that, residential neighborhoods scattered amongst decaying industrial districts, boarded-up storefronts.

But like I said: working on the ambulance was partially an excuse to have new experiences that I wouldn't have otherwise. A nursing home in the middle of the night can be a terrifying place. With no light but the red glow of emergency exits, the halls fill with the sound of people crying from darkened rooms. The staff leads you to a woman who has been exhibiting stroke symptoms for the past ten hours and who, for whatever reason, has only now become a concern. You drive to the South Side, where a teenager is ODing on the floor of an unfinished house with pipes and insulation still exposed on the walls, plastic-covered windows that shake in the wind. Like playing connect the dots between nightmares, each call lands you in some hallucinatory new landscape. The homeless shelter on Oxford where half of the people are dying from AIDS. The projects on East Fayette where you have to step over puddles of piss in the staircase, where the cops refuse to enter in groups of fewer than three. But no matter where you go, you always end up back in the ER, watching convoys of stretchers roll up and down the perfect white halls.

My boss tells me stories about "the good old days," before the mid-90s, when small cameras that hang beneath the rear-view mirror were installed in each of the trucks. The cameras are activated by G-force—anytime you hit a pot-hole, accelerate or brake too quickly, or clip the curb rounding a tight corner, a red light comes on and the camera saves one minute of footage spanning thirty seconds before and after the activation. The cameras are mostly for insurance purposes, to make sure we're driving safely, but the broader effect is stress, paranoia. Back in the good old days, my boss tells me, there were no cameras, nothing to worry about. If a patient got combative or out of hand, he says, you punched him. A black eye presented no risk. You were friends with the nurses, so in your report, you noted that the patient had bumped his head while climbing into the truck. Who would you believe: the guy who is tied to a stretcher, shouting and bleeding from his head, or the calm, collected gentleman in uniform whose job it is to save lives?

The good old days.

In 1950, Syracuse reached its peak population and entered what has since been a period of steady decline.[7] The construction of Interstate 81 began in 1957 and throughout the early 60s, under President Eisenhower's federal Urban Renewal Program, the city of Syracuse razed a number of landmark properties, including a historically black neighborhood known as the 15th Ward. The erection of the highway was an attempt to jump-start the city during a time when many of its primary businesses were collapsing or relocating, taking jobs and people along with them.[8]

The construction of I-81 in Syracuse forced the eviction of nearly 1,300 people.[9]

A 2003 article by Maureen Sieh quotes Fred Murphy, who was employed by the Urban Renewal Agency in Syracuse between 1965 and 1970: "We didn't have a good understanding of the consequences of this mass scale of moving people around," Murphy says. "We were beginning the fight for attracting people to retail and fighting suburban malls. Why else would people come to cities if we didn't have shiny and glitzy buildings for people to work?"[10]

Revision: the first thing you learn when you become an EMT is geography. A book of maps is kept in the front cab of each truck. You learn the main roads that bisect the city, the short-cuts that run between them. You learn the high-traffic spots, the one-way changes. You invent mnemonics to memorize cross streets in areas of high call volume. You learn how to find your bearings no matter where you are. You learn where to get on and off the highways, 690 East or West, 81 North or South.

---

[7] "Syracuse, New York Population History," biggestuscities.com, last updated May 23, 2014, https://www.biggestuscities.com/city/syracuse-new-york.

[8] "Maureen Sieh, "15th Ward Stood Tall, Fell," The Post-Standard, September 21, 2003, accessed April 2, 2012. http://syracusethenandnow.org/UrbanRenewal/15th_Ward.htm (hereafter cited as Sieh).

[9] Ibid.

[10] Ibid.

You learn the fastest routes to each of the five hospitals, three of which are on top of The Hill, each within a radius of less than one square mile.

It is 2009 and appendicitis has me dry-heaving in the passenger seat of my father's old Mazda en route to the emergency room at Upstate University Hospital. I stumble through the walk-in entrance while my father circles the block for parking. It's a packed house and the registration nurse informs me that I'll be waiting at least two hours. I stand up to leave but barely make it back out to the parking lot before collapsing from pain. The RN sees me and brings out a wheelchair, pulls me up off my hands and knees and wheels me back inside. She bumps me up to next in line for triage. You don't have to do that, I tell her, I was just going to crawl around the corner to the ER at Crouse.

In his 1967 memoir, *At Ease: Stories I Tell to Friends*, Dwight D. Eisenhower includes a chapter titled "Through Darkest America with Truck and Tank," in which he recalls his time as a young army officer on the Transcontinental Motor Convoy of 1919. Eisenhower, along with hundreds of other troops, embarked on one of the first ever cross-country automotive road trips, driving military trucks from Washington, D.C. to San Francisco, California. This was an experience that would directly inspire his later creation of the Federal Aid Highway Act of 1956, one of the many elements of the president's vast Urban Renewal program.[11]

Eisenhower devotes much of this chapter to descriptions of military vehicle accidents due to poor road conditions. Likewise, part of learning geography as an EMT is learning which roads never get repaired. They say that the G-force experienced with every pot-hole or sharp turn is multiplied by ten when you're

---

[11] Richard Weingroff, "Federal Highway Act of 1956: Creating the Interstate System," Federal Highway Administration, last modified November 22, 2011, accessed August 18, 2013, http://www.fhwa.dot.gov/publications/publicroads/96summer/p96su10.cfm (hereafter cited as Weingroff).

in the back of the truck. If your paramedic needs to get an IV, you definitely don't take South State Street, and a patient whose head is duct-taped to a backboard will always complain when a poorly paved street makes his or her teeth vibrate.

I work from 6 PM until 6 AM and ride my bike home in the morning with the sunrise like some strange afterglow of everything I'd seen overnight. From the station, which is on the West Side, I pedal through downtown, through The Bricks, and beneath the dripping I-81 overpass, where, during the day, homeless men and women stand in winter coats, holding signs made from old pizza boxes, like stubborn ghosts of those that were dispossessed half a century ago. Riding up The Hill feels like climbing out of purgatory. It is a steep slope and near the top, it always feels as if I am in danger of sliding back down, as if I must pedal faster or my front wheel might arc over my head and send me summersaulting backward toward The Bricks and the empty streets of downtown.

★

The Bricks. A neighborhood of low-rise, low-income apartments that kneel down beneath the shadow of I-81. A maze of courtyards and dead end streets. I grow accustomed to my partner complaining any time a call brings us there. "My feet were sticking to the floor in that place," or "I thought I was going to die from the smell in there," or "What a fucking niner."

The word "niner" is common slang amongst ambulance, firefighters, and police in Syracuse. A coworker tells me that the etymology comes from a particularly crime-ridden neighborhood on Syracuse's North Side that used to fall under the fifty-ninth police precinct. A shortened version of old cop slang, "five-niner."

It is 2009 and I am lying in a hospital bed, afraid. Not of the tiny organ inside my stomach which the doctor tells me is threatening to explode and spread infection throughout my innards, but of my lack of insurance and the crushing financial circumstances of my immediate future. Steeped in morphine, I am only half-joking when I tell my father that, no, I'd rather not get an x-ray, that unless they can figure out a less expensive way to confirm my diagnosis, I'd rather just go home and take my chances.

Two days later, I am still lying in a hospital bed, stitched shut, waking to find that a social worker from the billing department has left a blank Medicaid application on the bedside table.

At work, the word "niner" is used rather liberally, a blanket term to describe a variety of different patients. Alcoholics. Drug addicts. Psychiatric patients. Anyone who is particularly combative or eccentric. Anyone with poor hygiene or an unkempt living space. I often hear the word used to describe frequent flyers: people who abuse the system, who call the ambulance for ailments that are very obviously not emergencies—a sprained wrist, a lingering headache.

The majority of patients I treat on the ambulance, it seems, have either no health insurance or are enrolled in Medicare or Medicaid programs. After a few months on the job, I find myself automatically checking the "No Insurance" box on my patient care reports before I even bother to ask any of those questions.

It is 2010 and according to the U.S. Census Bureau, 15.1% of the population of the United States lives below the poverty line. In Syracuse, this number doubles to 31.1%, approximately 47,000 people living on roughly the cost of one appendectomy per year.[12]

A common thread that goes unrecognized amongst my coworkers is that the word "niner" is almost always used to describe poor people.

It is 1955 and President Eisenhower has declared that "our unity as a nation [depends on] individual and commercial movement over a vast system of interconnected highways crisscrossing the country and joining at our national borders with friendly neighbors to the north and south."[13] It is 1955 and the Civil Rights Movement is fighting to end racial segregation. Emmett Till has just been murdered. Rosa Parks

[12] USCB.
[13] Weingroff.

has refused to leave her seat. Three years from now, critics of the highway system, such as sociologist Lewis Mumford, will be conspicuously left off the guest list at the First National Conference on Highways and Urban Development, a five-day gathering of city officials and urban planners that takes place in Syracuse.[14] It is 1955 and several of Syracuse's biggest employers—the Onondaga Litholite Company, the Prosperity Laundry Company, the Frederick Marty Candle Company—are going bankrupt, shutting down, or being bought out and relocated to other cities.[15] Schools are being desegregated and suburbs across the nation are beginning to grow. It is 1955 and everyone is trying to get out of Syracuse.

In his 1964 article, "Portrait of a City," John A. Williams, an African-American novelist and native Syracusan who grew up in the 15th Ward, describes his old neighborhood: "We had one binding thing in common," Williams writes, "we were all poor."[16]

★

You learn the names of streets. Delaware, Otisco, Cayuga. Oswego Street, West Onondaga. Seneca Turnpike. Hiawatha Boulevard.

I know from my own experience: in most cases of emergency, Medicaid will completely cover you. For smaller things—a check up with your physician, an eye exam—you usually have to shell out. A ride in the ambulance is generally considered by insurance companies to be an emergency.

What happens is this: people who are on Medicaid and are unable to afford the cost of a visit to their physician end up calling the ambulance for small problems. The ER nurses roll their eyes and make jokes about the upcoming Oscars. The paramedics ask their questions in loud, sarcastic voices. But it's a free ride, an easy solution. I can't say I wouldn't do the exact same thing.

---

[14] Earl Swift, *The Big Roads: the Untold Story of the Engineers, Visionaries, and Trailblazers Who Created the American Superhighways* (Boston, MA: Houghton Mifflin Harcourt, 2011), 233-234.
[15] Edward Hutchison, "Former Employees of the Prosperity Co., Syracuse, NY," Edward Hutchison, 2014, www.erhutchison.com/Prosperity.html.

Revision: the first thing you learn when you are working as an EMT is to smell bullshit. You learn that these patients—the woman who is trying to score a new prescription, the guy who is homeless but healthy and wants to spend the night indoors—are niners and that their complaints are not to be taken seriously.

A rule of emergency medical practice is that you can't provide care for someone who doesn't want to be cared for. Just because a person has a broken leg does not give you the right to splint it. If someone doesn't want to be taken to the hospital, what you are allowed to do is strongly recommend your professional opinion. You can list for them all of the possible risks involved in their refusal, up to and including death. Then, you call your supervisor, you spend ten or fifteen minutes filling out the paperwork, acquiring the necessary signatures.

The exception in the case of a refusal is if the patient can be deemed mentally incapable of making decisions based on his or her own best interest: if the patient is intoxicated, is a minor, has a degenerative disorder such as dementia, has suffered an obvious trauma to the brain or spine, is unconscious, unresponsive. In these cases, permission doesn't matter and you are obligated to transport the person to the hospital using whatever means necessary. Sometimes this means contacting police, having the patient physically subdued and forced into your ambulance.

Maureen Sieh describes the protests of the residents of the 15th Ward during the time the neighborhood was being torn down: "Hundreds picketed City Hall and tried to block wrecking crews as homes and businesses were being demolished in September 1963. Some chained themselves to construction chains. One person scaled a dilapidated building and waited for police to escort him down. In a span of one week, 77 people were arrested for crossing the police line. The protests were organized by CORE, the Congress of Racial Equality, which held freedom rides and rallies nationwide to protest urban renewal and racial discrimination."[17]

---

[16] John A. Williams, "Portrait of a City: Syracuse, the Old Home Town," Syracuse University Library Associates Courier, Volume 28, Numer 1 (Spring 1993), accessed August 27, 2013, http://syracusethenandnow.org/UrbanRenewal/Williams/Williams15thWard.htm.

[17] Sieh.

Despite protests, I use canvas restraints to tie the wrists of a man on PCP to the metal rails of the stretcher. Another man who is cooperative but admits he has been drinking becomes suddenly agitated and I sit on his legs, hold one arm down while the paramedic stabs the other with a needle. I dodge punches, absorb insults, listen to patients swear at me, tell me that they hate me, that they are going to kill me.

It's 2010 and I'm lying in bed after work, trying to fall asleep, running my fingers over the scars on my stomach and thinking about how I've never told any of my coworkers that I was on Medicaid, that it probably saved my life.

It's 2010 and I'm smoking cigarettes outside of the station with a coworker. I'm leaning over the hood of the truck, running my fingers over the lines on a map and wondering who decides where to build the roads. They don't seem to make any sense in this city—there's nothing resembling a grid and few of the arterial roads can be travelled far without suddenly veering in a new direction or turning into a one-way. I'm half-listening to my coworker describe a call he went on earlier and it sounds like he says the word "nigger," though later, he will claim to have said "niner." I'm still not entirely sure that I misheard him, or that the words would have made a difference to him either way.

It's 2010 and everyone I know is trying to get out of Syracuse. I'm lying on a stretcher in the back of the ambulance in an empty parking lot in the middle of the night. The radio mumbles quietly from the front cab. It will be another year and a half before I quit my job and move away to attend graduate school in Pittsburgh, where I'll accept a position that provides me with healthcare for another two years. I close my eyes, wait for a call, think about how it doesn't matter where you're standing, there's always some violence buried under your feet. There's no such thing as a spot of ground where nobody has ever died, where nothing has ever collapsed or been ripped apart or buried or forgotten.

Brief History

Now it is time for the brief history
of the day my uncle's turkey shed burned down.
I remember walking through the wet
debris after the fire, corrugated metal

and scorched carcasses, and stepping
on a nail—a rusty, gnarled,
fire-scalded nail that slipped through
the sole of my old tennis shoes

like a pin through a pear.
That same morning my uncle's horse
gave birth standing in a creek
and the colt drowned. Though I was young,

I knew many things, how to turn a charred
glove into a bird, for example.
Also the long narrow leaves of the willow
into a blaze of white butterflies.

Robert A. Fink

Trailerville (1940)

print, lithograph
Charles T. Bowling, 1891–1985

The house trailers squat opulent as a loaf of bread.
It is 1940, no lines of men, their hands extended.
No chalked outlines on pavement, crumpled
double-breasted suits, pinstriped lapels still fluttering,
flightless birds plummeted from twelfth-floor windows.
Were it not for the trees, the trailers might seem companionable.
The trees say *denizens* of a Dante nightscape, squid-tentacled
limbs writhing, whipping the darkness visible.

I do not believe in the woman walking between the trash cans
huddled like mother and child and the sign promising M I L K,
two 1 x 4s nailed beneath, pointing the same direction—*away, away.*
Maybe it's her Popeye calves beneath the corrugated skirt,
her tight-necked blouse loose enough to conceal a .38,
and the hat—man-ish, a private eye, a wiseguy.
Is that a tin of hard candies in her hand? Cream-filled chocolates?
Roosevelt's heart? It's payment for the dark figure
behind the wheel of the charcoal sedan, engine idling . . .

from Staying Alive

When the culture passed over:

we bathed   in its light   in its fear   in its

mountain stream. We left mountains

of carts full of junk behind. We bade them

farewell. They bade us weep

and know shame

They bade us be hard.

Without power, I wielded

my body

———— ◆ ————

Star wars & ax wars & the letting of blood. The last beast dies. And under the "starry arch of heaven" and in the "stony Middleworld of earth," and even in the "dark waters of the underworld," we celebrate over the phonograph. How the tune it plays echoes wetly. Like we're underwater again in the days when the sky was a crocodile, like we're the ones thinning the membrane: the beast comes back, comes slithering

The present sheared

asunder from its parent cliffs and all the past was just

the sound of metal

warming

at the edge of space

at dawn. Who'd hump

the wretched future now? To every blasted city

numbed and stilled—

the light! It came from *underneath*—inside the earth—and shining upward, through

the rocks, the ground, and everything

Matt Morton

Not the Wind, Not the View

Two thousand miles away from here, my dad
is lying in a strange room, being tended to.
It is always getting later. No matter
if it's morning dampening the earth,
or burnt orange evening rending itself apart,
the doldrums of afternoon stuck in between.
This morning, I was sifting through
a famous nearly-dead novelist's letters,
wondering why he'd kept them all
so neatly filed away. I wasn't certain,
but I had an idea. An idea
cannot fix a heart. It cannot douse
a house on fire, which earlier I thought
my neighbor's was, but no, he was burning
wood in his backyard. Right now, I'm heating
a frozen dinner. In the studio next door,
a woman is singing, and a voice on my radio
is trying to resuscitate itself beneath layers
of static. I had an idea that each day seems
the same, yet somehow shorter.
Slight variances in the weather.
Rhythmic substitutions in the traffic's pulse.
I'm not sure what, but something
is long overdue. Do you understand
what it is I am saying? Somewhere
in America my father is dying and I am
sitting here, listening to the radio.

Battening Song

Doing daily shit while waiting
to swing the axe. To sing a lullaby
about doing dishtowels while looking

atrocious. To cinch the lariat
around the vocal apparatus
while doing nothing but proposing

paradise. Its microclimate
and solar array. Doing a mylar
helium balloon then reciting

The Pledge of Allegiance.
Proposing to believe. To routinize
failure into a form of hoping

to take the auspices
seriously. To follow them
out of the idiolect, motioning

toward forgiveness in that place
where doubtless it rains, but weather
is small and lenient. Along the way

to burden the sentence. To be
that burden, merging into traffic
with the precision of a bird.

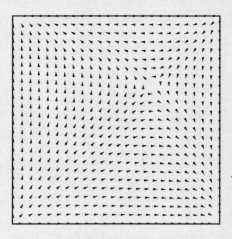

Odd Splendor: A Conversation with Early Career Poets of Color

The idea for this roundtable discussion originated in last summer's Bread Loaf Writers' Conference where David Tomas Martinez, Natalie Diaz, Roger Reeves, Tarfia Faizullah, and Jamaal May were fellows and where I was on faculty. As I got to know each of these amazing poets, what struck me was not just how different their individual voices were but, despite or maybe because of those differences, how generous they were with each other and with regards to varieties of poetry that they themselves didn't write. That generosity, that love of difference, that eagerness to engage in robust, uninhibited conversation about poetry in all its manifestations and life in all its rich diversity seemed to me then and seems to be now something unique to these particular poets, to their particular generation.

These poets share what Jamaal May has described as an assimilationist agenda, a desire to bring together and integrate what until recently we have mostly seen in isolation: lyric and narrative modes of expression, "closed" and "open" forms, spoken word poetry and poetry of the page, intellectual range and emotional intensity, engagement with contemporary experience and keen historical awareness. Many of the arguments that beset poets of my generation have been thankfully superseded by a commitment on the part of these poets to regain some of the ground that poetry has lost to other artistic disciplines in the hope of establishing a richer more creatively contentious / inclusive / honest dialogue about equality, race, sex, human decency, and the place of poetry in American culture.

—Alan Shapiro

1: BECAUSE I JUST LEARNED HOW TO IDENTIFY THE CONSTELLATION ORION DOESN'T MEAN IT HASN'T ALWAYS BEEN THERE.

Alan Shapiro: For much of my writing life, and certainly throughout the seventies and eighties, the conversation about American poetry has been hampered by a series of false dichotomies: free verse versus traditional verse, closed forms versus open forms, image versus idea, tradition versus individual expressiveness, popular (meaning non-university based) poetry versus "academic" poetry, intellectual skepticism versus sincerity and impulse. One of the more hopeful developments in the past ten years or so has been the emergence of poets of color who despite their different aesthetics share one powerful ambition: to integrate their various ethnic/racial traditions with the literary traditions of English poetry, and to redefine those literary traditions not by simple opposition and resistance, but by engagement and mastery. That is, in your work I see a powerful and productive confrontation with the literary past, which may in the end turn out to be a more durable form of resistance to it. You all seem, each in your own way, to have sought out the excluded middle term between the dichotomies I've mentioned above. You seem to treat what for my generation were mutually exclusive alternatives as mutually entailing ones. Is this how you see yourselves? And if so, how has this assimilationist moment in American poetry come about?

Despite your many differences from each other, how do you think you got to this similar place? What happened, not just in poetry but cultural life in general, to make you all possible?

David Tomas Martinez: The rise of Postmodern theory and thinking—techniques such as breaking free of binaries, disproving established dichotomies, and attention to a decentered perspective using fractured voice and polyvocal speakers—are devices that we use regularly because they are just part of the zeitgeist. Closely watch a movie that braids multiple stories together and you'll have learned a semester's worth of Postmodern theory. Also, being considered an "other" necessitates a fluidity of identity. As a minority, I have to move in a white world, a world that distinguishes itself from me by my skin, speech patterns, and hellacious swag. As a brown man, a whole closet full of assumptions come with me. Some I have rejected and some I have embraced. For instance, I am pretty heavily tattooed in a black and gray style associated with prison culture, and I knew this would lead some people to have certain assumptions about me, but I didn't care. Honestly, and this answers the question of assimilationist in part, I have to be who I am, and if some people are going to be offended or put off, oh fucking well. Now that doesn't mean I'm going to be salacious or impudent or arrogant, but I am going to be comfortable in my own skin because the dominant perspective has told each of us participating in this roundtable, at one time or another, that we are not quite right, and I reject such thinking. Every morning I wake up and twirl and marvel at the beauty that is me (albeit with an eye closed so I don't notice my nalgas are getting bigger). I'm being a bit facetious, but the basic idea is true because we are not arriving at a place of assimilation; we have been here, writing and reading and living, and the dominant perspective is now only beginning to recognize. Because I just learned how to identify the constellation Orion doesn't mean it hasn't always been there.

★

As far as my dealing with the literary past, nothing moves me the way a strong poem can move me, not even the movie *Steel Magnolias*. That being said, I love Tupac just as much as Shakespeare, but for different reasons, and place value in both of their contributions to our society.

This type of embracing of multiple registers of language and various levels of culture floods throughout *Hustle*. For instance, the book begins with a poem that addresses poetry's rich history of loving nature. There are poets that know

"AS A MINORITY, I HAVE TO MOVE IN A WHITE WORLD, A WORLD THAT DISTINGUISHES ITSELF FROM ME BY MY SKIN, SPEECH PATTERNS, AND HELLACIOUS SWAG."

every tree and flower and bird by sight, exhibiting this knowledge in their poetry. I know nothing about nature. I hate camping. What is called a canyon in *Hustle* is a dusty area along a freeway. I used to walk a giant gutter that ran underneath my neighborhood; we also called that a canyon. Because I know nothing about nature I'm constantly engaging with it, and in that way, engage with all those nature-loving poets. To the point of how it became possible that we all came to a similar place, I think that we are all well-educated people that are not entrenched completely in our own culture. I can say that about each of the members of this roundtable, and you Alan, as well. We are aware of other cultures and comfortably move within the standards of multiple cultures. Now that may be a personality quirk, or a high EQ, or we are all chameleons and sad people. Strike that; we're poets, so sad is redundant.

"MY BRAIN WAS SHAPED BY THE UNDERSTANDING THAT HISTORY WAS MYTH — WE NATIVES KNOW TOO WELL THAT HISTORY IS BRUTAL BUT NOT NECESSARILY TRUE."

Natalie Diaz: I'm with you on the "false dichotomies" wagon, Alan. Often, when I find myself in conversations about poetic traditions, what I realize people mean is, "I need to define you to figure out if I can understand you or should even bother trying to understand you," or "I need to feel defined myself so I can be recognized as a real writer." This reliance on poetic tradition troubles me because I see it as the practice of legitimizing a writer because she or he is writing in the vein of a poet who has been claimed by academia as noteworthy or authentic. Most importantly, and most dangerously, in my opinion, this thinking allows us to ignore or marginalize writers whom we don't "understand" or who don't subscribe to a "tradition" we recognize. It allows us to keep some writers, such as writers of color, locked out of the academic machine that tends to establish what is "good" writing or what is "legitimate" writing. It can also act as a strange cloning machine. It's like spending millions of dollars "proving" natives are Asian and came across the Bering Strait when we keep trying to tell you we actually came from this mountain or this lake or this place.

The majority of my engagement with poetic "traditions," at least in the classical or academic sense, is directly informed by a flipped script. The script I am referring to is the one that defines and teaches us the meanings of "history," "myth," and "tradition." My brain was shaped by the understanding that history was myth—we natives know too well that history is brutal but not necessarily true. And since myth was the word used to refer to and discredit our creation stories and our own versions of the world and our lives, I understood that "myth" was true, was a thing that really happened. "Tradition" was a word used to talk about certain aspects of my culture that were allowed or accepted by white America as definitive of native identity. The characteristics that white America did not want us to keep were called "savage," instead of "tradition."

Poetic tradition and poetic history exist the way all history does to me in that it is all myth. Myth became tradition for me and tradition/history became myth. This blur has allowed me to move into any poem or any book and exist in it because I don't feel left out of any of it. It can all be my truth. This is the real magic of poetry for me, that I read a poem of yours, Alan, from a life I do not know, from a lineage I do not know, from a time I have not been a part of, and I still leave your page with a newness about me that I carry into my own small life. As well, I take what I want and need from it. I feel like I have a right to speak to any poet and to interpret her words the way I need them in my life and poetry.

I was raised in a culture where it is proper etiquette to trace where your story has come from or where you have come from. For me then, I am always in dialogue with who has come before, who has passed this story down to me, even more so than I am in dialogue with those I am speaking directly to. How this translates into my poetry is that I feel I am talking to everybody. I want the energy of what they've done but not the rules of what they've done. I don't have the same fights as those who've come before me, and in some ways, my fights are eased by their work, and in other ways, my fights are heightened by this new world. I am loyal to my poetic ancestors in terms of respect, in terms of understanding my language has come through them, but I am not loyal to their rules. I cannot be—they are not my rules—those ancestors changed the rules, and I am lucky enough to be writing at their heels.

AS: I'll wait to comment at length until everyone else has had a chance to but, David, regarding your comment about hating to camp—if I were a Native American, my Indian name would be Hard to Camp With. My wife refers to me as a rugged indoors man.

ND: Alan, maybe, just maybe if you were a Native American, your name might be "Sounds-Like-Wild-Bill-But-Still-Means-White-Boy."

AS: You got me. If the shoe fits! If I had a shoe line, I'd call it Air Shapiro's. The ad slogan would be, "If your vertical leap is zero, buy Air Shapiro."

Regarding rules, though, I don't think there are any. Rules of thumb, maybe, certain effects following certain choices, but nothing in my experience that's prescriptive. I view tradition(s) as both pervasive and insufficient, and at its liveliest it inheres in the very arguments about tradition that tradition fosters. A tradition, in other words, is always emergent, never settled, always evolving in ways one can't predict. In fact, a tradition's vitality in my view is inversely proportionate to its predictability. Predictability, in other words, is the enemy not only of art but of tradition itself. I grew up, as you all did, in multiple traditions: some Jewish, some mercantile, some Bostonian, some literary, some folk, traditions of pop culture, rock and roll, biblical, Yiddish, and American and British. High cultural influences through college and "low" cultural influences from the streets, not to mention biological traditions and chemical traditions. If any principle governs my life on and off the page it's the Coleridgean one of bringing the whole soul into activity, getting as much life into the art as I can, as much vitality, as much impurity. As a poet I'm never happier than when I can bring high and low registers of language together in a single poem, when I can put King Kong in conversation with King Lear. I think this mongrel appetite is something we all share, despite our different backgrounds and different ages. Another way to put this would be to say that the enemy of tradition is the traditionalist, the one who wants to "purify" the art, to codify it, or cage it with a bunch of rules.

DTM: Alan, I think you make some very valid points concerning tradition, especially considering the need for "new blood" to keep traditions interesting, though we do have to be careful of exocitizing traditions outside academia's hull because in that form of mild othering comes an implicit mitigating of significance. For instance, the first word used to describe a poet of color is usually their skin (though I get "ex-gang member"), and this in a way sets apart and distinguishes (ironically) poets of color immediately. That Chican@ Literature is even a category separates it from the main hallway of American poetry. Natalie, I think your points about a smeared idea of myth and history is something all people learn, just to deal with the hypocrisy, at times, of our society, and people of color are just more aware of our society's hypocrisy because of the inevitable engagement with a history, a person of color must do, just to stay sane in a country that has not been kind to people very similar to you for no other reasons than they are just like you. Also, Alan I'm pretty sure Natalie and I would both rock the Air Shapiros.

Tarfia Faizullah: I want to begin with something you said later, Alan: the notion of never being happier than when you can bring "high and low registers of language together in a single poem." That to me directly gets at writing between those dichotomies that you named. I grew up in a bilingual, religiously conservative household in West Texas, exposed to everything from Tagore and Nazrul Islam to country music to Nietzsche to the Qur'an to hip hop. I also grew up in a culture that really privileges poetry. When I was in Bangladesh for a year, and people asked what I did, I would say that I wrote poetry. "Sure," they'd scoff. "We all do. But what do you really do?" they asked. That was a valuable lesson for me—the essential democratic nature of poetry, and how sometimes, in the middle of all of those conversations about dichotomies, or amid reading articles about whether or not poetry matters, we can forget that poetry is available to the illiterate as well, which is part of its power. Elsewhere, writing poetry can get you imprisoned, assassinated.

In that way, writing between those dichotomies wasn't something I was even aware of until much later when I found myself in those conversations. I found those conversations ultimately baffling—what was everyone fighting about? It's poetry, isn't it? Don't we all just use all the gifts we have at our disposal, and don't we all just ultimately end up writing what compels us, what doesn't relent? I love what you said, Alan, about tradition being both pervasive and insufficient— and what you said, Natalie, about your loyalty to your ancestors, but not to their rules. It brings to mind a talk I heard the novelist Elif Shafak give recently—she used a compass as a metaphor to talk about the way she thinks about writing. I

> "WHEN I WAS IN BANGLADESH FOR A YEAR, AND PEOPLE ASKED WHAT I DID, I WOULD SAY THAT I WROTE POETRY. 'SURE,' THEY'D SCOFF. 'WE ALL DO. BUT WHAT DO YOU REALLY DO?'"

loved that—the idea of having a fixed place from which you can draw circles. The word that comes to mind is lineage, which in biology, also refers to a sequence of species thought to evolve from its predecessor. I like that word a lot because it gets at the way tradition is both a fixed snapshot of a moment as well as a place from which to draw wider and wider circles.

There's been a new word popping up in the creative-writing spheres: agency. I'm still trying to figure out what people mean when they use it, since it doesn't bear much resemblance to what the word actually means. But I think people mean that they are willing to take hold of what they feel is theirs with regards to their own poems. I think about Adrienne Rich's poem "Diving into the Wreck," the notion that "these are the materials." For me, poetry is the language of magic, of spell-casting, of wonder, and poetry has always been a place that can and will bear the weight and nuance of my many vocabularies and lineages. It's about the arrangement, the approach. The materials are all there.

★ **Roger Reeves:** Tarfia, you bring up the word arrangement, and I think that word might be quite useful in thinking about "tradition" and "canon"—to think about tradition as an arrangement of derangements and influences (I am borrowing the phrase an "arrangement of derangements" from Terrance Hayes). What I mean is that one's personal "tradition" or "canon" is a compilation of influences, writers, styles, senses of sound, wit, intelligence, images, poses, personas, and tones. For instance, I have a few friends that love Ashbery, Keats, and Rilke. How each of these writers deploy what they learn from these poets, the materials of poetry, is quite different.

"WHEN WE BEGIN TO INTEND TOO MUCH FOR THE POEM, AS OPPOSED TO ATTENDING TO THE MATERIALS OF THE POEM, THE POEM LOSES ITS ABILITY FOR SURPRISE, FOR DISCOVERY."

different. This might be the hidden bounty of poetry. That we might all love Larry Levis, for instance, but how we employ his sense of history, place, image, and the line might be quite different.

I also believe this period of assimilating many different types of aesthetic stances, poses, and dispositions into one poem comes about in my own work because I don't believe anything should be dismissed as outside of my wheelhouse. I believe whatever makes the best poem should be utilized. Also, these prior aesthetic debates—New Formalism versus Confessional Poetry, L=A=N=G=U=A=G=E Poetry versus Academic Poetry (and Acceptance)—partly come about because of intention rather than attention. When we begin to intend too much for the poem, as opposed to attending to the materials of the poem, the poem loses its ability for surprise, for discovery. Alan, you called it predictability—that which hampers a poem's ability to gain any flight. And isn't that why we write poetry: to discover something new (aesthetically, intellectually, politically)?

AS: I think this conversation itself illustrates what you all have been saying. Out of our own materials and inheritances and accidents, we forge our own way. That way never emerges in isolation, but from always being in tension with wherever we are—wherever we've been—individually and collectively.

ND: And maybe it is important to think of this as something other than assimilation, which is a loaded word for many of us. It is an erasure of some proportion, sometimes large, sometimes small. Maybe this isn't so much an assimilationist moment, as what Roger refers to as a refusal to dismiss or be dismissed.

AS: YES, this makes a lot of sense to me. How about Admissible? A moment in which nothing is inadmissible.

2: RAGE ON

AS: As MFA programs have proliferated, the distinction between inside and outside, avant-garde and rear guard, academic and nonacademic poetry has become harder and harder to determine or maintain. Spoken Word poets notwithstanding (and I want to talk about them in a minute), nearly everybody, no matter what their political or poetic stripes, or their aesthetic affiliations, to varying degrees is a member of the establishment. We all teach. We are all members of AWP. We all attend, for the most part, the same writers' conferences and festivals at which we give talks, and conduct workshops, and if you haven't done so yet, you all will soon be sitting on panels giving out awards and fellowships. Resistance to the status quo has been an essential part of your lives on and off the page. Now that you're being recognized by the very institutions and power structures that excluded or discriminated against poets of color who came before you, do you worry about maintaining and cultivating your creative independence and productive rage?

How do you think you yourselves can avoid in twenty years becoming the very establishment that the next generation of innovative writers will need to oppose?

And related to this, what other poets of color your age could you name who should be part of this discussion, whose aesthetic differs from yours but who are truly doing something distinctive and valuable (even if it's something not to your taste), something not yet accepted by the world that has accepted you?

★

DTM: Man, I personally struggle with balancing my private and public personas everyday. I can't be the same person I am teaching a poetry workshop as I am on the basketball court; however, my goal is to be as close as possible in these personas. Part of this is never wanting to become too assimilated in the dominant culture, yet to be fully familiar with the dominant culture. Being fully familiar with dominant culture is not really difficult; as a member of academia and a person that spends most of his time with other writers, my world now is completely different from the one in which I grew up. My childhood was spent in an urban environment, with working class parents, and that is a world I try to hold on to, but it isn't easy. Staying in touch with old friends, family, playing basketball, any space where people aren't impressed by the fact that I am a poet are spaces that help keep this writing world in perspective because it is such a small, insular world, and it is easy to forget in poetry that what we call problems are often just trifles. It's not the end of the world because I didn't win a prize or didn't get published in a journal or I'm not mentioned as a great writer or any of the small ways writers seek validation.

But these are really just concerns that all people share; we must each assemble ourselves each morning, trying to please the world while still making ourselves happy. One of my variables just happens to be race. One happens to be gender. My sexuality. And despite the increasingly specialized society, in which any type of subject, entertainment, or information one desires is available, there still seems to be difficulty for some writers to integrate the various aspects of their personalities into their writing. I know I have struggled with integrating the various aspects of my personality into my writing (hell, I started this question by admitting my difficulty navigating the various spaces I inhabit) but as I became more comfortable with the various aspects of my personality, I began to

> "ALSO, THE FACT THAT I WAS A TEENAGE FATHER, WAS IN A GANG, AND I SOLD DRUGS — THIS IS NOT THE NORMAL BACKSTORY OF A COLLEGE PROFESSOR, OR A POET."

see the ways I didn't fit into academia as strengths, distinguishing quirks of history or character. For instance, my ethnicity. There are not a lot of Latin@s in literature, but also my working class background. Also, the fact that I was a teenage father, was in a gang, and I sold drugs—this is not the normal backstory of a college professor, or a poet. All of these personal histories have made me feel like an outsider since I began my academic and writing career. So I expect to eventually to be railed against. Considering I didn't expect to live beyond 25, it's a blessing to be in academia and not dirt-napped somewhere or incarcerated. So, come at me, bro.

★

ND: I think something that keeps me grounded is remembering that "this is just poetry." While it is a lucky gift—the gift to tell a story, the gift to slow down long enough to ask a question of this world—it is also just a small part of this big world and my personal world. I wrote a rack of poems about a brother who suffers and makes his family suffer, and it didn't solve my own real-life brother who is suffering and making my family suffer. Poetry is what I do when I don't know what else to do. I can't explain the aches and desires in me, so I put them on the page. It is one of many things I do that makes me a slower, more thoughtful, more emotional, maybe even a better person. The only thing I want my poetry to do is to offer to some other person like me a story they can find themselves in, a question they might not ask, a beautiful thing they maybe missed because they averted their eyes.

I have been the receiver of so many gestures of generosity and kindness from people of all colors. It is my responsibility, and I still believe in responsibility, to return that to someone else when I have the opportunity to do so. Knowing how small I am in this world is important in keeping me in a "giving" mode and not in a "measuring" mode. What I mean by this is too often in our smaller communities we begin to count the prizes and the opportunities available to us. Instead of realizing the sum of opportunities for Native writers or writers of color or female writers or queer writers is "too few, which means we all need to push each other toward the top until we have just as many as everyone else," it seems we get greedy or afraid and arrive at "too few, which means I have to start scrapping with the only people who can help me change this, who are other Native writers or writers of color or female writers or queer writers." If I ever get like this, I hope someone will pull me outside, like my mom used to do at Mass when we were misbehaving, and set me straight (well, I hope they set me straight without taking their sandal off and swatting me with it—that was embarrassing, plus my mom has like a size eleven shoe, so that was one giant sandal).

> "KNOWING HOW SMALL I AM IN THIS WORLD IS IMPORTANT IN KEEPING ME IN A 'GIVING' MODE AND NOT IN A 'MEASURING' MODE."

The academic "establishment" of poetry has always been a little strange to me, in that we credit it with keeping poetry vibrant and alive, but it is also part of the cage that separates poetry from real-life people. That being said, I came to poetry through a university. However, if basketball had not taken me to that university, I would have been one of the people on the other side of the cage. I don't worry that I will be deprogrammed in some way when I arrive at a university to teach, if I do. The rez is not a place I have left—I carry it with me, and it keeps me humble. I realize that this life is part hard work and a lot of blessings and luck.

AS: Fair enough. So, what poets should we have included in this discussion whose work differs from yours or represents in some ways aesthetic choices you don't particularly embrace but still feel are important?

DTM: I would have been interested in what francine j. harris would have had to say, probably really interesting stuff. She's a craftsperson. Besides I just really like her work, which makes interesting moves I wouldn't usually do. Also, Eduardo C. Corral and Jamaal May would have amazing answers to these questions. I am always entranced by his perspective and his work.

TF: Alan, I'd like to answer this question first from the perspective of an editor. Journals and presses have funny little lives in and around the establishment. They are often supported by the universities they are attached to, though they operate independently as well. They are spaces that feature and spotlight the work of writers from multiple corners of the world, both within and outside of the institutions that be. Often, they are misunderstood: their goals, the reasons they do what they do. Behind closed doors, the conversations about what to publish and why are thoughtful, impassioned, anxiety-provoking. Are we representing the full breadth and depth of poetry, then and now and in the future? Do these poems move/challenge/connect, or do they do the opposite?

These questions are what I consider both as a writer and an editor, and in that way, I am also a spy. Like all spies, I'm interested in survival: of my own strange and individual nature, for those of my tribes, for our many and varied stories. I'm interested, as a writer and editor and teacher, in moving between the boundaries, and moving the boundaries around. In that way, academia is one space of many in which people are asking the questions about what language to use to survive between and inside of those boundaries. I support, and always will, other spies: artists who are doing the good work here, there, and everywhere.

A few good spies doing some audacious work: Michelle Chan Brown, Nandi Comer, Rajiv Mohabir, Marcelo Hernandez Castillo.

RR: Alan, I want to go back a bit to the question that you asked: "How do you think you yourselves can avoid in twenty years becoming the very establishment that the next generation of innovative writers will need to oppose?" I hope not to avoid it. I hope that my answer doesn't come off churlish or a bit maverick. But, honestly, I hope to produce something that the next generation of innovative writers feel compelled to be in conversation with, to speak back to. I swapped out the term "oppose" at the end of your question for the terms or phrases "be in conversation" and "speak back to." I think this question that you asked has residue from the former question on tradition. I think the goal of writing is to produce something that continues, augments, challenges, converses with what has been said, written over this very long

"I HAVE PLENTY OF POETRY MENTORS AND ELDERS, THOSE THAT WE MIGHT CALL THE ESTABLISHMENT, THAT SUPPORT AND CRITIQUE AND LOVE AND CORRECT MY WORK DESPITE IT CALLING INTO QUESTION THEIR OWN POETIC AND AESTHETIC LEANINGS AND DISPOSITIONS."

transnational, transhistorical tradition called poetry. In our own very American context, you don't have Gwendolyn Brooks "Anniad" without "The Aeneid." You don't get the Black Arts Movement without the Harlem Renaissance and their opposition to what they felt were the bourgeoisie aesthetics and the lack of revolutionary politics of the Harlem Renaissance. You don't get Gwendolyn Brooks post the poetry conference at Fisk University without the Gwendolyn Brooks that's championed by *Poetry Magazine* in her early career. What I mean is that we, writers, become the establishment through age and living. However, there are many ways of manifesting establishment. For instance, I have had plenty of poetry mentors and elders, those that we might call the establishment, that support and critique and love and correct my work despite it calling into question their own poetic and aesthetic leanings and dispositions. I hope to provoke. Provocation is one of the few imperatives of art.

I don't worry too much about keeping or maintaining my creative independence or "rage," because this country will probably not stop shooting black boys and men that look like me in the very near future. This country will probably not stop shooting and killing my sisters and mothers. This country will continue to look at me as though I am not here, that weird moment of both invisibility and hypervisibility, which offers me "second-sight," as DuBois might say. I will constantly have to write my way into existence. I am always a disappearing country of sorts. My country is always in need of a new myth. Otherwise, we might never be born.

The writers of my age, who write from this disappearing country, that should be in this conversation are: Solmaz Sharif, Rickey Laurentiis, Phillip B. Williams, Jericho Brown, Wendy Xu, Aracelis Girmay, Ladan Osman, Donika Ross, Danez Smith, T'ai Freedom Ford, Cristina Correa, Dawn Lundy Martin, Evie Shockley, Carolina Ebeid, Eduardo Corral, Ocean Vuong, Terrance Hayes, Natasha Trethewey, Carmen Gimenez-Smith, Laurie-Ann Guerrero, Frannie Choi, Claudia Rankine, Saeed Jones. This is a rather short list, but I think it's a good start.

AS: Roger, I hope you're right. I hope the generation after you feels compelled to push back against something in your work or assimilate it or both. What I hope doesn't happen is that they ignore it or that currents arise in the literary landscape that you dismiss or ignore or simply "write off" as not interesting or worth your while. Maintaining this kind of attentiveness and self-distrust, or vigilance against one's own complacency gets harder to do the older one gets. Trust me. I'm an old guy. The kind of stance you describe is of course what all of us hope for.

3: MANY MANSIONS, MUCH BEEF

AS: As teachers and artists, we strive to promote the best possibilities of poetry, in the classroom and on the page (and on the stage). At the same time, poetry has never been more available to so many people. I think we'd all subscribe to the notion that the wider and more diverse the audience, the richer the art will be. But is our commitment to art in tension with this democratic ideal? How do we balance the necessity for making judgments, or distinctions between good and bad, more interesting or less interesting ways of writing, with the competing necessity to be as inclusive as possible, so that as poets and teachers we remain open to the widest range of possibilities on and off the page? How do we foster excellence (however broadly conceived) and broadness of appeal?

DTM: For me, any conversation I have, regardless of the topic, is about poetry. I don't believe we can make one perfect poetry; no Socratic ideal floats in the sky waiting for me to fetch it down and call it my own. Therefore, if we are all making poetries, each its own animal, each having a different intended audience, then as evaluators we must be aware of the various writer-to-reader traditions, and judge each poetry on its own merit and intent. That being said, as a Chican@ poet, if I see another brown person write the trifecta Latin@ poem containing grandma's hands, tortilla making, and butter running down a wrist, I might spontaneously explode from hate. Poems such as these employ scenes that have been hollowed out of anything but sentimentality by the sheer number of times this type of scene appears in poems written by Latin@s, making it cliché. It is a taxidermy of emotion. Yes, it is a shared experience by many Latin@s, but it is not, as Pound asked for, an emotional complex in an instant in time because it is familiar, thus lacking complexity. The sentimental, tortilla-making grandma is an unsuccessful poem because it does nothing within the tradition. In part what makes this poem fail is that the poet speaks only inwardly, to their own self. For me, some of the most successful poems are the poems that address the many. I believe it is human nature to want to be addressed, not be ignored, and this is why I try to speak to as many people as possible by engaging with as many different traditions and conversations. To accomplish this, I utilize allusion to myth, slang, references to various cultures, the syntax and diction of various cultures, and images from everywhere. I assume this to be a highly democratic act.

ND: David, I guess now I have to throw away that poem I just wrote about my big-handed grandmother whooping your normal-sized-handed grandmother at a tortilla-making contest. Don't mess with Mojave tortillas—we burn a handprint into them!

When I read poems, I can't help but read them through my particular head and my particular experiences. I come to poetry for emotion. If I don't feel anything in a poem—not that deepening well in the stomach, not the empty bucket scraping the bottom of that well, not that small hurt in the back of my throat, not that urge to talk back to the poem or argue with it, and if I leave the poem empty handed, with nothing to echo in me through the days, I think the poem has failed in some way. What I try to deliver to my students when I teach is the commitment to making our language, our image, our every word, mean something to us as writers first. I think when the words and images are meaningful to the poet, it creates a possibility for meaning in the reader. That is the deal we make when we decide to write poetry: we say, I am going to write a poem that creates some sort of response in a reader. I always start with language and image, so the questions I ask my students are, "What are your images?" "What is your lexicon, the language that you find meaning in?" And I push and push and push them to discover it. I have to write my poems—I cannot write poems like David or Roger or Tarfia or Alan. I have to mine my set of images from my life—where I've been, what I've read, what I fear, what I love, and on and on. And I have to do that with language that carries emotion and energy in a way that affects my readers' energies and emotions. This is true for formal poetry, language poetry, white-people poetry, poetry of color, experimental poetry, Spanish poetry, basically everything except "mash-up" poetry. I still don't get "mash-up poetry." If they just called it "mash-up" I'd be okay with it, but "mash-up poetry"… I just can't.

> "WHAT I TRY TO DELIVER TO MY STUDENTS WHEN I TEACH IS THE COMMITMENT TO MAKING OUR LANGUAGE, OUR IMAGE, OUR EVERY WORD, MEAN SOMETHING TO US AS WRITERS FIRST."

I had the luck of learning poetry from Tim Seibles and Luisa Igloria at Old Dominion University. They taught me the hard work of poetry. They taught me in a straightforward way—they didn't pad their conversation with me or "go easy" on us. They talked poems and poetry and craft to me. They talked feeling and world and life. They believed I should know what my poems mean to me. It is not very different from basketball—you don't just set a random screen for no reason; you don't pick someone up on defense full court if you don't have to; you don't go in for a dunk if you can't dunk the ball; and you don't pull up from half court unless the time is ticking off the clock. That being said, it doesn't mean you can never shoot a three-ball if you aren't a good three-point shooter. Precision, not perfection is what I try to stress to my students—that comes through hard work and being honest with yourself. It's no secret that I know a lot more about basketball than I do about poetry. My hope is that my students end up knowing a lot more about their own poetry than I can tell them about poetry in general.

DTM: I'm not saying that we don't all have flying chancla stories, just that personal myths we create as writers don't necessarily resonate with all readers, and I definitely have a for-the-masses approach to poetry. That doesn't mean I write "commercial" poetry (does that even exist?). I take pride that readers up and down the scale of sophistication seem to have gotten something from my work. I am definitely not trying to exclude the type of people I write about (working-class/non-college educated) from reading my poetry. The difficult question, for me, is how to construct a poetry that interests the reader while still stretching the limits of my own aesthetics, the limits of my own personal narratives, and the limits of my intellectual knowledge. Testing the boundaries is the only way I know, as of now, to construct a poetry I find pleasing. Maybe in time, this will change. I sure as-yellow-melted-snow-on-the-sidewalk hope so.

RR: This question of keeping the room of poetry as inclusive as possible as well as keeping poetry as rigorous as possible requires us to dismantle the notion that there is one type of poetry and that there are such things as tastemakers, gatekeepers, etc. There are many rooms in the mansion of poetry. In fact, there are many mansions. And villas. And garages. And barrios. And split-level homes. And caves. And alcoves. And crevices. And forts. And tree houses. And dojos. And temples. The democratization of poetry requires us to allow it to be democratic—that we not feel that a poem not done in the manner, style, aesthetic, tone of our liking be dismissed as shrinking or besmirching the value of POETRY. If abuelita poems are not our bag, but they produce meaningful feeling for someone else, for another community of poetry lovers, even if these poems don't move the "Tradition of Abuelita Poems" along, let those communities that need those poems have them, and let them call these poems poetry without any snark from those that don't love those poems. Here, I am specifically speaking to writers of color. I don't believe this piece of advice works in all cases across poetry, particularly when it comes to writers of color trying to pierce the membrane of established poetry venues (read: historically white). Often, I catch myself rolling my mind's eyes during a reading because of well-trod or worn subject matter, and I have to remind myself to stop that judgmental bullshit. As Natalie noted earlier, poetry requires us to slow down, to examine words, situations, images that we thought we knew as if for the first time.

"THERE ARE MANY ROOMS IN THE MANSION OF POETRY. IN FACT, THERE ARE MANY MANSIONS."

I try to foster this slowing down, this defamiliarization of the familiar in my classroom through a suspension of dislike. Often students, particularly graduate students, come into the classroom with pretty developed palettes, sometimes over-developed in fact. I don't like Pilsners; I'm an IPA sort of girl. I'm not into Beyoncé, more of India Arie, Erykah Badu sort of dude. What I do in the classroom is to not allow this type of discussion about poetry. I ask my students to tell me how does the poet, say Ashbery or Baraka, deploy the materials of poetry. How does Ashbery or Baraka use line, metaphor, surprise, image, persona, argumentation, and to what effect? Moving the discussion away from likes and dislikes immediately opens up the analytical heart chakra (corny, I know) and allows for the conversation to become about what the poet reading the poem can use, borrow, steal. I believe every poet has something for us to steal, to take back to the cave that will help us better-make our poems and weapons. Likes and dislikes are inevitable, human in fact. However, I think alongside Whitman. I contain multitudes.

AS: Well, Roger, I agree with all of this in principle, but again as with your earlier answer, this is not as easy to do as one would think. And to some extent your comment that there are many rooms in the mansion of poetry, true as that is, begs the question because within those rooms one does make value judgments and evaluations. We still say in class you might try this and not that, or you might try putting the period at the end of the sentence instead of in the middle. When we write our own poems we revise in the direction of what we think will make a better poem. And I for one don't think our decisions are always or only personal or subjective. I think within the room of a certain kind of poetry we can say with some confidence this is better than that. What I can't do (whatever my preferences are) is say that one room is better than another room. I can't say basketball is a better game than football. But on a basketball court with its own rules and arrangements ("derangements" too), I can say that there are ways

> "THERE'S A GREAT DANGER IN BEING TOO CONFIDENT ABOUT ONE'S JUDGEMENTS. BUT THERE'S AN EQUALLY DISABLING DANGER IN HAVING NO CONFIDENCE IN JUDGEMENTS WHATSOEVER."

of playing that are better, more useful, and creative than other ways. I can say with confidence that LeBron James is a better basketball player than I am (I can hear you all saying, "Don't sell yourself short, Al"—no worry, my shortness sells itself.) It would be foolish to say though that he's a better athlete than say Tiger Woods at his best or Roberto Clemente. I try to teach in the manner you describe, Roger. All I'm saying here is that it's hard and probably on some level not advisable to avoid all judgment in describing student work. Or even work that is first rate but very different from what one does. Even to say "first rate" already brings evaluation into the discussion. I'm a better reader for certain kinds of poems than for other kinds of poems. And for the poems I can read with confidence I'm good at making suggestions for how those poems could be better. There's a great danger in being too confident about one's judgments. But there's an equally disabling danger in having no confidence in judgements whatsoever. At least in my experience as a reader and writer.

DTM: Alan, you make some wonderful points, much more eloquently than I could have said in my thumbed manner. Roger, I think you make a strong point by attempting to recognize the importance of inclusivity in poetry because as you say, there is no one poetry. As POCs we understand the difficulty of being excluded at times; however, I would argue that the dominant perspective has a familiarity with African-American poets' culture and have well-established impressions of black culture, for better and for worse. The dominant perspective does not have this familiarity with Latin@s. I think this, in part, is where the subtlety of our difference begins. And while I would be a madman to rail against inclusivity, I am a bit too aware of myself as an individual to think I can understand the poetries of another experience, which is why a myriad of experiences is important. I accept all perspectives, valuing no one over another; I just write a poetry of experience, rooted in the way that I see the world. And I have certain points of entry into this world. All I can do is hope to see the world in a way that results in some sort of pleasure for the reader. I am going to make judgements. I am not afraid of my judgements, and I will stand by them. There must be some distinctions made in my mind, and I will write or express these distinctions. And though, Roger, the point you make, as far as not devaluing traditions outside of the canonical tradition (white) is an important aesthetic rule of thumb, it is not a tool that I can use with total confidence because I know that my aesthetics are skewed to my tastes and experiences. Furthermore, I refuse to like something because it is brown. Or black. Or white. I like what I like, and I will strip down whatever I like from the poetries I like. (Admittedly, I am most attracted to sensibilities outside of the dominant perspective.) I will take the hubcaps and steal the radio to make a good poem, to pimp together a language I find appealing. But this is also a distinction of choice that is emblematic of our books. *King Me* has a real beauty in the multiplicity of voices, a genius in the ability to put on other personas. *Hustle* is one fallible dude walking in the world, jacking his life and trying to learn from these mistakes. My poems are me. The way I think. Good and bad.

TF: I'm going to steal a word from your question, Alan, and a word from your answer, David, and put them together: excellence and fallibility. They have such a tricky relationship, and yet circle around each other constantly. In order to achieve excellence, one must risk fallibility. I encourage myself and my students to pay attention to what we're doing well, and to what we could do better. I am in awe, often, of how well my students know themselves once encouraged to acknowledge themselves. Even barely-hatched writers acknowledge the truth when someone points out to them what they could be doing better. The truth—its messy imperfections, its fleeting revelations—is how I define excellence. And if the truth is real, then it has to be delivered thoughtfully, right? And there has to be a way to communicate to the people you're delivering the truth to that you have been honing your techniques of truthtelling all along. It is that collision of craft and vision, to feel as though someone is speaking to you alone, because they have figured out the best, most honest way, most intimate way to speak to themselves that makes me awake to a world both familiar and new.

AS: Beautifully put.

RR: David, I'm not asking you to like poems because they are written by brown, black, white, purple, green, or red people. In fact, dislike them. However, what I am petitioning for is a nuanced way of discussing and inhabiting one's "dislikes." We, people of color, cannot pretend as though our canons, writers, artists carry the same political, aesthetic, social clout as the greater American (read: white) tradition. Our traditions are always-already read as funky, recalcitrant, unlearned, dirty, foul, and reprobate. Think about what Louis Simpson wrote about Gwendolyn Brooks in the 1960s, something along the lines of, "if being black is all that Gwendolyn Brooks has to write about, then she doesn't have much to write about." I bring up this "critique" of Brooks by Simpson as an example of the precarious footing that our "experiences" have in the world of literature and art. I also bring up this moment because we must be careful about dismissing work, critiquing work without exploring its potential efficacy and rigor because we might be re-inscribing the very boundaries, borders, oppressions, and racisms that we seek to implicitly and explicitly dismantle. We cannot pretend as though our critiques occur in a bubble. They, our critiques, occur in the very public space of America, poetry, academia, criticism, and all of its rife, disingenuous, and racist history.

Also, David, you speak of experience as though it arrives in front of us like a hamburger or a steak—whole and ready for us to eat. Yes, we will always see the world from our particular vantage point, from our lens, our eyes. And, yes, we can only write from that particular understanding and vision. However, our vision of the world is constantly changing, evolving and being influenced. Flaubert once said that you talk on the first floor differently than you talk on the fourth. Our selves are constantly in flux. We are constantly seeing and re-seeing. This process is what makes writing such a beautiful art—vision then revision. Then, the revising of the revision. This is not just the making of art or poetry. It is the making of our lives, the "human."

AS: I agree with this, Roger. And everything you say here speaks to the need for and is an example of careful, scrupulous judgment, judgment that's hyper-sensitive to context. We should distrust our dislikes but not pretend we don't have them. That conversation about our differences which of course entails negotiating competing likes and dislikes is itself what constitutes a vibrant and always emergent tradition.

DTM: Tarfia, I agree wholeheartedly with your assesment of truthtelling, and the often cumbersome attempt at getting there. Roger, you make an astute point considering how the experiences of poets of color are often discounted, exoticized by the dominant perspective. I acutely feel the sting of this fact because I am often considered the "gangster" poet or the memoirist in verse, which to a certain extent puts in captivity my "experiences." And obviously the Simpson critique of Brooks is a horribly flat interpretation of Brooks. Also, I do agree that we talk differently on the fourth floor than the first; however, our poems are written in an instant in time, a shard of experience that we process in that moment. Let me make an analogy: my neck is tattooed with the phrase "Homme de Lettres." I got this tattoo when I entered my MFA program, and it was, admittedly, a rather pretentious tattoo to get, but I got the tattoo as a goal to aspire towards. This may or may not explain or mitigate the obvious grandiose gesture to some, but my thought process could not allow for that. I had a "by any means necessary" mentality. I had

"THE TATTOO IS LIKE A POEM I HAVE WRITTEN; IT IS WHERE I WAS AT THE MOMENT, AND I CAN ONLY JUDGE IT IN ALL THE SUCCESSIONS OF MOMENTS WHERE I ENCOUNTER THE POEM LATER, NEVER FIXED."

to make it. I had to survive. I still feel that way. I hope I always do. Obviously, I am in a much different place, able to see subtleties that I was numb to before. But that is not revision, but a changing of meaning over time because of circumstances and events. And the tattoo is like a poem I have written; it is where I was at the moment, and I can only judge it by all the successive of moments where I encounter the poem later, never fixed. But it never changes. You can call your steak chicken, but it ain't. And I think this is the difference, and maybe a bigger poetic truth: beef is indeed different than po(e)ultry. I know about beefs. Trust me.

4: TO LEARN BY HEART

AS: Every stylistic choice we make as writers entails a bias. To write in some particular form brings certain aspects of experience into focus by ignoring others. To do this is not to do that. Different forms and different kinds of poems reckon with life and language in different ways. In fact, one could argue that we live in a time not of poetry but of poetries, each with its own set of rules and procedures, its own opportunities and risks.

The most popular form of poetry in the world right now is Performance Poetry, or Spoken Word. It reaches an incredibly wide and diverse audience. It has done more to democratize the art of poetry than any other literary or popular movement I can think of. Some of you in fact have a significant and distinguished background in stage-based poetry. I've heard some of you talk about the value of performance poets learning from the poetry we associate with academic study. But what lessons can page poets, so to speak, learn from stage poets? What things can one do in a performance medium that isn't possible on the page? How can our practice be enriched by theirs?

ND: I'm not a spoken word poet, so I am speaking from the only side of this I've got. The reading of my poems is important to me—whether we call that performance or reading or recitation or whatever floats your boat. I practice reading my poems. I enjoy reading my poems. I don't know why people are embarrassed to say that—but I love words and the way I put them together on my page has as much to do with the way they feel and sound in my mouth as it does with the meanings of the words and the word orders. But the work of my poems happens on the page. I don't usually craft sound by itself. Sound is part of my attention to the energy a word carries—this energy is part feeling in my mouth and throat, part feeling in my ears, and this energy is also built up over the course of the word's existence. In my experience of spoken word poetry, control of sound—tone, volume, rhyme, alliteration—are leading the way for the narrative or the emotional impact. One of the

"SOUND IS PART OF MY ATTENTION TO THE ENERGY A WORD CARRIES."

best young spoken word poets, in my opinion, who is doing the hard work of the page is Danez Smith. You can see him grow from poem to poem. You can see him learning his craft—not my craft or your craft. He is making poems.

DTM: I think page poets can learn dramatization from our spoken word brethren, who have a flair for pleasing the crowd. Unfortunately, the unsuccessful poetry readings I attend are often given by poets with a lack of interest in the audience's level of enjoyment. I find this problematic. There are nervous people, who are much less gregarious than myself, and I don't fault them for stage fright or social anxieties; however, I do feel an obligation to entertain anyone who has taken time out of their busy schedule to hear me read. They could be watching "Hoarders" with their valuable time, so I do my best to convey my appreciation by putting on a good show. Spoken word poets know how to put on a good show, and I admire the effort they put into their craft. I sure as shine can't memorize my poems like they do. Another virtue I find in spoken word is, due to the nature of oral presentation and judging, a tendency towards pleasing the crowd. When done right this just amazes me, though it can go off the rails fast. But that's the difficulty with any poem, so making the poem interesting should just be the start. But often page poets can get routed in one direction, and forget of all the ways that can make a poem interesting. A poem can be made interesting with intellectual discoveries, emotional discoveries, and formal discoveries, and these are only a few ways, and I feel like spoken word poets most often remember the ways their reading of a poem can please an audience.

RR: I want to complicate this notion of performance (poetry and otherwise) because there's a politics to bodies and their respective expressions. The question of performance and poetry is rather gnarly and thorny one for black poets because no matter what black poets do (even if they stare down into their book and read from the page) people (audiences) often see what they're doing as performance. What I have found is that black poets (bodies) perform and white poets (bodies) read. Black bodies embody knowledge while white poets create knowledge. In other words, there is a presiding intelligence in white poets' work that does not exist in black poets' work. This dichotomy is problematic because it often reifies racist notions of (the lack of) black intelligence and concretizes the hypervisibile invisibility that black

> "WHAT I HAVE FOUND IS THAT BLACK POETS (BODIES) PERFORM AND WHITE POETS (BODIES) READ. BLACK BODIES EMBODY KNOWLEDGE AND WHITE BODIES CREATE KNOWLEDGE."

bodies must contend with on a daily basis. If you ask me, all poems are performed, enacted to some degree, but that's not what you're asking Alan, and honestly, I wrote a whole dissertation on the thorniness, invisibility, sublimity, and opacity of black intelligence as manifested in poetry and the novel, and we don't really have time for that. And I don't want to bore. However, what I've learned from performance poetry is that our audience should be moved, should be disturbed. Again, art as provocation. Also, we page poets should not be scared that our poems mean less or are less intellectually rigorous if they sound beautiful coming out of our mouths. I believe that spoken-word poems are just as intellectually rigorous as any page poem.

AS: I agree with all of the above. I would only add (and this looks back to the question before this one) that most of everything is bad, most page poems are bad, most stage poems are bad. But the best stage poems are as good, as compelling, and as important as the best page poetry. I don't feel any need to choose between them.

TF: I'm in agreement with many of the points brought up. I went to a lot of slams in high school and college, always as an audience member who wanted to be a participant. Like you, Natalie, I love to read poems, the music of them, the movement of word to word, line to line. What is so powerful to me about performance poetry is that it fully embraces the love of that music, encourages poetry to be spell-casting. I think, too, that the memorization of poems leads to recitation, which feels closer to prayer and to war cry. Recitation, too, is democratic—even folks who can't read can memorize, and recite. Poetries—when they are at their best—are vengeful, worshipful, and available to all.

AS: Is there a more beautiful expression in the English language than "to learn something by heart"?

ND: Roger and I have had this conversation about "performance," and I think it is an important one. Something to keep challenging and questioning. Whether it is minstrel performance or black and brown/red face in television and theater, or once great chiefs whittling miniature bows and arrows at world's fairs and in human zoos, performance can be a charged word, a violent word. I am very interested in this side of the conversation about performance. But there is also another side of the word for me. I do feel the "performance" when I am reading, much as I felt the "performance" of game day—meaning, I had a mindset, a physical demeanor, a different head and heart space to exist in for the duration of a reading or a basketball game. There was a time when my anxieties had me in a grip, and I began to get extremely anxious before readings, almost to the point of hyperventilating. A friend of mine suggested I treat poetry readings the way I once treated basketball games. I would actually bring an extra set of Chucks, a "game pair" in a bag and change them immediately before the reading, either in the bathroom or in a side room if one was available, and somehow that helped me to prepare for what I needed to do. In this instance, it feels like performance to me, like basketball. However, we have all had those questions after a reading, where someone in the audience says, "I loved the cadence of voice, did that come from your Navajo songs?" or, "Your voice sounded like a ceremony chant I heard on the Pueblo reservation." And well, that makes me realize something very different. (Note: I am not Navajo or Pueblo, and I do not chant.)

5: *FIRST YOU MUST CHARM YOURSELF*

AS: And this of course leads to the question of audience and community. When you write, to whom or what, if anything, do you feel responsible? To your families or the communities you come from? To the literary community including not just contemporary poets but the poets of the past? Or to your own imagination? And as a corollary to this question, how do you maintain your imaginative freedom and independence (which in my view is essential to artistic expression) and at the same time still honor whatever communal obligations and responsibilities you might feel?

ND: In my everyday real and average life, I am always responsible for my family, for my community. But that responsibility is not one that affects what I write or how I write. My responsibility is to not be silent. To use whatever gifts I have. Once, that gift was basketball. Today, that gift is working with my Elders to save our language. Some days, that gift is telling stories—I tell stories by writing poems. We poets have a magical type of hunger, one that can never be sated. We want to say things that we cannot possibly say. We want to ask questions that have no answers. We want to understand what no human has yet been able to understand. It is lucky work and lonely work. It makes us sad a lot of days. It makes us anxious with the world. But it also eases us into the world. Throughout my life, I have held in and suppressed so many questions that I had—questions with teeth, questions that will eat you up. On the court, I ran from those questions. Now, poetry has allowed me to stop running, to rest or be restless on the page, to not always have my heart interrogated by those questions, but to be the interrogator. The way I see it, my questions cannot possibly be that different from those of my brothers and sisters or mother and father, from those of my family and community. The difference is I have been given the gift of a passion for language, a gift to see it as electricity in me and in everything, and the way I was taught, my responsibility is to use that gift.

AS: Lovely.

DTM: Lovely indeed. Like Natalie, in my everyday life I feel responsible for many things beyond just my own self and those that I love, and I used to consider my writing apolitical, even if it was addressing political issues indirectly, but now I feel compelled to be political in my writing because my voice has chased me there. The mob has reached my door and I have refused to give up my guests, and I won't offer my daughters to the mob of Babylon either, so I can only write and try to change my part of the world. By hook or crook, my friends. As long as I am writing work addressing more than flowers or birds or some hypothetical situation I have constructed. I find so much to be problematic with the poetic mask, or the adoption of an identity to hide behind. It's not that I don't see the benefits of the mask, but often this poetic mask is used to occlude interiority to the point of rendering poetry flaccid. But think of what a mask does: it gives anonymity so that the wearer can move in freedom, or as with the Greek chorus, it allows the wearer to speak truths. This, for me, is the power of poetry; the ability to speak from behind a speaker, but if we, as poets, are not challenging ourselves to tell truths or aren't on the verge of revealing something embarrassing about ourselves or the human condition then why the fuck are we writing? I have little patience for pretty poetry or poetry that is no more than masturbatory. Ok, I just exhaled. But somebody had to say it.

> "THROUGHOUT MY LIFE, I HAVE HELD IN AND SUPPRESSED SO MANY QUESTIONS THAT I HAD — QUESTIONS WITH TEETH, QUESTIONS THAT WILL EAT YOU UP. ON THE COURT, I RAN FROM THOSE QUESTIONS."

TF: Every time I think I understand the answers to these questions, I realize I don't. I read your answers, Natalie and David, and I think, "Yes, that too." Sometimes the communities I represent have both nurtured and hurt me. Those lesions and lessons have made their way into poems, and from those poems grew understanding, and tenderness. Sometimes the pain flares, and never resides, and I try to write that too, but also the laughter in between. It's not just, after all, pain that we pass on and perpetuate. I feel curiously responsible to everyone—the villains and the heroes—and the list grows when I meet or read about someone else lost, someone else fighting beautifully to remain. Poems both help me remember where I came from, and yet, they also give me space and room to forget that I am anything but a teeny little speck of a thing against the vast backdrop of the universe. I revel in the poem's ability to contain it all.

RR: Tarfia, I really love your answer—the notion that we write for a community that both hurt us and loved us. Yes, yes, yes, to that. Like everyone else, I write for Earl, Lil' Nene, Uncle Ricky, grandparents, and the children that have yet to be born. I remember, in graduate school, Marie Howe reminded us every class to write for the

> "I FEEL CURIOUSLY RESPONSIBLE TO EVERYONE — THE VILLIANS AND THE HEROES — AND THE LIST GROWS WHEN I MEET OR READ ABOUT SOMEONE ELSE LOST, SOMEONE ELSE FIGHTING BEAUTIFULLY TO REMAIN."

★

children that have yet to be born, write for fifty years into the future. Something about that appealed to me. But I must say that I also write for myself. Recently, I read this short interview Antonya Nelson gave, and she said: "First you must charm yourself." I love this notion that first we must write something that keeps our attention, keeps us, the writer, intrigued, baffled, wanting more. One of my favorite writerly pieces of advice is from Robert Frost: "No tears for the writer, no tears for the reader. No surprise for the writer, no surprise for the reader." This Frost quote reminds the writer that his first audience is him or herself. Often, I write to keep the world's beauty in front of me. I write to oppositionally gaze back at the world that would tell boys and men and girls and women that look like me that we are not beautiful or worthy of love. When I write, I write towards these things.

ND: Yes, Roger Reeves, we are worthy of love. I think we are all writing toward this, toward learning to love each other better, especially for writers of color. We know how to love hard, but we must learn how to love each other better.

6: ODD SPLENDOR

AS: I would love to hear your thoughts on this definition of sentimentality by James Baldwin, and how it connects, if at all, with your understanding of race and representation: "Sentimentality, the ostentatious parading of excessive and spurious emotion, is the mark of dishonesty, the inability to feel; the wet eyes of the sentimentalist betray his aversion to experience, his fear of life, his arid heart; and it is always, therefore, the signal of secret and violent inhumanity, the mask of cruelty."

ND: I am not afraid of the word "sentimental." I am a sentimental person—I am enthralled by emotions in such a way that I make it my job to render them on the page. I am nostalgic—for my brother, for lovers, for that sweet ass jump shot I used to let fly like a passenger pigeon, for every lost thing that ever existed even if I wasn't the one losing it. And while I have never been a big crier—wet eyes don't do you much good on the rez—I have large, unruly sadnesses that I must work hard to drive through these too bright days. "Sentimentality" is like the word "autobiographical" in that it has become a dirty word in some writing circles. I don't mind that word either—I will never write a thing that isn't autobiographical because I only have one set of eyes/mouth/ears with which to filter this world and spit back onto the page from the same eyes/mouth/ears. I am also okay with "excessive," because I think there has to be an element of hyperbole in every poem. By that, I mean that a poem must make the word, the image, the emotion more of itself than it could ever truly be in order to let it be what it is and to let it be what it was when it first meant itself. I don't seek the honest image when I write a poem, I seek to destroy the honest image, to rebuild it so I can feel it again. Francis Bacon sought to annihilate the image that came before the image he was building in that moment. He wanted to return the nervous system to the image more violently. I interpret "more violently" as "more emotionally," as a way that might make some part of you tremble or ache.

On the other hand, I think writers can be lazy, and when they are lazy, I think the images can be weak, and the language and verbs can be static. We all know how easy it is to pat yourself on the ass for a line that sounds good—everyone likes their ass patted. But I don't think these poorly executed poems or moments of prose are a result of excessive emotion, rather they are the result of laziness or fear of looking a thing in the eye for what you might see in yourself. This blue-blue world needs excessive emotion, especially now. I bury my own excessive emotions in my images.

We have even designated certain words as "sentimental." And language is too beautiful to let words get swept up by The Department of Waste and Sentimentality Management—I am not ready to give up on

"I SEEK TO DESTROY THE HONEST IMAGE, TO REBUILD IT SO I CAN FEEL IT AGAIN."

words like beautiful and sorrow and desire and terrible and awful. I know they can mean to me what they meant the first time someone took them into their mouth. But, if I don't put the work into making those words mean something to me, then that is my failing—not at emotion—at good old fashioned work.

AS: I think there's an important distinction to be made between sentimentality and sentiment. I would never disparage sentiment, or feeling. Poems that aren't generated by and speak to powerful emotion aren't terribly interesting, at least to me. But sentimentality, at least as Baldwin defines it, and as I understand it, is a travesty of sentiment or feeling. As he says, to express emotion differs crucially (and morally even) from parading emotion. By sentimentality he means formulaic expression—pat, stale, generic language that does violence to the particularity of experience. By connecting it with racial bias as he does he makes an interesting and suggestive correlation: if sentimentality is an aversion to truth in all its irreducible complexity, a palatable and simplifying lie in the place of truth with all its jagged edges, then to write sentimentally about, say, our childhoods is to do to the perception of our own lives what a bigot does to the perception of another person when he sees that person through the simplifying and distorted lens of prejudice. Which would then make prejudice sentimentality writ large, and sentimentality prejudice internalized. In other words I do think that sentimentality in all its forms is something we do need to guard against, so as to honor and cultivate sentiment.

DTM: I think this is a question of craft; I already spoke to the function of masks, so I will spare y'all that spectacle, but I feel as though sentimentality, in Baldwin's sense, means the crude expression of an idea, or as Pound thought, an emotional complex. It is in our rush to move the reader (or maybe ourselves?), that we quickly assemble an emotion from a scene or an idea that hasn't warranted that emotion. Racism then is the crude expression of a person's identity by another person drawing from a shallow experience of assumptions. But this crude blanketing of people is something we can recognize as happening in many of the relationships in our lives; such as, Tio Pepe is drinking too much again at a family party, so I assume all the family from Guerrero are drunks. The difference is the transition from the private to the public, and the sort of institutionally sanctioned violence that happens to so many minorities, to men and women, in places across the United States. The examples are too inexhaustible to even name. So again, it is the craft, or the complexity of thought, which as I think about it are not very far from each other, that can we make our art, our lives better, richer.

★

TF: What comes to mind for me, reading what y'all have all said, is the word indulgence. Sentimentality doesn't seem like truth-telling because it's excessive, and it moves us away from the just and gorgeous articulation of the truth, which is never too much. When I revise my own poems, I'm always asking myself: What is necessary and what is indulgent? I think about theoretical physicists, how they know that an equation is correct when it is both precise and elegant.

Avoiding sentimentality to make room for sentiment, like y'all have said, isn't easy—it's harder work to not be on autopilot. It's harder work to stand up and say, "This is the truth," and it's not all handkerchiefs being daintily pressed to our eyes. It's the wailing alone late at night, too. I think why Baldwin believed that it's the "signal of secret and violent inhumanity" is because you can see allegiance to sentimentality in all of the worst events of the world: Hitler's bucolic notions of Aryanism, for example, or widespread riots and warring between religious or ethnic groups, based on loyalty to abstract ideas of difference.

It's the difference between representing yourself, and just being. The poems that wreck me the most just are—they do not try to be anything but themselves, and their makers have applied their skills so that the truth, naked of its ornaments but not of its complexity, can move us away feeling alone or afraid.

I think, too, that sentimentality must hang out at the same bar as fetishization. Both sustain and perpetuate stereotyping and prejudice, like you pointed out David, and because both are irrational, and gain in power by fixating on a single idea to the detriment of others.

This is what seems so amazing about this current moment in poetics in terms of race and representation. We aren't seeing just the received stories—we're seeing individual stories, in all their odd splendor. The accumulation of individual stories can defeat the persistence of a stereotype. By avoiding sentimentality, we're announcing our names, one by one, loud and clear.

AS: "Odd splendor"—I can't think of a better way of capturing the essence of a story told honestly and truly.

★

7: *FLAWED CRYSTALS*

AS: The philosopher and classicist, Martha Nussbaum remarks that "great art plays a central role in our political lives because, showing us the tangled nature of our lives and commitments, showing us ourselves as flawed crystals, it moderates the optimistic hatred of the actual that makes for a great deal of political violence, moderates the ferocious hopefulness that simply marches over the complicated delicacies of the human art." Does this statement resonate with your vision of the political role of poetry in America right now?

To think that poetry can put an end to evil (in all its myriad forms, political and otherwise) is of course naive in the extreme. But how, in what small ways, can it prevent the victory of evil, or constrain it? How in our own work does it attempt to promote a plurality of human values?

ND: I am speaking generally, but I think poetry has an ability to hold a reader in a way that prose cannot. Poetry exists in an altered space, by the simple construction of lines and whitespace. A reader of poetry must leave the prose-ruled world, the start-here-end-here-go-at-this-pace-I'm-going-to-tell-you-exactly-how-it-is world. When a reader comes to a page, already we have invited them to a space where a different sensibility is king, or where there is no king, or where the king loses his head (Roger Reeves's *King Me* plug). On a page of poetry, there is space for the reader to feel, to bring her own life to the page. The image a poet delivers to the page is never the image the reader sees. The emotion that image allows our reader to bring into our poem

> "WHEN A READER COMES TO A PAGE, ALREADY WE HAVE INVITED THEM INTO A SPACE WHERE A DIFFERENT SENSIBILITY IS KING, OR WHERE THE KING LOSES HIS HEAD."

is the magic of language. Poetry is just another way to tell a story, and stories are how we learn and how we remember, even how we hope or want for something more. The poems in my book will not change the world but they tell stories that say, "Hey, this isn't right," or "This doesn't have to be this way," or even, "This is hard to survive." Sometimes they say, "The only way to make it through this is to put my hands on a body and remind myself of tenderness." They say, "I am human, and you are human too." In a world like this, we need to remind each other of these things as much as we can.

AS: Amen.

DTM: Natalie your book is wonderful, as are Roger's and Tarfia's books, and Alan is a Jedi, and I would say each of you highlights some sort of social ailments in your writing, which was one of the things that really struck me about each of your books, the way they attack things that matter to me. My own work also attempts to show "the cracks in the crystals," though often they are only my own. I just hope the reader can see the same cracks within themselves. I have felt very grateful to many readers who have identified with my book and have felt moved enough to contact me or talk to me after a reading. I really do not know how much my book can or will change a reader. But I do know that I write because I read, and I read because books have changed the way that I see myself and the way that I see the world. If books can change me, a pretty obstinate heel, then there is hope for a good portion of the population. I just hope that the work we all do can resonate with some readers. This really shows why it is important to have a multiplicity of voices, writing about different experiences because we need to be reaching the various sectors in society not just who we assume reads poetry. I think the biggest impact I have is not my writing but as a visible embodiment that there is a different way out of the 'hood, gangs, and all the entrapments many minorities experience in this country. If I can show that you don't have to play ball to succeed, then I have succeeded.

RR: Something about the Nussbaum quote doesn't quite sit right with me. I think it might be in the notion of "moderation," particularly in the area of political violence. I can't help but think about this quote in terms of Ferguson, Missouri, Michael Brown, New York City, Eric Garner, the demonstrations and riots to protest the killing of black folks across this country by police officers and vigilante policing agents. It seems that right now, one person's political violence is another's call for justice. Now what can poems, poetry, poets do in all of this—provide more discomfort with the easy and smooth killing of black bodies. Seeking justice is not a moderate act. Seeking justice requires tenacity, ruthlessness, bravery, selflessness, and humility. Nothing in moderation. Now, I don't require poems do this, but if they can, that would be great.

"WHAT CAN POEMS, POETRY, POETS, DO IN ALL THIS — PROVIDE MORE DISCOMFORT WITH THE EASY AND SMOOTH KILLING OF BLACK BODIES."

AS: Okay, I can see why you would balk at the word moderation. But if Naussbaum had said "Art obliterates the optimistic hatred of the actual" wouldn't you have thought that she was herself indulging in optimistic hatred of the actual? All I can say in defense of the word as Nussbaum employs it is that art does moderate or attempt to moderate, minimize, counter, take issue with the political clichés that do corrupt political discourse. Back in the sixties, at anti-War demonstrations and political sit-ins sloganeering often passed for political debate and even policy making. Slogans are fine when it comes to mobilizing political energies. But in the poems we read and write, in the representations of experience we admire, don't we look for something more respectful of the truth with all its jagged edges than say, "Smash Racism," as though racism were something like a vase that could be smashed. Likewise, the optimistic hatred of the actual which we see in American politics—in presidential debates (if you can call them debates), in defenses of "free enterprise" or "competition" or "individual responsibility"—is the kind of simplistic horseshit that Nussbaum and Baldwin have in mind, the replacement of truth with palatable lies.

8: BEYOND POETRY

AS: Aside from poems and stories, what kind of non-literary reading do you do? How important is it for poets to read not just outside their aesthetic preferences, but outside the discipline itself?

ND: I read anything that interests me. I am often reading several things at once. I get so excited that one thing leads me to another and another. I read a lot of stuff for my job as a language revitalist, such as historical texts and documents—I am currently transcribing notebooks from 1907 written in a mix of Mojave and English. I like science, so things about electricity or brains or hysteria or redshifts. But I am like a Galactus—I just devour whatever I am drawn to and then absorb those little electric bits that I need to survive my life and move on.

DTM: I read a lot about sports. I read blogs. Autobiographies about athletes. I see some carryover between sports and writing, so I like to read about athletes' process for their craft. I also like cookbooks. I read a lot of theory about writing and literary criticism because I feel like those books really help generate ideas for me. It also helps introduce writing I was unfamiliar with before. That's really why I read literary theory and criticism. My secret is out. Damn.

TF: I encourage my students and myself to read all over the place. I roll around in language everywhere, in gas stations and museums, and like Natalie, I'm usually reading a number of things at once.

I love comic books (shout out for *Saga*, which is the best thing that has happened to my life recently/ever) and science too, especially physics and brain stuff. There are two beautiful psychological studies I love by Aleksandr Luria, this 1970s Soviet neuropsychologist, called "The Man with a Shattered World" and "The Mind of A Mnemonist." I like reading about social theory and anthropology, why people behave the way they do, and about memory. I also like rereading books I read as a kid: A Wrinkle in Time, for example, by Madeleine L'Engle is my jam.

9: ALL CAMPS BUT NONE

AS: If economic considerations didn't matter, what would your ideal MFA program or poetry academy look like? How many years of training would it entail? Who would the faculty be? What texts would be required? What kinds of courses would comprise the curriculum? What would you want your graduates to have learned when they leave the program?

ND: I was in a three-year program at ODU, and that was perfect for me. I didn't write a poem-poem until my third year. It took me that long to learn to read poetry—I had come from an athletic background, so I came late to poetry. I didn't own any poetry books until graduate school. I would recommend a faculty like I had: Tim Seibles and Luisa Igloria. They believed in the work of reading and writing. I don't think I realized how lucky I was to have them. I thought everyone had mentors like that. We read many writers of color.

If I were building an MFA program, I would stress the importance of literary criticism—it can't be left in the hands of so few people, people who largely don't live in the diverse, multi-voice, multi-cultured, bi-or tri-lingual world that most of us write from. However, we can't simply complain about reviews or critiques of literature if we continue to sit on the sidelines and let them "make the decisions" so to speak, about what good writing is. But more than that, if we care so much about this art of ours, we should be willing to engage in it in a way that moves beyond our own personal connection and toward a wondering about the connections others make to it.

AS: I agree. This goes along with the importance of conversation and argument, with a vision of tradition itself as a robust, uninhibited and

"LITERARY CRITICISM ... CAN'T BE LEFT IN THE HANDS OF SO FEW PEOPLE, PEOPLE WHO LARGELY DON'T LIVE IN THE DIVERSE, MULTI-VOICE, MULTI-CULTURED, BI- OR TRI-LINGUAL WORLD THAT MOST OF US WRITE FROM."

wide open argument about what exactly tradition is, what exactly a poem is or can be. I sometimes think that poems exist for the conversations they generate about what it means to be alive. Our private experience of the poems we read is one part of the process but the process doesn't realize itself fully unless we talk about the poem to other people, unless we share our experience of it, and in the sharing come to a better understanding of experience itself, in and through the poem. In fact, I'd connect the conversation poems generate to the kind of tenderness, Natalie, you were talking about—as a cultivation of active tenderness in the form of conversation.

TF: I was in a three year program too, at Virginia Commonwealth University and was lucky to have Claudia Emerson and David Wojahn and Kathleen Graber as teachers. I always felt like they were in the trenches with us, doing the work alongside us. They didn't act like they knew everything, but they were generous with all the wonderful and wise things they knew. I learned that it is worth it to continue to learn as much as you can about what you love doing.

I would incorporate that idea of poetry as practice into a poetry academy, as well as the rigor of reading deeply and broadly. I agree so very much, y'all, about the importance of conversation and criticism. It is always a joy to return to a poem and see new wonders, and an added joy to share in those revelations with others. And to learn about the limitations of poems, what they don't do and could.

I would add wonder to that too—a school where tenderness is cultivated, and wonder too. Criticism seems so important to me because it also leads to learning discernment, which is not just a tremendous poetry tool, but is also a life skill. Being an adult is so challenging because it's all about discerning between choices. Poems work similarly.

"IF YOU HELP PEOPLE LEARN FOR THEMSELVES, THEY WILL HAVE A RICH AND NUANCED LIFELONG RELATIONSHIP WITH THEIR OWN INTERIOR LIVES."

I find the competitiveness I sometimes see among students in MFA programs so disheartening for that reason, because it's so antithetical to that practice of tenderness and wonder. I think that if you help people learn for themselves, they will have a rich and nuanced lifelong relationship with their own interior lives. That's another reason why teaching discernment is so important: so that they learn to think for themselves with increasing spark and courage.

AS: Amen.

DTM: I have been through a three year MFA (I took five years to graduate though I was done with credits after three) and I am finishing a five year PhD program, so I know something about graduate writing programs. I have been fortunate to work with poets such as Glover Davis, who taught me about formalism and encouraged me to write exclusively in metrics for two years. Very few poets get to cut their teeth by writing in form, and this really served me as I moved into free verse later. Then I studied with Sandra Alcosser and she instructed me to read widely and deeply, as Tarfia suggested, by "being in all camps but none." I was able to work with Ilya Kaminsky, and he pushed the beauty of the image and the sound of a line. These poets were all on faculty at San Diego State University when I was there. At the University of Houston, where I have been working on my PhD, I have worked with Tony Hoagland, who has just been a wizard at generating poems in me. I owe Tony a lot. I worked with Kevin Prufer, and he has been a great advocate and oversaw a good portion of the heavy construction of *Hustle*. I also worked with Martha Serpas, using her keen eye to develop a clean line. I am indebted to all of these professors, as well as the classmates and colleagues I was able to share poems with. I was lucky that I was able to have such a varied experience in my graduate studies, so I would want a program that teaches many approaches and techniques to poetry. A program that can serve the intellectual and emotional needs of the student. Often, the person gets left behind for the poet in CWP's, but I would hope that we, as professors, can serve all of their needs. I know the biggest gift graduate school gave me was the experience of a different way of living. It allowed me time to grow and mature. Ultimately, the ideal program would benefit all sense of personhood of a writer.

10: SO MANY SUPERB MUTANTS

AS: Outside of reading and writing, I found athletic discipline great preparation for a life in poetry. I learned the game of basketball on the playground by imitating kids who played it really well. I assimilated the moves I saw them do into my own expressive repertoire. I learned the value of rote work, of practice, how sometimes the most inspired moments of improvisation arise from or depend on hours of practice and grunt work. Also, as a basketball player, well, if you were the kind of player I was, you got used to failing in public, a lot, and you never got too high when things were going well or too low when they were going poorly. Basketball prepared me for the vicissitudes of a writer's life, the ups and downs, the frustrations and disappointments. What non-literary activities or disciplines in your lives have prepared you for the life you're living now? What things do you still do to stay in shape, poetry-wise?

ND: I couldn't have said this better, Alan. The values and strengths that made me good at basketball are the same ones that make me work hard at writing. One of the interesting things about me, that most people seem surprised by since I was a high-caliber competitive athlete is that I am not at all competitive when it comes to writing. I don't understand at all how we could be. It doesn't mean that I don't read writing that I admire or writing that makes me want to write better and deeper into myself. Instead, what I mean is that I don't understand what there is to win or lose against another poet and how we can actually battle one another in a competitive way. Even for a prize or a fellowship. It would be one thing if my body were up against your body, my hand on your lower back, or trying to turn your hip, my forearm counting your ribs as you tried to drop your shoulder and make a lane to the basket—that is competing. That old, dirty trick my dad showed me of yanking the opponents arm down and clamping my armpit closed and around their hand down in the paint as we fought for a rebound—that is competing. But to put our work before a group of people trying to read their own lives in our poems, and for one of your poems to speak to those people more powerfully than mine, well, that isn't competition. Competition is something that I can prepare for and adjust to. If you start going left, then I can cut off your left. If you start going back door, I can drop to the rim. If you start trying to post up, I can foul you hard enough to make you not want to come back down there—just kidding. But, the way I see it, the thing that keeps me "in the game" of poetry is that I think we are all competing against this world that crushes the tenderness in us and tries to make us hurt each other.

> "I THINK WE ARE ALL COMPETING AGAINST THIS WORLD THAT CRUSHES THE TENDERNESS IN US AND TRIES TO MAKE US HURT EACH OTHER."

I mean, if you really want to compete, challenge Roger Reeves to a footrace. Then, when he beats you, go home and write a poem about it.

I feel lucky for the athlete in me. It makes me work hard. It doesn't let me "lose" to other writers. It allows me to see other poets and writers as part of my team, not as my opponents. It means that I will never lose at poetry or win at it. I'll just be there in the dim room, alone, shooting jumper after jumper, trying to find that one shot that will rip open the net of myself.

TF: Natalie, I love what you said about seeing other poets and writers as part of your team. I feel like there's the team on one side of the chess board, and the universe at its worst on the other side. To go back to comic books—I really like being on the X-Men team with so many superb mutants.

I'm not an athlete, but I'm a game player. I actually appreciate the relationship between opponents: it requires trust and a commitment to see it through and an implicit expectation of enjoyment for both sides. I really love chess, for example, and other games where your brain has to do so much at once, and make a decision from that assessment.

Photography is another activity that keeps my brain writing-ready. It's an act of noticing, with an extra eye that is sensitive to all of the conditions around it. I learn a lot about light: how and why it matters. I listen to and play music. That act keeps me thinking about the nuances of sound and breath.

I also think that being very still with your eyes closed for a long period of time is training. Our lives are ones of perpetual distraction in some ways—email, texts, social media—and I really think the act of sitting or lying still alone with your thoughts takes practice. I used to joke that writing a poem and taking a nap look a lot like each other. Okay, I still joke about that, because it's still true.

DTM: One does not challenge Roger to a run. But even on a team, we practice and we "compete," but as you know that is only to make ourselves better. At the end of practice, we sit back and joke and compliment each other. We are all in the same gang, for real.

REVIEWS

READ A BOOOOOOOOK

READ A BOOOOOOOOK

In the Garden of the Body

Eula Biss, *On Immunity: An Innoculation*
Greywolf Press, 2014. Hardcover, 216 pp, $24.00

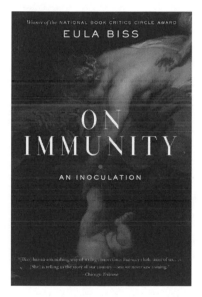

I'm reading Eula Biss's *On Immunity* at the same time I'm hearing about Ferguson. It's the morning after Darren Wilson has avoided indictment and I'm in the airport, traveling from Houston to Minneapolis. I read to keep myself awake. Over my head, there's a man on TV shouting about the riots. "The question," a dumbed down reporter issues, "is why they would want to destroy their own." It's five in the morning, and I'm feeling vulnerable, unfiltered enough to swear audibly so the woman behind the desk at the gate shoots me a disapproving glare. A week later, I will recount this moment to a classroom of poetry students who have spent the majority of the semester learning to converse about the various ways in which America expertly promotes the practice of silencing and marginalizing, learning that it is the job of the poet to give voices to people who otherwise struggle to get heard. "Othering," I will say in the classroom, "is the most effective way of shutting down a difficult and threatening discourse."

In the airport and throughout the ensuing days, I feel lucky to have Biss's book in my hands. I hold it on my lap on the plane, put it on the table in front of me at a café in Minneapolis, place it next to the cutting board as I make dinner for friends who have just returned from a protest where a man in a car ran into a group of people who had stormed the highway. Biss's book makes me feel safer amidst all the anger and confusion, not because she dismisses and dissolves a larger problem, but because she struggles throughout her book to create a language and a framework to talk about the issues of communal safety in a world where the individual is problematically valued above the society that surrounds it.

Biss's examination of vaccination comes out of her own personal course of inquiry: "we must live the questions our children raise for us," she says, and, in that regard, she asks herself if she should or should not vaccinate her first-born son. In the book, she quickly lands on the side of yes. This project, then, is not an exercise in cataloging the pros and cons of each side; rather, it is a serious study of why we humans are so skeptical and resistant to the idea of inoculation. Biss is persistent and relentless, coming at the center of this book from what would seem like the most unlikely of places: she addresses the ways in which we view the environment, our citizenship, trust in government, and, ultimately, the book becomes a critique of how we humans, throughout time and space, from Achilles to Dracula, from variolation of smallpox to the flu shot, from the personal to the global, have been hell-bent on separating the self from the non-self.

This book works best by giving its reader enough information and then leaving space to allow her to make her own connections to, say, Ferguson or Ebola or whatever is going on in the world at the time you are reading this review. As I tell my students, the only way to get at the broader truths is to nail down the particular ones.

So what truth is Biss revealing here? It's tricky. As she reminds us, "knowledge is, by its nature, always incomplete." This statement, she says, is as true for science as it is for poetry. (Here, in the same, expert breath, she calls on both Feynman and Keats.) Questions only lead to more questions, if you're doing it right, and to pin down an argument from Biss would be to miss the entire point of the book.

Because what she's trying to promote in these pages is an entire reworking of the ways in which we think and talk about disease, immunity, politics, war, citizenship, story, personhood. "Our understanding of immunity remains remarkably dependent on metaphor," she says, and much of these pages are packed with the unpacking of these comparisons. For instance, in a discussion of the word germ, she says, "We use the same word for something that brings illness and something that brings growth. The root of the word being, of course, seed."

"Metaphors," she says later, "flow in two directions—thinking about one thing in terms of another can illuminate or obscure both." It seems to me that Biss executes an elegant and illuminating exploration of the ways in which we can use language to promote either injustice or justice. Biss, thankfully, advocates for the latter, and she does this by opening up a space instead of closing it down. She does not say "they," or angrily run a car into a crowd of people; instead, she reveals her own inability to come to any concrete conclusion. "In the garden of the body," she says in her concluding pages, "we look inward and find not self, but other." She does not pretend to know exactly what this means, to pack up the statement in a tidy bow; instead, she leaves the statement on the table, unpacked, ready for the reader to pick it up and roll it around a while, to start a conversation, entirely new and exciting and voice-giving.

Adrienne Perry

Brutal Business: Coming of Age in 1970s Houston

Thomas McNeely, *Ghost Horse*
Gival Press, 2014. Paperback, 266 pp, $20.00

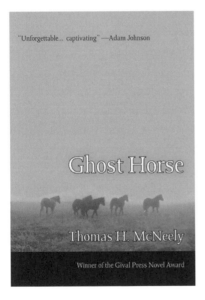

In the summer of 2013, I moved from Wyoming to Houston. My loved ones warned me against it; they were wary of heat and humidity, cockroaches as big as your thumbs, traffic jams, sex trafficking, and oil spills in the Gulf. Now I realize these friends were working with an image of Houston circa 1970, a decade that witnessed Houston schools' (long overdue) desegregation, Dean Corll's killing spree, and a truck carrying ammonia that crashed into the Southwest Freeway, releasing clouds of toxic fumes. Mercifully, the Houston that greeted me, though not without its woes, was nothing so grim. Think: *complicated beauty*.

Thomas McNeely's first novel, *Ghost Horse*, reminds me why Houston put my nervous Nellies on edge. While nothing in the novel is grotesque, both psychological and literal violence smolder throughout. At times, that violence arises from the environment: a man has been dragged out of the nearby bayou, the characters carry the memory of boys murdered in a field, a husband hits his wife. More often the novel's tensions feed on divisions—racial, class, gender, and geographic rifts—present in the Houston of then and (somewhat less so) now. Add to those divisions compressed prose delivered in the present tense, and the reader hurtles forward into a productively unsettling story that involves the rupture of virtually every aspect of a budding adolescent's life.

Ghost Horse is in good company with other novels that reveal what a brutal business coming of age can be. For Buddy Turner, the novel's protagonist, imagination is the number one way to find reprieve from his parents' unraveling marriage, uncertain friendships, and the shifting, tested allegiances at home and school. When the novel opens in the summer before sixth grade, the mythic superheroes and monsters of Buddy's favorite films and television shows mold his brain and its imaginative landscapes. *Star Wars*, vampires, *Godzilla*, and the B movies radiating out of boxy televisions amp Buddy and his friend Alex Torres up on hefty doses of horror-delight and inspire the boys to make *Ghost Horse,* their own movie.

These two working-class boys growing up in Houston in 1976 see their movie and "the Horse" at its core as a ticket to a Technicolor life where the bullies who call them fat and gay can no longer touch them. Though Alex spends hours drawing the mysterious Horse and Buddy promises a script, Buddy urgently needs an escape that movie making cannot provide. Their film, though integral to the novel, is not the predicament at the heart of *Ghost Horse*. Buddy is not simply caught between two worlds; he is being asked, forced really, to choose—by friends, parents, relatives—who he is and will be. Mom or dad's house, if his parents separate? Should Buddy forsake Alex and his diverse school for Simon and the well-heeled white boys at St. Edward's, his new private school? Will his life best unfold in the wealthy, oak-lined boulevards surrounding Rice University near Gramma Turner's house? Or in the East End, where the bayou, factories, and Houston's looping highways provide the backdrop to his mother's and his Gramma Liddy's homes?

Ghost Horse undertakes daring work when it explores the intersection of white and nonwhite immigrant communities, changing assumptions about working women, and the stigma then associated with divorce. The emotional tumult in these intersections power the novel. In a scene between Alex, Buddy, and his new friend Simon, Buddy acts as interpreter, sliding between English, Spanish, and Latin. Although no earthshattering exchange occurs, this tense negotiation sews the seed for one of the novel's most searing, violent scenes.

The relationships between men and boys in this work are charged, especially Buddy's relationship with his father. In one telling scene, we feel Buddy's fear and confusion when his father forces him to run laps around the Rice University track:

> He keeps his face turned from his father, listening to the rain whisper on the track. "Get up," his father says, nudging him with his shoe. "We'll have to do it again." He kneels on the ground, squeezing his eyes shut. "Is this what you want?" his father says. "To lay out here in the dirt?"

On the ground, soothed by the rain and refusing to rise, Buddy is like Sisyphus watching his boulder roll downhill. The pause, the slow walk behind the boulder before hoisting it again, offers Buddy solace and a momentary act of rebellion against a man who both loves and hurts him.

In late October, I met Thomas McNeely and asked him about this love. We were at Bohemeo's café, a brightly painted coffee shop in the Tlaquepaque Market, smack-dab in the neighborhood where much of *Ghost Horse* takes place. It became clear that the fraught relationship between Buddy and his father was linked to Houston's complicated beauty. A native Houstonian, McNeely mined the city of his childhood and adolescence for the details animating *Ghost Horse*. But the setting of 1970s Houston also allows the novel to wrestle with major changes to the social fabric in which Buddy, his parents', and his grandparents' generations were wrapped. The novel dwells in historical time, giving the impression that even forty years later, these events represent the "now" of Buddy's life. That present comes through slightly distorted, as "Buddy wonders if what he is watching is his real life, or the movie of his life, or something else that he can't even imagine." Through McNeely's imagination, what becomes real in *Ghost Horse*, for Buddy and the reader, is Houston and the acute ache of a boy caught in the grip of life.

Distributed in Space, Inside the Body, and on the Page

Stéphane Mallarmé, *A Roll of the Dice Will Never Abolish Chance*
Translated from the French by Robert Bononno & Jeff Clark
Wave Books, 2015. Hardcover, 66 pp, $25.00

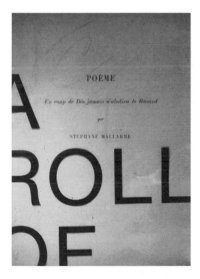

Before I begin, dear reader, a confession: I am not a speaker of French. I invite you, however, to ignore this shortcoming in your judgment of my capacity as reviewer, for though fluency may be prerequisite to the act of translation, it could be said to obviate the necessity of the resulting object. Translation, after all, is more than the mere harvesting of "meaning" and placing its fruits into the basket of an alternate language (what then of the tree, the leaves, or the bridge?). No, a book of translation is an active object that permeates and is permeated by its environment—it is born, then, not only by its translators, but by the eye and touch and neurons of its readers, as well as by all objects with which it comes into contact (the table, say, or the internet, or the totality of human language).

This book in particular involves translation not only from English into French, but from Language into Design (and the other way around), and the result is not only aesthetically moving, but inventive, and infinitely pleasurable. But I digress. All translation, assuming it is noble (which I believe this book to be), will carry along the essence of the departing work, in this case evidenced not only by the choice of words but by their arrangement on the page, and by the lack of punctuation, and by the variations in font and style, and it is in this capacity as one who is deeply immersed in the gravitational pull of language, insofar as it is distributed in space, inside the body, and on the page, that I feel I might be worthy of the task of reviewing this book.

Another point before I begin: enough of French remains in English that even the monolingual can find pleasure in the relationship between the arriving (English) and departing (French) texts. In fact, the young child who stands at the precipice of language will undoubtedly benefit from the experience of this book, as it will remind her that language is not so certain and staid as she has been taught in grammar school, that it trembles and marches across the page and grows larger and smaller and contains ever more playfully intricate and serious pieces of itself: that it is in fact its own ecosystem, or economy, or jungle gym. And perhaps still an animal who is entirely without language is likely to take immense meaning from this book as a whole, from the feel of its paper to its considerable heft and balance and beautifully interspersed black and white images, and reader, I would go so far as to say that a fly, if it found itself, having landed on an open page, wandering amongst the words displayed before it like a two-dimensional staircase or a textual representation of the double-helixes that swirl and communicate within its very own body, might find itself both terrified and delighted by the contents of this book, as it would be sure to engage with its many-lensed eyes at least a few of the varied and variegated ontological realities and dappled things presented here, even taking into consideration the relative flatness of the page and monochromatic nature of ink.

It seems necessary as well, before I move on to review this book, to mention that the preface to the poem (necessarily) does not begin until a full thirty-two pages into the book itself, and it is equally necessary that the preface urges the reader not to read it, "or that, once perused, it be forgotten." (Perhaps a similar warning should be included in this review.) I call it necessary because the poem, which occupies only twenty-three pages, including the preface, is as much about scale and time and space—in the sense of the quantum correlation between matter and emptiness as well as in the literary sense of "white spaces" or to use

Mallarmé's word, "*blancs*"—as it is about the text itself. "The [physical] paper," writes Mallarmé through his translators:

> intervenes whenever an image, of its own accord, stops or withdraws, accepting the others that follow, and since it is not a question, as always, of regular lines of sound or verse—but rather of prismatic subdivisions of the idea, the moment they appear and for the duration of their convergence, in some exact spiritual setting, it is in variable positions, near or far from the latent theme, through their verisimilitude, that the text establishes itself.

Quite soon, I assure you, we will begin to review the poem itself, but before we do, I fear we must acknowledge that the poem, insofar as one tends to think of a poem as an accumulation of ideas and images that marches forward through time in stanzas and lines and words, containing one predetermined order and understood vehicle, eventually arriving upon a place to rest, does not exist. Rather, it is Mallarmé's phrase the "prismatic subdivisions of the idea," that commands me, as one simple reader, to recognize that we must look upon the poem not as we look upon our own lives—which is to say one slice of time at a time—but as one looks contrapuntally and nonlocally upon a culture of organisms through a microscope, refocusing and reconfiguring the dials to find ever deeper valences of meaning and form and structure, or as one views a shipwreck, first from a great distance and through the gray haze of the sea as a single object, but then with a gradual coming into focus of its texture and failure and complex systems of life. *A Roll of the Dice Will Never Abolish Chance*, then, carries its readers not only through (and into) time, but through (and into) space, and in fact the poem is an exploration (or an explosion) of the title of the poem as it expands and breathes and is explored and mined and weighed and balanced and given meaning both across the pages and, individually, within them. The poem, then, must be read infinitely and by infinite readers to find itself complete.

And now, as have I promised, I will present to you my review, without melodrama or philosophy, telling you only the facts: Read this book, reader, and step deeper into your life. Then, having taken that step, reopen the book, and begin anew.

Aimee Bender is the author of five books, including *The Girl in the Flammable Skirt* and *The Particular Sadness of Lemon Cake*. Her most recent, *The Color Master*, was a *New York Times* Notable book of 2014. Her work has been translated into sixteen languages. She lives in Los Angeles, where she teaches creative writing at USC.

Juliette Bianco is Deputy Director of the Hood Museum of Art at Dartmouth College, Hanover, New Hampshire. She has organized and curated numerous exhibitions, including *Nature Transformed: Edward Burtynsky's Vermont Quarry Photographs in Context* (2012), and published on leadership and pedagogy in college and university museums.

Emma Bolden is the author of *Maleficae*, a book-length series of poems about the witch trials in early modern Europe (GenPop Books, 2013), and *medi(t)ations*, a book-length poem forthcoming from Noctuary Press. She's also the author of four chapbooks of poetry—*How to Recognize a Lady* (part of Edge by Edge, Toadlily Press), *The Mariner's Wife* (Finishing Line Press), *The Sad Epistles* (Dancing Girl Press), and *This Is Our Hollywood* (in The Chapbook)—and one of nonfiction—*Geography V* (Winged City Press). Her poetry and nonfiction have appeared in such journals as *The Rumpus, Prairie Schooner, Conduit, Indiana Review, Harpur Palate, The Greensboro Review, Redivider, Verse, Feminist Studies, The Journal, Guernica, Spoon River Poetry Review*, and *Copper Nickel*. She was the winner of *Spoon River Poetry Review's* 2014 Editor's Prize Contest and the Press 53/*Prime Number Magazine* 2014 Award for Flash Nonfiction.

Daniel Borzutzky's recent books and chapbooks include *The Performance of Becoming Human* (2016), *In the Murmurs of the Rotten Carcass Economy* (2015), *Bedtime Stories for the End of the World!* (2014), *Data Bodies* (2013), and *The Book of Interfering Bodies* (2011). Poetry translations include Raúl Zurita's *Song for His Disappeared Love* (2010) and Jaime Luis Huenún's *Port Trakl* (2008). His work has been supported by the PEN American Center, the National Endowment the Arts, and the Illinois Arts Council.

Sharon Butler is an artist and arts writer who blogs at *Two Coats of Paint*.

May-lee Chai is the author of seven books of fiction and nonfiction and the translator from Chinese to English of *The Autobiography of Ba Jin*. Her short stories and essays have been published in various publications including *The Missouri Review, North American Review, ZYZZYVA, Seventeen, Many Mountains Moving, Christian Science Monitor*, and *Dallas Morning News*. She is the recipient of an NEA Fellowship in Prose. She teaches in the MFA. program at University of North Carolina Wilmington.

MRB Chelko is the recipient of a Poetry Society of America Chapbook Fellowship for *Manhattations* (PSA, 2014). Her work has appeared in many journals and chapbooks—publications include *AGNI Online, Forklift, Ohio, Indiana Review, Poetry International*, and *Washington Square Review*. A recent John Ciardi Tuition Scholar at the Bread Loaf Writers' Conference, Chelko holds an MFA in Poetry from The University of New Hampshire and lives in Central Harlem.

Patty Yumi Cottrell's work has appeared or is forthcoming in *Denver Quarterly, LIT, Birkensnake*, and *Caketrain*, among other places. She lives and works in New York.

Julia Kolchinsky Dasbach emigrated as a Jewish refugee from Dnepropetrovsk, Ukraine in 1993. She holds an MFA in Poetry from the University of Oregon and is in the University of Pennsylvania's Comparative Literature Ph.D. program. Julia's poetry has appeared in *Green Mountains Review, Tupelo Quarterly, Guernica,* and *Nashville Review,* among others journals. Her manuscript, *The Bear Who Ate the Stars,* won *Split Lip Magazine's* Uppercut Chapbook Award, and can be purchased from Split Lip Press. Julia is also the Editor-in-Chief of *Construction Magazine.* Visit her website at http://www.juliakolchinskydasbach.com/.

Natalie Diaz was born and raised in the Fort Mojave Indian Village in Needles, California, on the banks of the Colorado River. She is Mojave and an enrolled member of the Gila River Indian Tribe. Her first poetry collection, *When My Brother Was an Aztec,* was published by Copper Canyon Press. She is a 2012 Lannan Literary Fellow and a 2012 Native Arts Council Foundation Artist Fellow. In 2104, she was awarded a Bread Loaf Fellowship, as well as the Holmes National Poetry Prize from Princeton University, and a US Artists Ford Fellowship. Diaz teaches at the Institute of American Indian Arts Low Rez MFA program and lives in Mohave Valley, Arizona, where she directs the Fort Mojave Language Recovery Program, working with the last remaining speakers at Fort Mojave to teach and revitalize the Mojave language.

Kristin Dykstra's translation of *Other Letters to Milena,* by Reina María Rodríguez, was published by the University of Alabama Press in December 2014. Two more of her translations are forthcoming from UAP in 2015: *Breach of Trust,* by Ángel Escobar; and *The Counterpunch (And Other Horizontal Poems),* by Juan Carlos Flores. She previously translated several books of poetry from Cuba, including works by Rodríguez and Omar Pérez, and is now working on full books by Pérez, Marcelo Morales Cintero, and the Uruguayan writer Amanda Berenguer. With Kent Johnson, Dykstra is also currently co-editing an anthology dedicated to Berenguer. She co-edited *Mandorla* from 2004-2014 with Gabriel Bernal Granados and Roberto Tejada. Dykstra taught in the English department at Illinois State University from 2002-2014, beginning as Assistant Professor and leaving as Full Professor. She is now Distinguished Scholar in Residence at St. Michael's College.

Turkish poet and essayist **Haydar Ergülen** was born in Eskişehir in 1956. The winner of multiple awards, his most recent book is *Vefa Bazen Unutmaktır.* Among the most prominent poets of his generation, his work is only beginning to appear in English. He frequently reads and lectures throughout Turkey and makes his home in the Cihangir neighborhood of Istanbul with his wife and daughter.

Tarfia Faizullah is the author of *Seam* (SIU 2014), and *Register of Eliminated Villages* (Graywolf 2017). Her honors include a Pushcart Prize and a Great Lake Colleges Association New Writers' Award. She is the Nicholas Delbanco Visiting Professor in Poetry at University of Michigan's Helen Zell Writers' Program and co-directs the Organic Weapon Arts Chapbook Press and Video Series with Jamaal May.

Robert A. Fink is the W. D. and Hollis R. Bond Professor of English and Director of Creative Writing at Hardin-Simmons University, Abilene, Texas. His sixth book of poetry, *Strange You Never Knew,* was published in April, 2013 by Wings Press, San Antonio. Bob Fink's previous five books of poetry include *The Tongues of Men and of Angels* (Texas Tech University Press 1995) and *Tracking The Morning* (Wings Press, San Antonio, 2005). His literary nonfiction book *Twilight Innings: A West Texan on Grace and Survival* was published by Texas Tech University Press in 2006.

Chitra Ganesh received her MFA from Columbia University in 2002. Her works have been widely exhibited internationally and are held by prominent collections such as the Museum of Modern Art(NYC), Saatchi Collection (London), & Devi Art Foundation (New Delhi). She is the recipient numerous awards and fellowships including a 2012 John Simon Guggenheim Memorial Foundation Fellowship in the Creative Arts, and her solo exhibition *Eyes of Time* is currently on view at the Brooklyn Museum through July 2015. Her installation, text-based work, and collaborations suggest and excavate buried narratives typically absent from official canons of history, literature, and art. She is widely recognized for her experimental use of comic and large-scale narrative forms to communicate submerged histories and alternate articulations of femininity to a broader public.

Marosa di Giorgio (1932-2004) was an acclaimed Uruguayan poet and novelist who wrote seventeen books during her lifetime. Born and raised in a rural area, di Giorgio studied law, acted in local theatre and worked for twenty years as a municipal civil servant before moving to the capitol city of Montevideo and devoting herself to full-time writing. Known for its startling imagery, odd syntactical turns, glorious depictions of nature and basis in a child's imaginative world, di Giorgio's writing is sometimes described as surrealist; however, she herself did not identify with any literary school. The poems included here are from her sixth book, *La guerra de los huertos (The War of the Orchards)*.

Ana Gorría (b. 1979, Barcelona) is an acclaimed Spanish-language poet, critic and translator. She has published several collections of poems, including the multimedia work *Araña (Spider)* and the chapbook *La soledad de las formas (The Solitude of Forms)*, from which the poems in this issue are drawn. Her work has been translated into French, German, Chinese and other languages, and has been featured in several anthologies, most recently in *Panic Cure: Poetry from Spain* for the 21st Century (Shearsman Books, 2013), edited by Forrest Gander. *Sky under Construction*, the first full-length selection of her poetry in English (translated by Yvette Siegert), is available for publication. Gorría is currently completing a PhD in literature at the Universidad Complutense de Madrid.

Rachel Howard is the author of a memoir about her father's unsolved murder, *The Lost Night*. Her fiction and nonfiction has appeared in *ZYZZYVA, Canteen, the Arroyo Literary Review*, the *New York Times'* "Draft" series, and other publications. She was the 2011-12 Joan Beebe Fellow at Warren Wilson College, and the next year served as Interim Director of Undergraduate Creative Writing. She lives in the San Francisco Bay Area, where she is writing a collection of essays.

Pablo Helguera (b. 1971, Mexico City) is an interdisciplinary artist working with installation, sculpture, photography, drawing, socially engaged art and performance. Helguera's work focuses on a variety of topics ranging from history, pedagogy, sociolinguistics, ethnography, memory and the absurd, in formats that are widely varied including the lecture, museum display strategies, musical and theatrical performances, and written fiction.

Adriana X. Jacobs is an assistant professor of modern Hebrew literature at the University of Oxford. Her translations of Hebrew poetry have appeared in various publications, including *Zeek, Metamorphoses, Truck, Poetry International*, and *The Michigan Quarterly Review*.

Paul Jenkins has recently retired from Hampshire College, in Amherst, Massachusetts, where he taught poetry writing happily for 29 years. His poems have appeared widely in magazines, from *Poetry Northwest* to *The New Yorker* to *The Antigonish Review*. His full-length collections include *Forget the Sky*, *Radio Tooth*, and *Six Small Fires*. A new manuscript, *Where When Here*, is currently being prepared.

In 2003 **Kim Kyung Ju's** literary debut won the Seoul Newspaper Spring Literary Contest for Poetry, then for several years he wrote pornographic novels and provided services as a ghost writer. Later he released his first collection of poems, *I Am A Season That Does Not Exist*. Already in its 30th edition, rarely in fine literature has a book achieved such enormous popularity in Korea. Critics have said, "he is a blessing and curse to Korean literature," and, "this is the most important poetry book written by a Korean." After such notable attention by critics, he has been seen as the progenitor of the Korean new-wave movement known as "Miraepa" (*future movement*). He has written and translated over 10 books of poetry, essays, and plays and is widely considered to be one of the most important younger writers in South Korea.

New poems from **L. S. Klatt** have appeared in *VOLT*, *Harvard Review*, *The Iowa Review*, *Colorado Review*, *32 Poems*, *Michigan Quarterly Review*, and *The Common*. His third collection of poetry, *Sunshine Wound*, was published by Free Verse Editions (Parlor Press) in 2014. He is the current Poet Laureate of Grand Rapids, Michigan.

Mark Labowskie is currently a Stegner Fellow in Fiction at Stanford University. His work has appeared in *Sou'wester*.

Kien Lam is an MFA candidate at Indiana Universeity. He has poems out or forthcoming in *The Journal* and *32 Poems*. He's also a catch-and-release oxygen hunter.

Lawrence Lenhart holds an MFA from the University of Arizona. His work appears or is forthcoming in *Alaska Quarterly Review*, *Prairie Schooner*, *Guernica*, *Wag's Revue*, and elsewhere. A former "Lifeguard of the Year" for Rehoboth Beach Patrol (2010), he currently lives in Sacramento, where he is reviews editor and assistant fiction editor of *DIAGRAM*.

Jake Levine edits poetry at Spork press and is pursuing a PhD in comparative literature at Seoul National University as a KGSP fellow. He is the recipient of many awards and fellowships, including a Fulbright Fellowship in 2010, and is the author of two chapbooks: *The Threshold of Erasure* (Spork) and *Vilna Dybbuk* (Country Music). He holds an MFA from the University of Arizona and is from Tucson.

Susan Lilley is a Florida native. Her poetry and nonfiction appear in *Poet Lore*, *The Southern Review*, *Drunken Boat*, *The Florida Review*, *CALYX*, *Sweet*, *Slipstream*, and other journals. She is the 2009 winner of the Rita Dove Poetry Award, and her two chapbooks are *Night Windows* (winner of Yellow Jacket Press Poetry Contest) and *Satellite Beach* (Finishing Line Press). In 2010 she received a Florida Individual Artist Grant. She holds an MFA in Creative Writing from the University of Southern Maine. She lives and teaches in Central Florida.

Rebecca Liu is currently a fellow at the Michener Center for Writers. She is the recipient of the Glascock Poetry Prize, an Academy of American Poets Prize, and a fellowship from the Stadler Center for Poetry. Recent work can be found in *Apogee Journal* and *The Columbia Review*.

Talia Mailman's fiction has appeared in *Bluestem, Flyway, Untoward*, and elsewhere. She received her BA at Williams College, her Masters in Music at Boston University, and is pursuing her MFA at University of Houston, where she serves as Nonfiction Editor for *Gulf Coast*.

MANUAL (Ed Hill / Suzanne Bloom) divide their time between their studios in Houston and Vershire, Vermont. In the spring of 2014, they completed construction of their website, www. manualart.net, a virtual catalogue raisonné of their forty-year collaboration. They are represented by Moody Gallery, Houston.

F.T. Marinetti (1876-1944), a poet, prose writer, dramatist, artist, and activist, is perhaps most widely acknowledged as an architect of the very concept of the avant-garde: a master of the incendiary manifesto, of the "happening," of collective action to reform "passéist" culture, who hailed the dawn of modern art by asserting the need to erase the boundaries between art and life. Born in Alexandria to a family from Piemonte, Italy, he was educated at an international school by French Jesuits, and then at the Sorbonne. After receiving his BA, he moved to Italy to earn a doctorate in law, but afterwards pursued the arts. Marinetti would devote his career to rejecting the culture of the salon and the masterpiece, perceiving earlier than most of his contemporaries the need for modern art to renew itself through engagement with the current moment, mass culture, and the mechanisms of everyday life. His major writings include a series of essential manifestos, *Mafarka the Futurist: An African Novel* (1909), *The Untameables* (1922), and *The Futurist Cookbook* (1932).

David Tomas Martinez's work has been published or is forthcoming in *Poetry Magazine, Ploughshares, Boston Review, Oxford American, Forklift; Ohio, Poetry International, Poem-A-Day, Poetry Daily*, and other journals. He has been featured or written about in *Poets & Writers, Publishers Weekly*, NPR's *All Things Considered*, NBC Latino, *Border Voices*, and in numerous other venues. He is a PhD candidate in the University of Houston's Creative Writing program, where he is the Reviews and Interviews Editor for *Gulf Coast*. He received his MFA from San Diego State University, and is the recipient of Breadloaf and CantoMundo Fellowships. His debut collection of poetry, *Hustle*, was released in 2014 by Sarabande Books, which won the New England Book Festival's prize in poetry and was an honorable mention in the Antonio Cisneros Del Moral prize.

Ted Mathys is the author of three books of poetry, *Null Set*, forthcoming from Coffee House Press, *The Spoils* (Coffee House 2009), and *Forge* (Coffee House 2005). The recipient of fellowships and awards from the NEA, NYFA, and Poetry Society of America, he holds an MFA from the Iowa Writers' Workshop and lives in Saint Louis.

Derick Mattern holds an MFA in poetry from the University of Wisconsin, Madison. Winner of the British Centre for Literary Translation's Young Translator Prize in 2012, his translations of Haydar Ergülen's work have appeared in *Guernica* and *Modern Poetry in Translation*. His own work has appeared or is forthcoming in *Subtropics, Whiskey Island*, and elsewhere. He lived in Istanbul from 2008 to 2013.

Tyler McAndrew lives in Pittsburgh, PA. He holds an MFA in fiction from the University of Pittsburgh. His work has appeared most recently in *Salt Hill* and *The Nashville Review*.

Gary L. McDowell is the author of *Weeping at a Stranger's Funeral* (Dream Horse Press 2014) and *American Amen* (Dream Horse Press 2010); he is also the co-editor of *The Rose Metal Press Field Guide to Prose Poetry* (Rose Metal Press 2010). His poems and essays have appeared or are forthcoming in *The American Poetry Review, The Nation, Green Mountains Review, The Journal, The Laurel Review, DIAGRAM*, and *Prairie Schooner*, among others. He is an assistant professor of English at Belmont University in Nashville, TN.

Jennifer Militello is the author of four collections of poetry: *A Camouflage of Specimens and Garments* (Tupelo Press 2016), *Body Thesaurus* (Tupelo Press 2013), named a finalist for the Alice Fay di Castagnola Award by Marilyn Hacker, *Flinch of Song*, winner of the Tupelo Press First Book Award, and the chapbook *Anchor Chain, Open Sail*. Her poems have appeared in *American Poetry Review, The Kenyon Review, The New Republic, The North American Review, The Paris Review, Ploughshares*, and *Best New Poets*.

Peter Mishler's new work appears or is forthcoming in *Poetry Daily, Web Conjunctions, Drunken Boat, The Literary Review*, and in *Best New Poets*.

El mundo como ser (The World as Presence) is the newest work by **Marcelo Morales**, addressing change and uncertainty in Havana in 2014. Dedicated to the slow development of his books, Morales (b. 1977) has won awards for segments of larger works in progress. For example, excerpts that reappeared in his 2006 poetry collection *El mundo como objeto* won the 2004 poetry prize from *La Gaceta de Cuba*, as well as an honorable mention in the national Julián del Casal prize competition and a finalist position in the international Casa de las Américas competition. Morales is the author of the poetry collections *Cinema* (1997, Pinos Nuevos prize), *El círculo mágico* (2007), and *Materia* (winner of the 2008 Julián del Casal prize), among others. Given to the exploration of prose-like fragments in his poetry, Morales is also interested in the motions of prose as such. His novel *La espiral* appeared in 2006.

Matt Morton has been a finalist for a Ruth Lilly Fellowship and a finalist in the *Narrative* 30 Below Story and Poetry Contest. His poems appear or are forthcoming in *Indiana Review, West Branch, Colorado Review, Forklift Ohio*, and *Quarterly West*, among others. The recipient of scholarships from the Bread Loaf Writers' Conference and the Sewanee Writers' Conference, he is a lecturer in the Writing Seminars at Johns Hopkins University. Originally from Rockwall, Texas, he lives in Baltimore.

Elisabeth Murawski is the author of *Zorba's Daughter*, winner of the 2010 May Swenson Poetry Award, *Moon and Mercury*, and two chapbooks: *Troubled by an Angel* and *Out-patients*. Hawthornden fellow, 2008. In her heart, she has never left the "city of the big shoulders" where she was born and raised.

Vaan Nguyen (b. 1982) was born in Ashkelon, Israel to Vietnamese refugees and raised in Jaffa, near Tel Aviv. She and her family are the subjects of Duki Dror's 2005 documentary *The Journey of Vaan Nguyen*, which documents the Nguyen family's efforts to reclaim ancestral land in Vietnam. The film also introduced Vaan's poetry to the Israeli public. *The Truffle Eye* (Ein ha-kmehin), a chapbook of poems, appeared in 2008. An expanded version, published by Ma'ayan Press, appeared in 2013 in both print and digital editions. Nguyen is affiliated with *Gerila Tarbut* (Cultural Guerrilla), a collective of Israeli and Palestinian poets, artists and activists, and also has worked as an actress and journalist.

Dave Nielsen lives in Cincinnati, OH with his wife and four children. His poems have recently appeared in *The Cortland Review, Cutbank,* and *Painted Bride Quarterly.*

Alexis Orgera is the author of *How Like Foreign Objects* (H_ngm_n Bks) and *Dust Jacket* (Coconut Books), three chapbooks, and a forthcoming full-length collaboration with the poet Abraham Smith. Her Agatha poems are part of a series that imagines the experience of Saint Agatha of Sicily. As the legend goes, Agatha spurned the advances of a Roman prefect, who subsequently had her breasts severed from her body as one part of her protracted torture. She is said to have been saving her virginity for God, but she was more likely fierce and brave in her desires.

Mike Ostrov hails from Florida, writes about music for Ninebullets.net, and has had fiction published in *The Lifted Brow, Metazen,* and elsewhere. He's spent the last few years in Boston, but by the time this publishes, he'll be somewhere else on the East Coast with his fiancée and maybe a dog.

Adrienne Perry is the editor of *Gulf Coast.*

Guy Pettit is the author of *My Life's Work* (Mindmade 2013) and *Love Me or Love Me NO1* (Minutes Books 2011). He lives and works in Western Massachusetts, where he founded the arts and publishing organization Flying Object.

Jeannine Marie Pitas is a teacher, writer, and literary translator currently living in Toronto. She is the author of a poetry chapbook, *Our Lady of the Snow Angels*, which was published by Lyricalmyrical Press in 2012, and the Spanish-English translator of Marosa di Giorgio's fourth book of poetry, *The History of Violets*, which was published by Ugly Duckling Presse in 2010 and will be reprinted in 2015 in a bilingual volume including three additional books by di Giorgio.

Richard Prins is a New Yorker who sometimes lives in Dar es Salaam. He received his MFA degree in poetry from New York University. His work appears in publications like *Barrow Street, Cimarron Review, Rattle, Southern Indiana Review,* and *Willow Springs.*

Awarded a 2014-2015 Hodder Fellowship from Princeton University, a 2014 Pushcart Prize, a 2013 National Endowment for the Arts Literature Fellowship and 2008 Ruth Lilly Fellowship, **Roger Reeves's** poems have appeared or are forthcoming in *Best American Poetry, Poetry, Ploughshares, American Poetry Review, Boston Review,* and *Tin House,* among others. *King Me,* his first book of poems, was published by Copper Canyon Press in 2013 and has been awarded the 2014 Larry Levis Reading Prize by the creative writing program at Virginia Commonwealth University and the PEN Oakland/Josephine Miles Literary Award. He is an assistant professor of poetry at the University of Illinois at Chicago.

Andrew Michael Roberts has a new book of poems called *good beast* from Burnside Review Books. He is also the author of *something has to happen next* from University of Iowa Press. He lives with his wife Sarah in Portland, Oregon, where he spends his time as a cardiac nurse, a cyclist, a sasquatch enthusiast, a library regular, and a poet.

Christopher Robinson's debut novel, *War of the Encyclopaedists*, co-authored with Gavin Kovite, will be published by Scribner in May 2015. His work has appeared, or is forthcoming, in *New England Review, The Missouri Review, Alaska Quarterly Review, Kenyon Review, Southern Review, McSweeney's Online,* and elsewhere. He is a recipient of fellowships from the MacDowell Colony, the Millay Colony, Bread Loaf, and the Djerassi Resident Artist program. His secret underground lair is located somewhere in Seattle.

Martin Rock's poems have appeared in publications such as *AGNI, Black Warrior Review, Conduit, DIAGRAM, Hayden's Ferry Review, Third Coast, Salamander* and *Best New Poets 2012.* He is co-editor, with Kevin Prufer and Martha Collins, of *Catherine Breese Davis: On the Life and Work of an American Master* (Plieades Press 2015) and is the author of the chapbook *Dear Mark* (Brooklyn Arts Press 2013). He has recieved writing fellowships from Mount Tremper Arts, the Port Townsend Writers Conference, NYU, and the University of Houston. Martin is the managing editor of *Gulf Coast.*

Anna Rosenwong is a translator, poet, editor, and educator. Her publications include Roció Cerón's *Diorama*, José Eugenio Sánchez's *Suite Prelude a/H1N1* and the forthcoming *Climax with Double Cheese,* as well as an original collection of poetry, *By Way of Explanation.* She is the translation editor of *Drunken Boat.* Her literary and scholarly work has been featured in *World Literature Today, The Kenyon Review, Translation Studies, The St Petersburg Review, Pool,* and elsewhere.

Raphael Rubinstein is a New York-based poet and art critic, and a professor of critical studies at the University of Houston School of Art.

José Eugenio Sánchez is an acclaimed poet and performer and the author of numerous poetry collections, including *Physical graffiti, La felicidad es una pistola caliente,* and *galaxy limited café,* which was a finalist for the 2010 Jaime Gil de Biedma International Poetry Prize. He calls himself an "underclown," and his aggressively playful work eagerly engages both pop and high culture with irreverence and insight. Originally from Guadalajara, Sánchez lives and writes in Monterrey, Mexico.

Jennifer Scappettone works at the juncture of poetry, translation, research and pedagogy, and the scoring of textual, visual, sonic, and gestural fields. Her books of poetry include *From Dame Quickly* and *Thing Ode / Ode oggettuale,* the latter translated in dialogue with Marco Giovenale. *Exit 43,* an archaeology of landfill and opera of pop-up pastorals, is in progress for Atelos Press, with a letterpress palimpsest, *A Chorus Fosse,* forthcoming from Compline. She edited and translated *Locomotrix: Selected Poetry and Prose of Amelia Rosselli,* and is at work on new translations of Carla Lonzi, as well as on the new Italian section of PennSound, which she is curating. Collaborative work includes performances of *Exit 43* with the Difforme Ensemble; digital and AR archaeologies with Judd Morrissey; libretti, scores, and vocal concepts for *PARK,* directed and choreographed by Kathy Westwater; and sonic documentaries for *X Locus,* an installation conceived with AGENCY architecture and composer Paul Rudy at the American Academy in Rome. *Killing the Moonlight: Modernism in Venice,* a study of the obsolescent city's influence on the aesthetic, social, and cognitive imagination of the modern world, was published by Columbia University Press in 2014.

Natalie Shapero is the author of the poetry collection *No Object*, and her writing has appeared in the *Believer, The New Yorker, Poetry, The Progressive,* and elsewhere. She lives in Columbus, Ohio and works as an Associate Editor of *The Kenyon Review.*

Alan Shapiro is author of twelve books of poetry (most recently *Reel to Reel,* from the University of Chicago Press, and *Night of the Republic* from Houghton Mifflin/Harcourt, a finalist for the National Book Award) and four books of prose (most recently *Broadway Baby,* a novel from Algonquin Books). He's published two translations with Oxford University Press and won numerous awards, including The Kingsley Tufts Award, LA Times Book Prize, an award in literature from The American Academy of Arts and Letters, two NEA grants, a Guggenheim, and a Lila Wallace Reader's Digest Award. He is also a member of the American Academy of Arts and Sciences.

Yvette Siegert is a writer and translator based in New York. Her work has appeared in *Aufgabe, Circumference, Guernica, The Literary Review, The St. Petersburg Review, 6x6, Springhouse* and other places. She has taught at Columbia University, Baruch College, and the 92nd Street Y, and has edited for the United Nations and *The New Yorker.* For her translations of the collected works of Alejandra Pizarnik, recently published by New Directions and Ugly Duckling Presse, she received fellowships from PEN Heim/NYSCA and the National Endowment for the Arts.

Laura Sims's fourth collection, *Staying Alive,* is forthcoming from Ugly Duckling Presse in 2016.

Gale Marie Thompson is the author of *Soldier On* (Tupelo Press 2015) and *Expeditions to the Polar Seas* (Coconut Books 2016), in addition to two chapbooks. Her work appears in *Guernica, Volt, Colorado Review, Phantom Limb, The Volta,* and elsewhere. She is creator and editor of *Jellyfish Magazine* and lives, teaches, and writes in Athens, GA.

G.C. Waldrep's most recent books are *The Arcadia Project: North American Postmodern Pastoral* (Ahsahta 2012), co-edited with Joshua Corey, and a chapbook, *Susquehanna* (Omnidawn 2013). BOA Editions will release a long poem, *Testament,* in May 2015. Waldrep lives in Lewisburg, PA., where he teaches at Bucknell University, edits the journal *West Branch,* and serves as Editor-at-Large for *The Kenyon Review.*

Jaren Watson earned an MFA at the University of Arizona and now teaches writing and editing in Idaho. He has a book of narrative nonfiction and a collection of essays forthcoming with Torrey House Press.

Diana Xin holds an MFA in creative writing from the University of Montana. Her work has also appeared in *Alaska Quarterly Review* and *The Masters Review.* She lives in Seattle, Washington.

Raúl Zurita's books of poems include, among others: *Purgatorio* (1979), *Anteparadise* (1982), *El paraíso está vacío* (1984), *Canto a su amor desaparecido* (1985), *El amor de Chile* (1987), *La vida nueva* (1993), *INRI* (2003), *Las ciudades de agua* (2007), *In Memoriam* (2007), *Los países muertos* (2006), *Sueños para Kurosawa* (2010), and *Zurita* (2011). Translations to English include *Purgatory, Antepariso, INRI,* and *Song for his Disappeared Love.* His numerous awards include the National Literature Prize of Chile and the Pablo Neruda Prize. He lives in Santiago, Chile, where he is a professor of literature at Universidad Diego Portales.

PAIGE ACKERSON-KIELY / MICHAEL BAZZETT / SEAN HILL / SANDRA BEASLEY / MARY BIDDINGER / MARK BRAZAITIS / TRACI BRIMHALL / TARFIA FAIZULLAH / JOEL BROUWER / JERICHO BROWN / CORSINO FORTES / JULIE CARR / MARTHA COLLINS / NATHAN OATES / CAROLINA EBEID / COPPERNICKEL / JOHN GALLAHER / ROXANE GAY / MARK HALLIDAY / TONY HOAGLAND / REBECCA HAZELTON / BRIAN HENRY / BOB HICOK / H. L. HIX / AILISH HOPPER / PATRICE DE LA TOUR DU PIN / HENRY ISRAELI / TROY JOLLIMORE / SALLY KEITH / DAVID KEPLINGER / LALEH KHADIVI / CIRCE MAIA / KENDRA DeCOLO / ALEX LEMON / NICK LANTZ / MELISSA KWASNY / ADRIAN MATEJKA / JILL OSIER / D. A. POWELL / JAMES RICHARDSON / PATRICK PHILLIPS / NICOLE SEALEY / MICHAEL MARTONE / ALEŠ ŠTEGER / G. C. WALDREP / NACHOEM WIJNBERG / CATHERINE PIERCE / JAN WAGNER / ALISSA VALLES / ERIKA MEITNER / CRAIG MORGAN TEICHER / ED SKOOG / ADA LIMÓN / HAILEY LEITHAUSER / SEAN O'BRIEN / RANDALL MANN / MARGOT SCHILPP / &c.

poetry / fiction / essays / translations / subscribe / submit / copper-nickel.org